MUTINY—

IN THE

—"BOUNTY!

AND

STORY OF THE PITCAIRN ISLANDERS.

BY

ALFRED McFARLAND, Esq.

(DISTRICT COURT JUDGE, NEW SOUTH WALES.)

Rediscovery Books

Reproduced by kind permission of the
Royal Geographical Society

Published by
Rediscovery Books Ltd
Unit 10, Ridgewood Industrial Park,
Uckfield, East Sussex,
TN22 5QE England
Tel: +44 (0) 1825 749494
Fax: +44 (0) 1825 765701

This edition © Rediscovery Books Ltd 2006

To find out more about Rediscovery Books
and its range of titles visit
www.rediscoverybooks.com

Published in association with

The **Royal Geographical Society with IBG** was founded in 1830 to advance geographical science. Today it supports geographical research, promotes geography in schools and through outdoor learning, in society and to policy makers. Geography connects us to the world's people, places and environments.
The **Rediscovery Books** series allow us to see how previous geographers and travellers understood and recorded the world.

In reprinting in facsimile from the original, any imperfections are inevitably reproduced and the quality may fall short of modern type and cartographic standards.

Printed and bound by Lightning Source

THE "BOUNTY" AT OTAHEITE.

To

THE MEN OF NORFOLK ISLAND,

I Dedicate this Account

of a

Daring Deed, and the Pitcairn Life,

of their Fathers.

ALFRED McFARLAND.

1st Sept., 1884.

Crows' Nest House,
    St. Leonards,
        Sydney.

PREFACE.

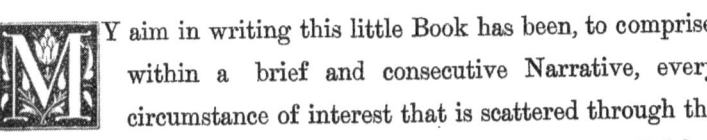

MY aim in writing this little Book has been, to comprise within a brief and consecutive Narrative, every circumstance of interest that is scattered through the pages of Lieutenant Bligh and Sir John Barrow, Lady Belcher and Mr. Brodie, the Rev. T. B. Murray and recent visitors to the main scene of it; and to present, at same time, a faithful, vivid, picture of a very remarkable incident in England's Naval annals—with which the history of Australia is also linked—of the occasion and sad consequences, in many respects, of that outbreak; of a notable voyage, and shipwreck, that sprung from it; and of the wondrous community it established, first at Pitcairn, and then within our own territory.

In doing so, I have submitted to the Australian reader a tale of bold enterprises, and terrible sufferings; of the impelling motives, acts, and fortunes, of Fletcher Christian, and his mates, on waters and isles of the Southern Pacific; of Bligh, their savage villifier, but dauntless leader of the *Bounty's* "Outcasts!" of the atrocities of Captain Edwards, the gaoler of Mr. Heywood, and thirteen others of the "mutineers;" and of the trial of ten of them, by Court Martial, at Portsmouth, after the loss of the *Pandora*, and drowning of the remaining four; of the wild deeds at Pitcairn, in the early days of its settlement, by Christian and the eight comrades who stood by him to the last; and of the happy, blessed, outcome of all—events that had their beginning on the shores of Van Diemen's Land, a mid-course on the great sea that girds the eastern and north-eastern coasts of New Holland, and by the reefs and sands of Torres Strait that realized, in their closing stage, the dream of poets—the aspiration of sages; that sent to Australia an early Governor; gave to New South Wales its hardy Norfolk islanders; and preserves their kindred stock in a still more distant and lovely isle of the ocean.

A. McF.

INTRODUCTION.

THE "Mutiny of the *Bounty*" is an expression common enough amongst Englishmen, and is sometimes heard amongst Australians; but few of either land know much about the real event, its origin, or consequences: There is an impression merely, with some, that it was a most unaccountable and barbarous—and, with others, a very intelligible—act, which excited great attention at the time, throughout England, and occurred not far from Australian seas.

Yet the blood of the mutineers runs even now in the veins of some of our people; nerving the arm of many a keen whaler, and giving to womanhood her noblest form, in Norfolk Island. Those, too, "who go down to the sea in ships," and happen to visit the yet lovlier, and more beautiful island of Pitcairn (whence the others came to us), must have felt a sympathetic glow as they beheld the early home, and persons, of a like goodly race—offspring of the same daring fathers, and dark-eyed mothers of Tahiti. While the Commander of the vessel in which the Mutiny arose, and the victim of it (as generally believed), or the undoubted and just cause of it (as others contend), became, eighteen years later, Governor-General of the New South Wales of that day—where he soon met, at the hands of the officers of its Military Corps, with somewhat similar treatment to that which the mutineers of the

Bounty visited him with—and for proceedings not unlike, though by no means so gross as, those which the latter attributed to him.

But, from the moment that he (with eighteen companions in misery) was cast away, in the *Bounty's* launch, off one of the Friendly Islands, until they reached Timor (that harbor of the fugitive, and the shipwrecked, in the early years of Australian settlement), his conduct of the intervening voyage, of some 3,600 miles in extent — amid the terrible sufferings which each endured, and he, by his prudence, skill and resolution, enabled all of them to overcome—sheds an imperishable lustre upon British pluck, power to command, and true seamanship : He was also the second English leader who forced a passage through the Great Barrier-reef, or sailed along the north-eastern and northern shores of New Holland ; where he found partial shelter, rest, and sustenance, on islands neighbouring same, that now constitute a portion of Queensland. And to Van Diemen's Land he was an early visitor.

Let him have his due, then ; and let me present, in so far as his own " Narrative " (published in 1792), contemporary evidence, of a character far less favorable to him, the records of the Court-Martial which resulted from the Mutiny, other authorities, and the light of subsequent events, enable me to state and weigh the facts.

The story of the maritime exploration of Van Diemen's Land, and Australia (in 1788-9), is necessarily interwoven in the account; for the *Bounty*, having reached our Southern Hemisphere, lay in Adventure Bay, and swept the south-eastern shores of the former, before proceeding upon the voyage that terminated in the Mutiny: And the launch, in which the outcasts were exposed, threaded her way amid islands and coasts of the latter, before gaining Timor :

So did "the boats' squadron" of the *Pandora*, wrecked on or near to the same Barrier-reef, when bearing to England fourteen of the alleged participators in that proceeding—and meeting at the same Timor with the intrepid William Bryant, his wife, little ones, and mates, after their flight from Port Jackson, its punishments, and frequent famine, and their unequalled voyage of 3,000 miles in a tiny fishing boat.

The investigation, too, of the circumstances preceding, accompanying, and ensuing on the Mutiny will largely relieve some, and completely exonerate others, of the four officers and twenty-one seamen charged with that act, from the aspersions and calumnies, cast upon them by Bligh—whose outrages, prior to it, were only surpassed by the later barbarities of Captain Edwards, towards certain of those unhappy men, after their surrender, or capture, at Otaheite—the rest of the party having, meanwhile, secured a safe retreat at Pitcairn Isle; where they and theirs have left a name that shall live through many an age.

And that interest is attached to the name of Fletcher Christian, the leader of the Mutiny, which is inseparable from a desperate deed, induced by foul usage, and followed by protracted suffering, and still sadder scenes—if not also by a mysterious end: Then, the story of young Heywood—a boy of fourteen, and on his first voyage when he joined the *Bounty*; insulted by her Commander, in common with every Gentleman on board; involved, by the force of circumstances, in a Mutiny at sea, sixteen months after sailing; a fugitive, an exile, and a prisoner, for upwards of three years later; bound in irons, hand and foot, and treated like a wild beast, by a King's Captain, for nearly half that period; tried for his life, at nineteen years of age, unjustly condemned, sentenced to death, pardoned but two days before the execution of three of his comrades in misfortune; and eventually becoming a Post Captain in the very Service in which he had been thus outraged—is, indeed, a most remarkable one.

In like manner, the incidents of the Mutiny itself; the wanderings, shipwreck, and varied settlements that followed it; the arraignment, trial, and fate in England, of alleged participators in it; with the lawlessness of many of the proceedings, and happy, waning, days of the last survivors—as well as the pure, hallowed lives, experiences at Otaheite, transfer to Norfolk Island, and return to the old home, of descendants of those of the mutineers who found a refuge at Pitcairn, afford materials at least for a graphic tale, with which every Australian should be familiar.

INDICIA.

OT love for island maid, but foul affront,
Fired the brain, and steel'd the heart,
Of Christian, and his mates.

"Hoist out the boat! was now the leader's cry:
And who dare answer 'No' to Mutiny,
In the first dawning of that mad hour—
The Saturnalia of unhoped-for power? . . .
The launch is crowded with the faithful few
Who wait the fallen Bligh — a saddened crew.
And 'twill be mine to tell their tale of grief,
Their constant peril, and their scant relief;
Their days of danger, and their nights of pain;
Their manly courage, e'en when deem'd in vain;
And sapping famine rendering scarce a son
To his own mother known."

Hither and thither, the outlaws sped;
From isle to isle they fled.

. . . . "The masts are cut away!
Both main and mizzen; first the mizzen went;
The main soon follow'd; but the ship still lay
Like a log, and baffl'd our intent. . . .

. . . . A wreck complete she roll'd,
   At mercy of the wave "—with her captured Mutineers.

Cedant arma togæ.

" 'Mid the mighty Southern Ocean,
    Stands an isolated rock;
  Whiten'd by the surf's commotion;
    Riven by the lightning's shock."

" My rapturous gaze o'er the prospect extending,
    I have fancied thee *Eden,* Fenūa Maitai ! " (*a*);
  Truth and, faith, worth and virtue blending,
    With daring keen; and fealty true for aye.

"Then fire the gun! the *Bounty's* gun!
    And set the bell a-ringing;
  And, with hearts and voices one,
    We'll all unite in singing,
        The Queen ! the Queen ! God bless the Queen !"

(*a*) The Good Land.

TABLE OF CONTENTS.

PART I.

MUTINY IN THE "BOUNTY!"

CHAPTER I.—The Deed ; and its Causes.

August, 1788—April, 1789 : Mission of the *Bounty*—Commander Bligh ; Fletcher Christian, Master's Mate ; and other officers, including Mr. Midshipman Heywood—The ship's visit to Van Diemen's Land ; and what was noticed there—Arrival at Otaheite ; doings at Matavai ; and departure thence—The Mutiny off Tofoa, one of the Friendly Isles ; its incidents ; and the "Castaways" in launch ; those who remained in the *Bounty* ; and whence the " conspiracy " sprang, according to Mr. Bligh's published " Narrative "—His story tested by the probabilities, by his true character, Billardiere's report, and his own private Journal ; Morrison's Journal ; and its picture of Bligh's treatment of his officers and men—Morrison's account of the Mutiny ; showing it arose from Bligh's own misbehaviour (outrages on Christian, and others), favouring circumstances, and a sudden impulse—Sir John Barrow's testimony ; Captain Heywood's ; and tradition among the Pitcairn islanders—The Cambridge Professor, and other friends of the mutineers—Bligh's savage letters to Mrs. Heywood, and Colonel Howell 1–27

CHAPTER II.—Bligh's Boat Voyage.

April,—Oct., 1789 : Intrepid voyage, sufferings, and endurance of Commander Bligh, and 18 other "outcasts," in launch of the *Bounty*, from Tofoa to Timor—Passage through, and touching at islands within, the Great Barrier reef, on the North-east coast of Australia, and in Torres' Strait (the Isle Direction, Restoration Island, and Sunday Island, Keys, or Lagoon Islands, Turtle Island, Bay of Islands, and Wednesday Island)—The supplies they yielded, the rest they gave, or troubles they brought—with glimpses of the main land; its features and natives. In the open sea, once again! events by the way; arrival at Timor; and reception there—England reached; Bligh performs on his own trumpet; the honors paid him; and a sketch of his subsequent life 28–42

CHAPTER III.—The Mutineers; and their Wanderings

April, 1789—March, 1791: Mr. Christian, and the 24 mutineers who remained in the *Bounty*, proceed to Isle Toubouai—Repelled from landing—Visit Otaheite, and procure live stock—All return to Toubouai, accompanied by Otaheitans, and form a settlement—Occurrences at Toubouai; occasioning another visit to Otaheite; where mutineers separate; Mr. Stewart, Mr. Heywood, with 14 others, remaining there; and Mr. Christian, with Mr. Young, the remaining 7, and some Otaheitans, &c., put to sea again, in *Bounty*—Fate of two, and occupations of the rest, of former band, during residence at Otaheite; till the *Pandora* appears—and her mission 43–55

CHAPTER IV.—" Pandora's Box ;" and Wreck.

March, '91—June, '92: Surrender or capture of the 14 " mutineers," who had staid, and survived, at Otaheite, and of the schooner they built— "*Pandora's* box;" and other agonies inflicted by Captain Edwards, and Lieutenant Larkin—The story of Peggy Stewart—Fruitless search for Mr. Christian, and his eight companions—Wreck of the *Pandora*, drowning of four of the prisoners (some of them in chains), and other loss of life, in or near to " Endeavor Passage "—On the reef!; and further inhumanities of Captain Edwards—Expedition of the saved, in ship's boats, to Timor- Trials of all, and fresh brutalities of Edwards to his captives, during it—Arrival at Coupang— Miseries there; and Mr. Larkin again !—Wretched voyage to Batavia; where they find gallant William Bryant, and his mates—The schooner is sold, and the ragged are clothed—To the Cape of Good Hope, and England !—Fate of Bryant, and party 56–73

CHAPTER V.—The Court Martial.

1792—Sep., Nov.: The trial by Court Martial, in England, of the 10 "mutineers" brought there by Captain Edwards—The Court; "Hamlet" and his " Uncle "—The charges, evidence, and defences— The verdict; and proceedings under it—After career of the chief witnesses, and parties, to the trial 74–88

PART II.

STORY OF THE PITCAIRN ISLANDERS.

CHAPTER VI.—Pitcairn; and its Refugees.

1789, September—March, 1829 : Pitcairn Island, and settlement there of Mr. Christian, the eight mutineers remaining with him, and Otaheitans, &c., who joined them—The dismemberment and sinking of the *Bounty*—Discovery of the survivors, and descendants of the party, in 1808, by the *Topaz*; and what her "log book" said about them—Visit, in 1814, of the *Briton* and *Tagus*, reports by their Commanders on the island and islanders; their appearance, manners, pursuits and customs; the climate, products, and village of Pitcairn—John Adams' account of occurrences in the island from 1789 to 1814, and comments thereon—Christian and his " cave ;" oppression and misconduct of the Englishmen towards the men of color; jealousies, plots, and strife; five of former, and all of latter, slain; violent end of two others of the mutineers—Conversion of Adams; its happy effect on the islanders and place; and death of Mr. Young—Accessions to the community (of Buffett and Evans) in 1823—Arrival of the *Blossom* in 1825 ; and Captain Beechy's picture of the happiness and comfort, simplicity of life, peace and purity, of the islanders—A fresh accession (of Mr. George H. Nobbs) in 1828 ; and sketch of his life—The death of " Father Adams," in 1829 89–121

CHAPTER VII.—The Otaheite business; and Queen's Deputy!

1830, March—Close of 1837—Visit to Pitcairn of the *Seringapatam*; and sketch of the islanders, by Captain Waldegrave—Their shipment, by British Government, from their own isle to Otaheite; how induced, and effected; the unhappy results; and return of the survivors to former (including incidents mentioned in reports of Captain Sandilands, of the *Comet*, and of Captain Freemantle, of the *Challenger*)—The usurpation of Mr. Joshua Hill; and subjection of the native islanders; his outrages upon " the three Englishmen"; and ultimate discomfiture 122–136

CHAPTER VIII.—Later History.

1838, Jan.—1850, Jan. : Restoration of harmony, election of "Chief Magistrate," and hoisting of the " Union Jack," at Pitcairn, in 1838—The " fossicking " Frenchman; and yearning for British nationality—

xviii   TABLE OF CONTENTS.

Lieutenant Lowry's Elysium ; land and people, in 1839—The gift-bearing *Camden*—Disease and relief—Death of Fletcher Christian's widow, in 1841—Inspection and features of "Elizabeth Island" (a proposed adjunct to Pitcairn)—A Queen to a Queen—The poor teacher—A portentous year ; hurricane of the next ; and rumor of war—An accident ; and the island's sympathy—A desire for Ordination—Fresh benefactions, and gratitude—Hieroglyphics on sea cliff, and descents to them—Other evidences of early occupants—The testimony of Worth—Arrival of live stock—Another man-of-war ! and celebration of the 60th year of the settlement 137–165

CHAPTER IX.— Mr. Brodie ; and Matters Domestic.

1850, March—April : Mr. Brodie's dilemma ; with his account of Pitcairn, and its people, physically and socially ; its agriculture, fish, and animals ; fruits and plants ; dwelling houses, dress, and aspect of islanders — Relics of the *Bounty* — House-keeping ; and house-warming—The picnic ; music lessons ; and "laws" 166–180

CHAPTER X.—By Land and Sea.

1851, July—close of 1853 : Daily occupations at Pitcairn—Reception of visitors—The Admiral, and his Lady petitioners—A flag-ship ! in the offing ; and consequent doings, arrangements, observations, and amusements—Anniversary Ode—Ordination of Mr. Nobbs—Second and third visits of the *Portland;* with "hard times," sickness, and endearments ; strolls by sunrise ; and ship's band ; evening adventure ; blind-man's buff ; and the parting—The Chaplain ; *Virago;* and Consul ; peace, and welcome ; song, and woe ; the funeral ; goat hunting ; and Nicolas' epitome 181–205

CHAPTER XI.—Parting Days ; and Removal to Norfolk Island.

1854—1868 : Suggestions for removal of Pitcairners to Norfolk Island ; and the grounds—Mr. Batchelor's description of its features, products, buildings, fish, and birds—A Post Captain's view of the position—Deaths of a little boy, and grown man, at Pitcairn—Duty and devotion—*Pro* and *con* on the removal question—The special mission, discussion, and decisive vote—Unavailing requests—Freemantle to the minority—Second visit of the *Dido*—Last days and departure (in 1856) of the islanders to Norfolk Island, in the *Morayshire ;* passage thither, first appearance, and landing there—Arrangements for their reception, and settlement—The "Ocean Hell," and "Earthly Paradise"—What the Bishop's Chaplain, and Mr. Augustus Robinson,

thought of the Pitcairners—Glance at their after history, on Norfolk
Island—Return to Pitcairn, in '58 and '63, of certain of them; and
instance of the pluck and devotion of the race 206-229

CHAPTER XII.—Pitcairn Re-visited, and Revived.

1858—1884: Pilgrims to the olden shrine—Captain Montreson's, and
Sir C. W. Dilke's, accounts of them, and it, in 1860 and 1866—that
of the shipwrecked sailors of the *Khandeish*, in '75—Rosalind Young's
letter; and Admiral De Horsey's report, in '78—A narrative of '82—
And tidings in '84—Parting suggestions 230-240

PART I.

MUTINY IN THE "BOUNTY!"

CHAPTER I.—The Deed; and its Causes.

August, 1788—April, 1789: Mission of the *Bounty*—Commander Bligh; Fletcher Christian, Master's Mate; and other officers, including Mr. Midshipman Heywood—The ship's visit to Van Diemen's Land; and what was noticed there—Arrival at Otaheite; doings at Matavai; and departure thence—The Mutiny off Tofoa, one of the Friendly Isles; its incidents; and the "Castaways" in launch; those who remained in the *Bounty*; and whence the "conspiracy" sprang, according to Mr. Bligh's published "Narrative"—His story tested by the probabilities, by his true character, Billardiere's report, and his own private Journal; Morrison's Journal; and its picture of Bligh's treatment of his officers and men—Morrison's account of the Mutiny; showing it arose from Bligh's own misbehaviour (outrages on Christian, and others), favouring circumstances, and a sudden impulse—Sir John Barrow's testimony; Captain Heywood's; and tradition among the Pitcairn islanders—The Cambridge Professor, and other friends of the mutineers—Bligh's savage letters to Mrs. Heywood, and Colonel Howell.

IN compliance with a request to George III., from the merchants and planters interested in his West India possessions, that the bread-fruit tree might be introduced there, from the South Seas, to serve as an article of food, a stout vessel, named the *Bounty*, of 215 tons, was provided for the service, by the Admiralty, in 1787, and placed under the command of Lieutenant William Bligh, on the 16th Aug. in that year.

Mr. Bligh was born of respectable parents, at Plymouth, in 1754, and had served as Sailing Master in the *Resolution*, under Captain Cook, in his last voyage (of 1776-9): But he seems to have entered the service in some humble capacity, and not to have had the advantage of an early association with officers; "it was his misfortune not to have been educated in the gun-room of a man-of-war, among young Gentlemen—which is to the Navy what a public school is to those who are to move in Civil society." Yet his appearance was prepossessing, and his well-known portrait is a good representation of him at about the age of 40 (or 5 years after the Mutiny in the *Bounty*). His complexion was naturally pale, or (as it has been described), of an ivory or marble whiteness. His hair was black. His face, though it had been exposed to all climates, and to the roughest weather, was far from coarse, even when weather beaten, or years began to tell upon him; and this was probably owing to his temperate habits, and fine constitution. *(a)*

The *Bounty's* establishment of men and officers amounted in all to 46 persons, including 23 able bodied seamen. The Master, or second in command, was Mr. Fryer; his Mates were Mr. Fletcher Christian, and Mr. Elphinstone; and there were five Midshipmen—Mr. Hayward and Mr. Hallet, Mr. Young, Mr. Stewart, and Mr. Heywood. Of these eight Gentlemen, the first, third, fourth, and fifth do not require any more special mention here; for they occupy but a secondary space in the following story. With respect, however, to the second, sixth, seventh and eighth, the case is different; they were the principal actors in the Mutiny, or marked victims of it; and a brief introductory notice of each is desirable.

Mr. Christian was of a good Cumberland family; had made two prior voyages with Mr. Bligh, and had been nominated Acting Lieutenant in this one, " his abilities being thoroughly equal to the task." He was ten years younger than the Commander of the *Bounty*, and must have been of singular attractiveness; for we are told that "he had a bright, pleasing countenance, and tall, commanding figure, well adapted to those feats of strength and agility which he so frequently exhibited on the passage to Otaheite." It is added, that a feeling of respect for him prevailed not only amongst those of his comrades who stood by him to the last, and died with him in Pitcairn Island (if *he did* die there), long after the Mutiny, but also with the other officers and men who remained in the *Bounty*, subsequent to that occurrence; till, having shared his

---

(*a*). Pitcairn, the Island, the People, and the Pastor, &c., by Rev. T. B. Murray, London, 1860.

fortunes at Toubouai, they separated from him at Otaheite; " and no act of his, even to the close of his days, appears to have diminished that respect."

Mr. Young was well educated, and "well recommended," writes Mr. Bligh in his "Narrative"; he had also "the look of an able, stout seaman;" though he "fell short," adds that veracious chronicle, " of what his appearance promised." Mr. Stewart was of "creditable parents, resident in the Orkneys; was a seaman, and had always borne a good character." And Mr. Heywood, or the boy "Peter," whose name will frequently appear in these pages, " was of excellent lineage in the north of England, and a lad of ability." He had a well proportioned figure, rather above the middle height; his features were regular and good—indicative of a calm, observant mind—and in conversation his countenance was lighted up with cheerfulness and vivacity.

Having taken in stores and provisions at Deptford, and being fitted up, under the inspection of Sir Joseph Banks, with proper conveniences for the reception of as many plants of the desired bread-fruit tree as she could contain, the *Bounty* sailed from Spithead on 23rd Dec., 1787; touched at Teneriffe; and arrived off Cape Horn, but, from the severity of the weather, was obliged to bear away for the Cape of Good Hope. On 24th May, '88, Simon's Bay was reached; and, after "refreshing," the vessel proceeded on her voyage; sighting the "Mewstone," on the southern coast of Van Diemen's Land, on 19th Aug.; and anchored, next day, in Adventure Bay, near to Penguin Island, where Bligh had been with Cook, in the *Resolution*, eleven years previously.

The "piratical convicts" who first swept the southern shores of the present Colonies of New South Wales, and Victoria, to the isles lying eastward of Wilson's Promontory, were still in chains at Port Jackson; and neither the ardent "Bass," who followed them, in his famous whale-boat voyage, from that settlement to Western Port—nor the gallant Flinders, who, with him, soon afterwards *circumnavigated* Van Diemen's Land, in the little *Norfolk*, and thus established its insularity—had as yet visited our Southern Hemisphere. The passage through the strait that now bears the name of the dauntless Surgeon (to whom Australia owes so much, and for whose memory she has done nothing,) was therefore unknown when Mr. Bligh sighted the coast, in Aug., 1788, and steered for the *southern* shores, of that land which Tasman had discovered in 1642, and named "Van Diemen" in honour of his friend Anthony, Governor-General of the Dutch East Indies, who had sent him on the mission—but which was considered, for upwards of a century and a half from that date, a portion of the "New South Wales" which Captain Cook had so styled in Aug., 1770, and the British Government had "occupied," at Port Jackson, in Jan., 1788.

After reaching Adventure Bay, the *Bounty* took in wood and water at the west end of the beach adjoining Penguin Island; many trees were observed that were fully 150 feet high; a sawpit dug; planks cut; and the trunk of a dead tree noticed on which had been inscribed (most likely by some of Captain Furneaux's people), "A.D. 1773": And upon the east side of the bay, apple and plantain trees, now brought from the Cape of Good Hope, as well as vines, Indian corn, and vegetable seeds, were planted. Thus, the peaceful shores of Adventure Bay were trodden and utilised by men, the tidings of whose bold outburst, or desperate voyage, and lengthened agonies, soon ran through England; and were followed in later years by the no less terrible accounts of the atrocities that blackened the island home of some of them—redeemed, however, by its wondrous transformation, through the influence and exertions of their last survivors, into an abode of order, and simplicity, purity, and Godliness, such, perhaps, as the world has never known elsewhere. Natives of the district were also seen, and spoken to (their voices are described as resembling "the cackling of geese"); and they included the one particularized by Captain Cook, in 1777, for his humor and deformity.

On 4th Sept., '88, the *Bounty* sailed out of Adventure Bay, rounded the "Peninsula of Tasman," skirted the little island which that amorous Dutchman has identified with his fair "Maria," stood clear of the land, steered for Otaheite, (where Bligh had also been with Cook, some years before), and on 26th Oct. made Matavai Bay there—on whose shores a large number of bread-fruit plants were collected and placed on board—shores

"Where all partook the earth without dispute;
And bread itself was gathered as a fruit." (a)

(a) Dampier's account of the bread-fruit is perhaps the best we have. "It grows" (he writes) "on a large tree as big and as high as our largest apple tree; it hath a spreading head, full of branches and dark leaves. The fruit grows on the

The vessel (after an unnecessary delay in that service of nearly five months), and burying the Surgeon (who had died at Matavai) (*b*), put to sea on the 4th April, '89, pushed westward, touched for water at Annamooka (one of the Friendly Islands); and on the 27th of same month was between Tofoa and Kooto (two of the south-westernmost of that Group): "Thus far" (writes Mr. Bligh in his "Narrative") "the voyage had advanced in a course of uninterrupted prosperity, and had been attended with many circumstances equally pleasing and satisfactory. But a very different scene was now to be experienced. A conspiracy had been formed which was to render all our past labour productive only of extreme misery and distress! though the means had been concerted and prepared with so much secrecy and circumspection, that nothing appeared to occasion the smallest suspicion of the impending calamity." (*c*)

Nor is there, up to this point, a word in that "Narrative" that suggests any act of the Commander which had occasioned dissatisfaction on board; unless the following admitted facts be evidence of such: At Otaheite, the ship's corporal and two of the seamen deserted, with their arms (that they might enjoy its seductions, Bligh says). What was their punishment, upon capture, is not mentioned by him; but we know, from another source, that they were flogged and put in irons—though Captain Cook, considering the temptations to which they were exposed, did not deem that the desertion of some of *his* men, at the same island, a few years previously, called for severe measures. Mr. Bligh does represent, however, that an attempt was there also made to cut the

---

boughs like apples; it is as big as a penny loaf when wheat is at five shillings the bushel; it is of a round shape, and hath a thick, tough rind. When the fruit is ripe, it is yellow and soft, and the taste is sweet and pleasant. The natives of Guam use it for bread; they gather it when full grown,—while it is green and hard; then they bake it in an oven, which scorches the rind, and makes it black; but they scrape off the outside black crust, and there remains a tender, thin crust. The inside is soft, tender, and white, like the crumb of a penny loaf. There is neither seed nor stone in the inside; but all is of a pure substance like bread. It must be eaten new, for if it be kept above twenty-four hours it grows harsh and choky; but it is very pleasant before it is too stale. This fruit lasts in season eight months in the year."

(*b*) One of the seamen had also died—during the outward voyage.

(*c*) A Voyage to the South Sea, in H.M.S. *Bounty*, Commanded by Lieut. W. Bligh; including an account of the Mutiny on board that ship; and the subsequent Voyage of part of the crew, in the launch, from Tofoa to Timor. London, 1792.

ship adrift; and though he "felt disposed, upon reflection," to attribute that offence to some of his own people, that "they might remain at Otaheite, without danger of being dealt with if the ship had been driven on the shore"—it can scarcely be supposed that British sailors would have risked a King's ship (not to speak of their own and comrades' lives), to attain such an object; and, at the same time (as he himself puts it), "to abandon every prospect of returning to their native country." Indeed, the better opinion seems to have been, that Bligh's after-thought "was wholly gratuitous" (as Sir John Barrow says); "and that the damage done to the cable was owing, in all probability, to its chafing on the rocky bottoms" over which the *Bounty* lay, during the many months spent on the waters of Otaheite, and against which she had once grounded.

And now, having left that island, as well as Annamooka, and reached the most south-western of the Friendly Isles, onward glides the ship o'er the Pacific wave; and as night sets in, the stars come forth, and the Southern Cross gleams in the heavens, high and bright: Scarce a breath of air greets the idle sail, or woos the deep; the officer in charge, and a few listless hands, hold the deck; the shadows of Tofoa loom in the distance, and the semblance of peace pervades throughout:

> "The morning watch was come; the vessel lay
> Her course, and gently made her liquid way;
> The cloven billow flashed from off her prow,
> In furrows formed by that majestic plough:
> The waters with their world were all before;
> Behind, the South Sea's many an islet shore."

But there was no peace in one heart, at least, of those who gazed on that fair scene; a smothered word is spoken: hurried feet break the silence; and arms begin to glisten; there is a rush below: the Commander is seized in his hammock, bound, and dragged on deck; his principal officers are imprisoned in their cabins; the mutineers are masters of the position; and the *Bounty* is lost to the King, and his heirs, for ever.

This is the account given by Mr. Bligh of what happened:—
"Tuesday, 28th April, '89: Just before sun-rising, while I was yet asleep, Mr. Christian (who was Acting Lieutenant, and had the morning watch—or from 4 to 8), with the master-at-arms, gunner's mate, and Thomas Birkett, seaman, came into my cabin; and,

securing me, tied my hands with a cord behind my back; threatening me with instant death, if I spoke or made the least noise. I, however, called out as loud as I could, in hopes of assistance; but they had already secured the officers who were not of their party, by placing sentinels at their doors. There were three men at my cabin door, besides the four within; Christian had only a cutlass in his hand; the others had muskets and bayonets. I was hauled out of bed, and forced on deck in my shirt—suffering great pain from the tightness with which they had tied my hands. I demanded the reason of such violence; but received no other answer than abuse, for not holding my tongue. Mr. Fryer (the Master), the gunner, the Acting Surgeon, Mr. Elphinstone (the second Master's Mate), and one of the botanists, were kept confined below; and the fore-holds were guarded by sentinels. The boatswain, carpenter, and clerk, were allowed to come upon deck, where they saw me standing abaft the mizzen-mast, with my hands tied behind my back, under a guard, with Christian at their head; and the boatswain was ordered to hoist the launch out, with a threat, if he did not do so instantly, to take care of himself.

"When the boat was out, two of the Midshipmen (Mr. Hayward and Mr. Hallet), and the clerk, were ordered into it: I demanded what the intention was in giving this order, and endeavoured to persuade the people near me not to persist in such acts of violence, but to no effect. 'Hold your tongue, sir, or you are a dead man this instant,' was constantly repeated to me. By this time, the Master had sent to request that he might be allowed to come on deck; the desired leave was granted; but he was soon ordered back to his cabin. Still, I continued my endeavours to turn the tide of affairs, till Christian changed the cutlass, which he had in his hand, for a bayonet that was brought to him; and, holding me with a strong grip by the cord that bound my hands, he, with many oaths, threatened to kill me immediately, if I would not be quiet; while the villains round me had their pieces cocked, and bayonets fixed. At the same time, particular people were called on to go into the boat, and were hurried over the side; whence I concluded I was to be set adrift with them: I therefore made another effort to bring about a change, but with no other effect than to be threatened with having my brains blown out.

"The boatswain, and seamen, who were to go into the launch, were allowed to collect twine, canvas, lines, sails, cordage, and a 28 gallon-cask of water; and the clerk got 150 lbs. of bread, with a small quantity of rum and wine; also a quadrant and compass; though he was forbidden, on pain of death, to touch either map, book of astronomical observations, sextant, time-keeper, or any of my surveys or drawings: but the mutineers having forced into the boat those of the seamen whom they meant to get rid of, Christian directed a dram to be served to each of his own (the *Bounty's*) crew. I then unhappily saw that nothing could be done to effect the rescuing of the ship; there was no one to assist me; and every endeavour on my part was answered with threats of death. Some of the officers were next called upon deck, and forced over the side into the boat; while I was kept apart from every one, abaft the mizzen-mast; Christian, armed with a bayonet, holding me by the bandage that secured my hands: And the guard round me had their pieces cocked; but, on my daring the ungrateful wretches to fire, they uncocked them. At the same time, one of the guard over me had (I saw) an inclination to assist me; and as he fed me with shaddock (my lips being quite parched), we explained our wishes to each other by looks; but this being observed, he was removed from me; he then attempted to leave the ship, by getting into the launch; but, with many threats, they obliged him to return.

"The armorer, and the carpenter's mates, were also kept contrary to their inclination; and they begged me, after I was astern in the boat, to remember they had no hand in the transaction. I am told, that Byrne, one of the seamen, also wanted to leave the ship: It is of no moment for me to recount my further endeavours to bring back the offenders to a sense of their duty; all I could do was by speaking to them in general; but it was to no purpose; for I was kept securely bound, and no one, except the guard, suffered to come near me. To Mr. Samuel, the clerk, I am indebted for securing my journals, and commission, with some material ship's papers. Without these I had nothing to certify what I had done; and my honour and character might have been suspected, whilst I had not a proper document in their defence: All this he did with great resolution, though guarded and strictly watched: He also attempted to save the time-keeper, and a box containing my surveys, drawings, and nautical remarks for 15 years past,—when he was driven away with, 'Dam your eyes, you are well off to get what you have.' But the carpenter on being ordered into the boat, was permitted, though not without some opposition, to take his tool chest." Mr. Bligh forgets to add, that Christian held over the ship's side, and placed in his hands, a book of nautical tables, and his own sextant, saying, "This book, sir, is sufficient for every purpose, and you know my sextant to be a good one."

"Much altercation took place among the mutinous crew during the whole business: Some swore, ' I'll be damned if he does not find his way home, if he gets anything with him '"—and (when the carpenter's chest was being carried into the boat), 'Dam my eyes he will have a vessel built in a month!' While others laughed at the helpless situation of the boat, and so little room for those who were in her. As for Christian, he seemed as if meditating destruction to himself, and everyone else: I asked for arms; but they laughed at me and said '*I was well acquainted with the people among whom I was going, and therefore did not want them;*' four cutlasses, however, were thrown in after we were veered astern. Meanwhile, the officers and men who were to accompany me being in the boat, they only waited for me—of which the master-at-arms informed Christian; who then said, 'Come Captain Bligh! your officers and men are now in the boat, and you must go with them; if you attempt to make the least resistance you will instantly be put to death!' And without further ceremony, with a tribe of armed ruffians about me, I was forced over the side, where they untied my hands; then, being in the boat, we were veered astern by a rope. At the same time, a few pieces of pork were thrown to us, some clothes, and the cutlasses already mentioned; and, after having undergone a great deal of ridicule, and been kept for some time to make sport for the unfeeling wretches, we were at length cast adrift in the open ocean" (as it is represented)—though two inhabited islands (to one of which they speedily proceeded) were close by; and the scanty supply of provisions, clothes, &c., allowed by the mutineers to the party in the launch, may be fairly accounted for, if the former believed (as all the circumstances show they did) that the latter would return to Otaheite (only 1,500 miles distant from the place of their outcast), or to Annamooka (which was much nearer still), and did not conceive that they would venture upon such a desperate alternative as they adopted.

The "Narrative" farther states, that Mr. Christian, and Mr. Heywood (one of the three Midshipmen remaining on board the *Bounty*), had been objects of Bligh's particular regard and attention; and that the latter had taken great pains to instruct them; "entertaining hopes that they would have been a credit to their country:" And it is added, that, "notwithstanding the roughness with which his Commander was treated, the remembrance of past kindness produced some signs of remorse in Christian. When the mutineers were forcing Bligh out of the ship, he asked if this treatment were a proper return for the many instances the other had received of his friendship;? at which Christian appeared disturbed, and answered with much emotion—" *That*, Captain Bligh; that is the thing—I am in hell; I am in hell!" But a much more reliable narrative than Bligh's (which will be quoted by and by) represents that the exclamation of Christian, here referred to, was made not in reply to any observation of the former, but in answer to an entreaty of the boatswain; and that what Christian said was really this— "No, it is too late, Mr. Cole; I have been in hell this fortnight past, and am determined to bear it no longer. *You know that during the whole voyage I have been treated like a dog* "—a charge which Bligh suppresses; but the force and truth of which will be presently seen.

For some minutes after the expulsion of the Commander, the two parties lay glowering, or sadly gazing, at each other; Christian, and his fellow mutineers, with those whom they detained in the *Bounty*, flushed with triumph over a hated oppressor, and a sense of unwonted freedom, or stunned by the past, and fearful for the future: while Mr. Bligh, from the launch, vociferated " his accusations, and vows of vengeance, against them all;" and the unfortunates, who were associated with him, cast in turn their mournful gaze on the vessel from which they had been expelled, and on the shores of the neighbouring isle—till the sails of the *Bounty* were filled by a passing breeze, and she stood to the eastward, amid a wild hurrah, and many a parting cry.

THE DEED; AND ITS CAUSES.

Mr. Bligh had with him in the Launch.		While there remained in the *Bounty*.	
Names.	Stations.	Names.	Stations.
Mr. Fryer	Master	Mr. F. Christian	Master's mate
,, T. Leonard	Acting Surgeon	,, Young	Midshipman
,, D. Nelson	Botanist	,, Stewart	do.
,, Wm. Peckover	Gunner	,, Heywood	do.
,, Wm. Cole	Boatswain	,, C. Churchill	Master-at-arms
,, Wm. Purcell	Carpenter	,, John Mills	Gunner's mate
,, W. Elphinstone	Master's mate	,, Jas. Morrison	Boatswain's mate
,, Hayward	Midshipman	Thos. Birkett	Able bodied seaman
,, Hallet	do.	M. Quintall	do.
,, J. M. Norton	Quarter-master	John Sumner	do.
,, P. Lenkletter	do.	J. Millward	do.
L. Lebogue	Sailmaker	Wm. McCoy	do.
John Smith	Cook	H. Hildebrandt	do.
Thos. Hall	do.	M. Byrne	do.
Geo. Simpson	Qr. Master's mate	Wm. Muspratt	do.
R. Tinkler	A boy	A. Smith	do.
Rob. Lamb	Butcher	J. Williams	do.
Mr. Samuel	Clerk and Steward	T. Ellison	do.
18 persons—and Bligh himself, Chief of the "outcasts."		J. Martin	do.
		R. Skinner	do.
		M. Thompson	do.
		W. Brown	Gardener
		J. Colman	Armourer
		C. Norman	Carpenter's man
		T. M'Intosh	do.
		In all 25.	

The only explanation given by Mr. Bligh of the circumstances occasioning the extraordinary transaction which he describes is this—"The women at Otaheite are handsome, mild and cheerful in their manners and conversation, possessed of great sensibility, and have sufficient delicacy to make them admired and beloved. The Chiefs were so much attached to our people, that they rather encouraged their stay among them than otherwise, and even made them promises of large possessions. Under these and many other attendant circumstances, equally desirable, it is now perhaps not so much to be wondered at, though scarcely possible to have been foreseen, that a set of sailors, most of them void of connections elsewhere, should be led away—especially when, in addition to such powerful inducements, they imagined it in their power to fix themselves in the midst of plenty on one of the finest islands in the world, where they need not labour, and where the allurements of dissipation are beyond anything that can be conceived." *(a)*

It is said, lastly, by Mr. Bligh, "The secrecy of this Mutiny is beyond all conception; thirteen of the party, who were with me in the boat, had always lived forward among the seamen; yet neither they, nor the messmates of Christian and Heywood, or of Stewart and Young" (two others of the Midshipmen remaining in the *Bounty*, or "involved in the business"—and who "always bore good characters"—), "had ever observed any circumstance that made them in the least suspect what was going on. To such a close planned act of villainy, my mind, being entirely free from any suspicion, it is not wonderful that I fell a sacrifice. Had the Mutiny been occasioned by any grievances, either real or imaginary, I must have observed symptoms of discontent, which would have put me on my guard; but the case was far otherwise. With Christian, in particular, I was on the most friendly terms; that very day he was engaged to have dined with me; and on the previous night he excused himself from supping with me, on pretence of being unwell—for which I felt concerned, having no suspicions of his integrity and honour."

In other words, it is represented by Mr. Bligh, that a daring and unprecedented act of Mutiny on the high seas, by British officers, of previous good repute, and by a number of seamen (whom he writes of, in another place, as "the best men in the ship"), is to be attributed, solely, to a desire on their part to lead a life of indolence and sensuality in a South Sea Island, and not to any cause of complaint against himself. He throws the entire blame on—

"The gentle island, and the genial soil,
"The friendly hearts, the feasts without a toil.
"The courteous manners, but from nature caught,
"The wealth unhoarded, and the love unbought."

(a) As evidence that the Mutiny was planned at Otaheite, and for the purpose of securing a residence there, Bligh absurdly relied upon the circumstance that several of the mutineers, "who had formed tender attachments in that island, had been marked in a tatooing process, to which they submitted," with the significant device of "hearts and darts!"

And he would have us believe that the mutineers were—

"Young hearts which languished for a sunny isle,
"Where summer years, and summer women smile;
"Men without country who, too long estranged,
" Had found no native home, or found it changed ;
"And, half uncivilised, preferred the cave
"Of some soft savage to the uncertain wave."

But it must be borne in mind, that the statement of the circumstances attending, and constituting, the Mutiny of the *Bounty*, which the Commander thus gave to the world, is an *ex parte* one ; and that the persons injuriously affected by it had no opportunity of ever meeting it (except as to those of them who were afterwards put upon their trial in England for that offence—of which a good deal will presently be said). The motives, too, assigned by Bligh, to the mutineers, for the flagrant violation of Naval discipline which they undoubtedly committed, are utterly insufficient to account for that act : Had they desired to remain at Otaheite, the offenders would scarcely have postponed the execution of the scheme, which was to have enabled them to gratify that wish, until they had sailed away, and were distant from that island about 1,500 miles. Neither did they proceed to Otaheite immediately after the Mutiny, when it *did* occur, but to a different island, and in order to settle on the latter : In like manner, when they made their first subsequent visit to the former, none of them then remained, nor did some of them ever seek shelter upon it : And, though the person charging them with those motives was a British officer, he is far from a reliable witness in a transaction in which prior harshness, and brutality in himself, towards others (though sedulously concealed in his story of it), really provoked the violence of which he complains in them, and in which the moral guilt of those others depends, to a large extent, upon the weight properly attached to his own veracity.

It is painful to be obliged to notice the fact ; but, having regard to the gravity of *his* charges against the officers and seamen who shared in the Mutiny, it ought to be stated that, upon Bligh's own showing, he failed in truthfulness to others on several occasions, prior to it : that is, to the natives of Otaheite, whilst he continued amongst them, in obtaining the bread-fruit plants by representing that he intended to return to the island, and would take some of them to England (as they desired); and by pretending that he was the son of Captain Cook (*a*): This, too, is the version which he himself cooly gives of the tale he fabricated, and directed his companions in the boat to repeat to the people of Tofoa, in explanation of their landing there after being outcast from the *Bounty*—" I was much puzzled in what manner to account to the natives for the loss of my ship: I knew they had too much sense to be amused with a story that the *Bounty* was to join me, when she was not in sight from the hills. I was at first doubtful whether I should tell the real facts, or say that the ship had been overset and sunk, and that we, only, were saved! The latter appeared to be *the most proper and advantageous for us*; and I accordingly instructed my people that we might agree in one story! As I expected, inquiries were made about the ship, by the natives; and they seemed readily satisfied with our account; but there did not appear the least symptom of joy or terror in their faces; though I fancied I discovered some marks of surprise "—as there well might have been. Thus we have, under Mr. Bligh's own hand, not only an unblushing avowal of falsehood, invented by him because it was "most proper and advantageous" to his purpose, but his shipmates in the boat made parties to that falsehood by him, their Commanding officer!

Again, it is mentioned by Mons. Labillardiere, in his Book on the "Voyage in search of La Perouse," that "one of the officers of the *Pandora*, who had arrived in Jan., 1792, at the Cape of Good Hope" (after the wreck of that vessel on or near to the Great Barrier reef, when returning from Otaheite, with some of the mutineers of the *Bounty* obtained there), "assured" the Gentlemen of the French expedition (then also at the Cape), "that Captain Bligh had behaved very ill to Christian; and that an abuse of authority by the former was the cause of his subsequent misfortunes. Christian, though a Master's Mate of the *Bounty*, had been maltreated according to Bligh's orders, as if he had been a common sailor of the lowest rank. If this be the fact, Bligh disguises the truth when he asserts, that he had always treated the other with the greatest liberality." And it is almost impossible to conceive

---

(*a*) See his own "Narrative," pp. 73, 112; Lady Belcher's "Mutineers of the *Bounty*," &c., pp. 42, 70; and Sir John Barrow's " Mutiny of the *Bounty*," &c., p. 54.

that the mutineers at large, would have preserved their secret so inviolably as they did, have treated him with the violence he attributes to them, and (as "unfeeling wretches") have jeered at him in the boat in which he was about to be cast away, if his prior conduct towards them had not been harsh, savage, and inexcusable.

Again, Mr. Bligh's behaviour at later periods of his life would justify the worst construction that can well be placed upon that which preceded the Mutiny. For there is conclusive evidence that, when Governor of New South Wales, between 1806 and 1808, he was exceedingly arbitrary and tyrannical in his proceedings; so much so, that the officers of its Military Corps arrested and deposed him: He was also very deceitful and false in his professions and conduct, from the time of his release from that arrest until his sailing for England. Nearly every Naval command, too, which he held subsequently to that Mutiny, was marked by oppression, and utter indifference to the feelings and reputation of others.

And Mr. Brodie, who, in the early part of 1850, spent some weeks, at Pitcairn, amongst the descendants of Christian, and his more resolute adherents, records that the account given by the islanders differs materially from that published by Lieutenant Bligh, after his return to England: " They flatly deny his assertion, that the original cause of the Mutiny was a connexion formed by the crew, while at Tahiti, with Tahitan women; and attribute it entirely to his own perverse temper, and tyrannical conduct. His language, particularly to his officers, is stated to have been habitually and inexcusably coarse. Of this, a single sample will suffice, which is set out in the words of the narrator. ' Some fruit, which had been sent on board at Tahiti, for the Commander's cabin, having been left on the quarter deck, disappeared; he was exceedingly angry; and, in rating Christian about the matter, made use of this expression, 'I suppose you have eaten it yourself, you hungry hound!' " Can we be surprised, adds Mr. Brodie, at insults of this nature rankling in the mind of a susceptible man, and driving him at last to the desperate deed by which he secured himself against their continuance. (*a*)

(*a*) Pitcairn Island, and the Islanders, in 1850, by Walter Brodie, London, 1851.

Mr. Bligh's representation of the circumstances that led to the Mutiny in the *Bounty*, must therefore be received with the greatest caution; and it is much more likely that that outbreak was occasioned by his own injurious suspicions, passionate disposition, and abuse and maltreatment of those concerned in it, than by love of idleness, or unworthy desires on their part. The portrait which is prefixed to his "Narrative" is that of a good countenance, with mild, humane expression; and his conduct in the boat, from the time of its being cast adrift, till its reaching Timor, showed the utmost solicitude for the life and comfort of every comrade—and is one of the most noticeable in the long line of famous services that mark the history of England's Naval officers: But all this is perfectly consistent with a foul tongue, ferocious nature, and tyrannous hand, in days of prosperity and command. Even during the fitting out of the *Bounty*, "the language he indulged in both to officers and men was so harsh, and offensive, as to be exceptionable at a time when it was deemed by many that discipline could not be maintained without the use of opprobrious and profane epithets;" and he often accused the men of purloining the ship's stores. Indeed, when we come to deal with the private Journals to be presently mentioned, and the disclosures made during the proceedings of the Court Martial held at Portsmouth, in Sept., 1792, upon some of the mutineers (though they were placed at a terrible disadvantage in those proceedings), conclusive proof will be furnished of the unbridled passion of the man, and of his infamous behaviour towards all on board (to Christian mainly), prior to the Mutiny: And Sir John Barrow expressly describes him, as a person " having an extremely irritable temper, of coarse habits, and entertaining very mistaken notions with regard to discipline ": While the dishonesty of his published " Narrative" is shown under Mr. Bligh's own hand; for he used to enter from day to day, in an original *manuscript* Journal, the events of the voyage of the *Bounty;* and there are many important passages in that Journal which do *not* appear in that "Narrative," but support the idea that the catastrophe resulted from his own intolerable misconduct, and from no such causes as he was pleased to assign after its occurrence.

There is also still extant a manuscript Journal, kept (both before and after the Mutiny) by James Morrison, the boatswain's mate—who was subsequently tried and convicted as one of the mutineers, but received the King's pardon, on the recommendation of the Court Martial. From talent and education, Morrison was far superior to the position he held in the *Bounty;* he had previously served in the Navy, as a Midshipman; and, after his pardon, was appointed gunner to the *Blenheim,* in which he had been in earlier years—and in which he eventually perished, with Admiral Sir Thomas Troubridge (who had been his former Captain), when that vessel went down off the Isle of Bourbon. This Journal was given to, and retained in later years amongst the papers of, Mr. Heywood; who though, himself, another of the pretended mutineers, tried and convicted with Morrison, was also pardoned, on a like recommendation, and rose to be a Post Captain; and various portions of it seem to have been corrected, either, by Mr. Heywood, or some other person; but none of the corrections alter the substance of its representations; which demonstrate that Mr. Bligh was a far greater culprit than Christian, and his mutinous mates, and brought upon himself all that he endured.

It appears from this important record, that the seeds of discord were sown at a very early period of the *Bounty's* voyage. As was then the case in all small vessels, the duties of Commander and Purser were united in the person of Mr. Bligh; and this, with the mode in which he discharged them, proved the cause of very serious discontent among the officers and crew, as shown by the following incident, which Morrison narrates: At Teneriffe, Bligh "had the cheese hoisted up, and exposed to the air—which was no sooner done, than he pretended to miss a certain quantity, and declared it had been stolen. The cooper informed him, that the cask in question had been opened by direction of Mr. Samuel, his clerk (who acted also as steward), and the cheese sent on shore to his (the Commander's) own house, prior to the *Bounty* leaving the Thames. Without making any further inquiry, Bligh immediately ordered the allowance of that article to be stopped both to officers and men, until the deficiency should be made up; and told the cooper he would give him a good flogging if he said another word on the subject."*

(*) In quoting this and other speeches of Mr. Bligh, I have purposely omitted *the oaths* with which he garnished them.

If that portion of Morrison's Journal stood alone, it would not carry much weight; for it could scarcely be supposed that a man of Mr. Bligh's shrewdness, if disposed to play the rogue, would have placed himself so completely, as it represents, in the hands of the steward and cooper, in a transaction, which, if revealed, must have cost him his Commission. But the Journal contains a statement (to be presently quoted) of two other incidents that depict Bligh's conduct, with respect to the ship's provisions, in an aspect almost as unfavourable as the other; and that statement is adopted in a book of high authority (a), as if it were free from question. It will also be seen, that, at the Court Martial of some of the mutineers, Mr. Fryer, the Master of the *Bounty*, gave evidence having marked bearing on this part of the case, and very adverse to the Commander. Morrison's further statement is this:—As the vessel approached the equator, some pumpkins, purchased at Teneriffe, were ordered to be issued to the crew at a certain proportion to biscuit, which they were reluctant to accept; and, on this being reported to Bligh, he rushed upon deck in a violent rage, turned the hands up, and directed the first man on the list of each mess to be called by name; at the same time saying, "I'll see who will refuse the pumpkins, or anything else I may order to be served out!"—to which he added—" You infernal scoundrels, I'll make you eat grass, or anything you can catch, before I have done with you!" This speech had the desired effect; every one receiving the pumpkins, even the officers. . . . Then, when a representation was made to Mr. Bligh, in a quiet and orderly manner (as prescribed by the Articles of War), respecting the mode of issuing beef and pork, he called the crew aft, told them that everything relative to the provisions was transacted by his orders; that it was therefore needless for them to complain, as they would get no redress, he being the fittest judge of what was right or wrong; and that he would flog the first man who should dare attempt to make any complaint in future—to which imperious menace they bowed in silence; but determined to seek redress on the *Bounty's* return to England. . . . And on the trial there of 10 of them, Mr. Fryer deposed that, on the day before the

---

(a) Eventful History of the Mutiny and Piratical seizure of H.M.S. *Bounty*: Its cause and consequences [By Sir John Barrow, Secretary at the Admiralty] 2nd Ed., London, 1835.

Mutiny, Bligh had challenged all the "young Gentlemen" with stealing his cocoa-nuts, as well as cursed them, and threatened their lives.

According to Morrison, also, " eternal discord was further sown between Mr. Bligh and some of his officers," while the *Bounty* was at Adventure Bay, Van Diemen's Land, where he censured them, and put the carpenter into confinement, without cause. And the relation that existed between the Commander and the superior officers during the passage may be inferred from the following extract from Morrison's Journal :—" Mr. Bligh and his messmates, the Master and Surgeon, fell out and separated; each taking his part of the stock, and retiring to live in his own cabin. Afterwards, they had several disputes, and seldom spoke to each other, except on duty, and even then with much apparent reserve." He is accused, too, of taking the officers' hogs, and bread fruit, on arriving at Matavai Bay, in Otaheite, and serving them to the ship's company; and when the Master remonstrated with him on the subject, he replied, he would "convince him that everything became *his* (Bligh's) so soon as it was brought on board; that he would take nine-tenths of every man's property; and let him see who dared to say anything to the contrary." As for the sailors' pigs, they were seized without ceremony; and it became a favor for a man to obtain an extra pound of his own meat. Further, when the *Bounty* had left Otaheite, and had anchored off Annamooka (as before mentioned), a watering party, in charge of Mr. Christian, though threatened by the natives with clubs and spears, were prevented by orders of Mr. Bligh from protecting themselves; and on Mr. Christian finding it, therefore, difficult to carry on his duty, and acquainting the Commander with the behaviour of the Annamookans, "he received a volley of abuse, was d——d as a cowardly rascal, and asked if he were afraid of naked savages, whilst he had weapons in his hands?"—a ruffianly taunt, to which he respectfully replied—" The arms are of no effect, sir, while your orders prohibit their use." This happened on the 23rd April, '89, or but five days before the Mutiny; and the only allusion made to the occurrence in Bligh's published "Narrative" is, that the then station "being *inconvenient* for watering, they weighed anchor on the 24th, and worked more to the eastward;"! but in his M.S. Journal, he writes of the disturbance on shore; and assuming, at first, that all the watering party were to blame for it, (an assumption for which there does not appear to have been any ground), adds, "the men cleared themselves, and they therefore merit no punishment. As to the officers, I have no resource, nor do I ever feel myself safe in the few instances I trust to them."

On the 27th April (or day immediately preceding the Mutiny), Mr. Bligh completed the measure of his insolence, and brutality; and included all his officers in the act of outrage. "In the afternoon of that day" (records Morrison—and this is the incident referred to in Mr. Fryer's evidence), "Lieutenant Bligh came upon deck, and missing some of the cocoa-nuts, which had been piled up between the guns, said they had been stolen, and could not have been taken away without the knowledge of the officers; all of whom were sent for, and questioned on the subject. On their declaring they had not seen any of the people touch them, he exclaimed, ' *Then you must have taken them yourselves!* '; and proceeded to inquire of them separately how many they had purchased. On his coming to Mr. Christian, that Gentleman answered, ' I don't know, sir, but I hope you do not think me so mean as to be guilty of stealing yours?': Mr. Bligh replied, 'Yes, you d——d hound, I do—you must have stolen them from me.'! Then, turning to the other officers, he said, ' You scoundrels, you are all thieves alike,' and combine with the men to rob me;! I suppose, you will steal *my yams* next; but I'll sweat you for it, you rascals— I'll make half of you jump overboard before you get through Endeavor Strait.'!! And this threat was followed by an order to the clerk, 'to stop the villains' grog, and give them but half-a-pound of yams to-morrow: If they steal them, I'll reduce them to a quarter.'!"

Supposing that Mr. Bligh was still in his senses, and not a raving lunatic, no one but a man of the lowest type of mind, and the most savage disposition, would have behaved in the manner thus attributed to him; and the Author of the "Eventful History" properly remarks, "It is difficult to believe that an officer in His Majesty's service could condescend to make use of such language to the meanest of the crew, much less to Gentlemen. It is to be feared, however, that there is sufficient ground for the truth of these statements. With regard to the last, it is borne out by the evidence of Mr. Fryer, on the Court Martial. This officer being asked, 'What did you suppose to be Mr. Christian's meaning, when he said, ' he had been in hell for a fortnight; Captain Bligh had brought all this upon himself?'—answered—' He referred to the frequent quarrels they had, and the abuse he had received from Mr. Bligh.' The Court, 'Had there been any very recent quarrel?' Mr. Fryer, 'The day before the Mutiny, Mr. Bligh had challenged Mr. Christian, and all the young Gentlemen, and people, with stealing his cocoa-nuts." But not a word about that charge is mentioned either in Mr. Bligh's daily Journal, or in his published " Narrative :" He prefers (as we have seen) to assert, in the latter, that there were no " grievances, either real, or imaginary," on the part of the officers, or men; that with "Mr. Christian, in particular, he was on the most friendly terms;"! that the other was to have " dined with him on that very day; and had excused himself from supping with him, the night before, on *pretence* of being unwell; for which the other *felt concerned.*"!

As additional evidence of Bligh's great "*friendliness*" towards the people of the *Bounty*, and of the *concord* which he afterwards pretended reigned on board, until the breaking out of the Mutiny! the following extracts from his Journal—each of which is suppressed in his " Narrative "—may be cited. The corporal and two seamen, previously alluded to, having deserted at Matavai Bay, on 5th Jan. (or about fifteen weeks before the Mutiny), the Commander made this entry in that Journal—" Had the mate of the watch been awake, no trouble of this kind would have happened. I have therefore disrated and turned him before the mast. Such neglectful and worthless petty officers never were, I believe, in a ship, as are in this: No orders are obeyed by them for a few hours together; and their conduct in general is so bad that no confidence, or trust, can be reposed in them: In short they have driven me to everything but corporal punishment, and that must follow, if they do not improve": (Nor was that " corporal punishment," or something closely approaching to it, long delayed : for Morrison tells us that, on the very day of that entry, Midshipman Hayward was put in irons, and confined to the 23rd of March,—seven weeks!) In the interval (17th Jan.), some of the vessel's sails being found very much mildewed, and rotten, Bligh writes in the same Journal: "If I had any officers to supersede the Master (Mr. Fryer), and boatswain, or I was capable of doing without them, and dealing with

them as common seamen, they should no longer occupy their respective stations: Scarcely any neglect of duty can equal the criminality of this." And on the 24th of Jan., after the deserters had been brought back, flogged, and put in irons, Bligh thus moralizes: "As this affair was solely caused by the neglect of the officers who had the watch, I was induced to give them all a lecture on the occasion, and endeavoured to show them that, however exempt they were at present from the like punishment, yet they were equally subject, by the Articles of War, to a condign one."
. . "It is only necessity that makes me have recourse to reprimand, because there are no means here of trying the officers by Court Martial,"—and who are branded "as having no feelings of honour, or sense of shame." . . . In a subsequent entry (under date 7th March), Mr. Bligh asserts, he has "such a neglectful set about him, that he believes nothing but condign punishment can alter their conduct;" and he attributes falsehood, and want of decency, to his officers.

Is it then to be wondered at, that when Christian, whom, chiefly, he had so grossly outraged, rose against him, Mr. Bligh received such little assistance either from the other officers, or from the seamen—or, as Sir John Barrow has it, that they "exhibited perfect indifference both to the Captain, and the ship, on the day of the Mutiny, ... when Christian, as fiery and passionate a youth as his Commander could well be in his manhood, and with feelings too acute to bear the foul and opprobrious language constantly addressed to him by the other, was the sole instigator of the Mutiny?"

Sir John expressly adds, that "the Mutiny was *not*, as Bligh in his "Narrative" states it to have been, "the result of a conspiracy; the minutes of the Court Martial show that the whole affair was planned and executed between the hours of 4 and 8 o'clock on the morning of the 28 of April, when Christian had the watch upon deck; that that officer, being unable to bear Bligh's abusive and insulting language, had meditated his own escape from the ship the afternoon before; choosing to trust himself to fate, rather than submit to the constant upbraiding to which he had been subject; but the unfortunate business of the cocoa-nuts drove him to the commission of the rash and felonious act, which ended, as such criminal acts usually do, in his own ruin, and that of a number of others—many of whom were wholly innocent."

And the following, as recorded in Morrison's Journal, is the account of the Mutiny, as given in his hearing by Christian, himself, to the Midshipmen Heywood and Stewart, when they were allowed to come upon deck, after the boat (in which were Bligh and his outcast companions) had been turned adrift. He said, that being much hurt by the treatment he had received from Lieutenant Bligh, he had determined to quit the ship on the preceding evening, and had informed the boatswain, carpenter, and two Midshipmen, (Stewart and Hayward) of his intention to do so, (by setting himself adrift on a raft, and making his way to the island of Tofoa, then in sight); that by them he was supplied with some provisions, nails, beads, and other articles of trade, which he put into a bag furnished him by the last named Gentleman; that he placed this bag in the clew of Robert Tinkler's hammock, where it was discovered by that lad when going to bed at night; but the business was then smothered, and passed off without any further notice; that he had fastened some stays to a stout plank, on which he intended to make his escape; but, finding he could not effect it during the first and middle watches, as the ship had no way through the water, and the people were moving about, he lay down to rest about half-past 3 on the morning of the 28th; that when Mr. Stewart called him to relieve the deck at 4, he had just fallen asleep, and was much out of order; upon observing which, the former strenuously advised him to abandon his purpose of flight; that, so soon as he had taken charge of the deck, he saw Mr. Hayward, the Mate of his watch, lie down on the arm-chest to take a nap; and finding that Mr. Hallet, the other Midshipman, did not make his appearance, *he suddenly formed the resolution of securing the ship* (a temptation prompted by the circumstances of the moment—as instantaneous acts of other men's lives frequently have been, though the uncharitable are pleased to ascribe them to deep-laid designs); that he declared his intention to Matthew Quintall, and Isaac Martin, each of whom had been flogged by Lieutenant Bligh; and they called up Charles Churchill (who had also tasted the cat), and Matthew Thompson, both of whom readily joined in the plot; that Alexander Smith [who afterwards figures in this story as the "John Adams," of Pitcairn Island,] John Williams, and William

McCoy, evinced equal willingness, and went with Churchill to the armorer, of whom they obtained the keys of the arm-chest, under pretence of wanting a musket with which to fire at a shark, then alongside; that finding Mr. Hallet asleep in the main hatchway, they roused and sent him on deck; that Charles Norman, unconscious of their proceedings, had in the meantime awakened Mr. Hayward, and directed his attention to the shark, whose movements the carpenter's mate was watching at the moment he (Mr. Christian), and his confederates, came up the fore-hatchway, after having placed arms in the hands of several persons who were not aware of their design; that Thompson was left in charge of the chest, and served out arms to Birkett and Lamb; and that Christian then proceeded to secure Mr. Bligh, the master-gunner, and botanist.

In corroboration of an important portion, at least, of the above statement of the events immediately preceding the Mutiny, and derived (Morrison tells us) from Mr. Christian himself, almost at the moment of its close, the former proceeds to state, in his Journal, that, "when the latter then related those circumstances, I recollected having seen him fasten some staves to a plank lying on the larboard gangway—as also, having heard the boatswain say to the carpenter, 'It will not do to-night.' I likewise remembered that Mr. Christian had visited the fore-cock-pit several times that evening; though he had very seldom, if ever, frequented the warrant-officers' cabins before." And "if that statement of Christian's be correct" (pursues Sir John Barrow), "and the greater part of it is borne out by evidence on the Court Martial, it removes every doubt of Christian being the sole instigator of the Mutiny, and shows that there were no conspiracy, nor preconcerted measures; but that it was suddenly conceived, by a hotheaded young man, in a state of great excitement of mind, amounting to a temporary aberration of intellect, caused by the frequent abusive and insulting language of his Commanding officer. Waking out of a short half-hour's disturbed sleep, to take command of the deck—finding the two Mates of the watch, Hayward and Hallet, asleep (for which they ought to have been dismissed from the service, instead of being promoted, as they afterwards were)—the opportunity tempting, the ship completely in his power, and a momentary impulse so urging, he darted down the fore-hatchway, got possession of the keys of the arm-chest, and made the hazardous experiment of arming such of the men as he thought he could trust."

In a letter, too, addressed, on 5th April, 1830, by the then Captain Heywood to Captain Beechy, R.N., it is stated, "that Christian informed the boatswain, the carpenter, and Messrs. Hayward and Stewart, of his determination to leave the ship upon a raft, on the night preceding the Mutiny, is certain; . . . . and I had the assurance of Christian himself the very night [22nd Sep., '89] he last spent at Otaheite [after the Mutiny, and on his being there for the second time], that the idea of attempting to take the ship had never entered his distracted mind until the moment he relieved the deck, and found his Mate and Midshipman asleep." Another extract which I shall quote from Morrison's Journal, would prove also, if there were no other evidence, that Christian (having been frustrated in his intention to quit the *Bounty*) was the only person who then conceived the idea of, and planned the Mutiny; and that pity should be mingled with censure in our consideration of it. When Mr. Bligh found he must go into the launch, he begged of Christian to desist, saying, "I'll pawn my honor—I"ll give my word—Mr. Christian, never to think of this, if you'll desist;" and urged consideration for his wife and family. Christian replied, "No, Captain Bligh, if you had any honor, things had not come to this; and if you had any regard for your wife and family, you should have thought on them before, and not behaved so much like a villain." Lieutenant Bligh again attempted to speak, but was ordered to be silent. The boatswain also attempted to pacify Mr. Christian—who replied: "It is too late, I have been in hell for this fortnight past, and am determined to bear it no longer; and you know, Mr. Cole, that I have been used like a dog all the voyage."

Naturally, then, after Mr. Bligh's return to England, at the close of the boat voyage which succeeded the Mutiny (and both before and subsequent to a second expedition, to whose command he was appointed, having a like object as that which had been frustrated by it), the friends of the missing mutineers freely charged him with overbearing behaviour and tyranny to the people of the *Bounty*, and maintained that his own misconduct was the cause of the event. Amongst these, was Christian's brother, Mr.

Edward Christian, a barrister, Cambridge Professor, and legal writer of eminence, who published his charges against Bligh; and though the latter "replied with much calmness," in a quarto pamphlet, the proofs which have been already given of his untruthfulness—with the facts supplied by Morrison's Journal—deprive that reply of all weight—especially as it consisted almost entirely of *affidavits* drawn up by himself, at London, in Aug., 94, for signature by his subordinates in the boat voyage, and of " such only of the *written* orders issued by him, in course of the *Bounty's* voyage, as were connected with the matter in question:" For affidavits so prepared, and sworn to by persons under *his* influence, and who could not be, or were not, cross-examined as to their contents, were of no real value; and from what has been seen of Mr. Bligh's tampering with his own earlier Journal, when he came to publish his " Narrative," it will be obvious that a selection by himself of his own written orders was a very idle and worthless proceeding. And one of his assailants does not hesitate to state, "not only was the 'Narrative' which he published proved to be false, in many material bearings, by evidence before the Court Martial, but every act of his after public life, from his successive command of the *Director*, the *Glatton*, and the *Warrior*, to his disgraceful expulsion from New South Wales, was stamped with an insolence, an inhumanity, and coarseness, which fully illustrated his character." (*a*)

Its blackness is best shown, however, by the following circumstances :—The evidence tending to connect young Heywood with the Mutiny, in any way (he was little over 15 years of age at its date), consisted almost entirely in the fact, that he was one of those left on the *Bounty*, after Mr. Bligh, and his 18 companions, were cast adrift; and the former does not charge him either in the " Narrative " or Journal, with having taken any active part in the transaction: Indeed, he and Stewart had been forcibly detained in the vessel by Churchill, the master-at-arms, as they were preparing to go into the launch. Yet when Heywood's widowed mother, having heard a rumour of the Mutiny, and that her boy was in some manner associated with it, wrote to Mr. Bligh, on his return to England, asking for some particulars, and expressive of her great

---

(*a*) " United Service Journal" for April, 1831.

misery, his reply was, the lad's "baseness was beyond all description; but I hope you will endeavour to prevent the loss of him, heavy as the misfortune is, *from affecting you too severely!* I imagine he is, with the *rest* of the mutineers, returned to Otaheite." And to Colonel Howell (the boy's uncle, who had also written to Bligh), the utterly unfounded accusation of Heywood's "ingratitude," and "baseness," was repeated—coupled with the savage, as well as hypocritical intimation, "it would give me great pleasure to hear *that his friends can bear the loss of him without much concern!!*" (*b*)

We shall now deal with an occasion on which Bligh's behaviour was as commendable, as it had been infamous up to the time of the Mutiny.

(*b*) In noble contrast to these ruffianisms of Mr. Bligh, was young Heywood's observation on hearing of them:—"I forgive him his cruelty; may God do the same." And in the first letter (of Nov., '91), the lad was able to send his mother, after his surrender, he declares—"I never, to my knowledge, while under Mr. Bligh's command, behaved myself in any manner unbecoming the station I occupied; nor so much as entertained a thought derogatory to his honor."

CHAPTER II.—Bligh's Boat Voyage.

April,—Oct., 1789: Intrepid voyage, sufferings, and endurance of Commander Bligh, and 18 other "outcasts," in launch of the *Bounty*, from Tofoa to Timor—Passage through, and touching at islands within, the Great Barrier reef, on the North-east coast of Australia, and in Torres' Strait (the Isle Direction, Restoration Island, and Sunday Island, Keys, or Lagoon Islands, Turtle Island, Bay of Islands, and Wednesday Island)—The supplies they yielded, the rest they gave, or troubles they brought—with glimpses of the mainland; its features and natives. In the open sea, once again! events by the way; arrival at Timor; and reception there—England reached; Bligh performs on his own trumpet; the honors paid him; and a sketch of his subsequent life.

AS we have seen, on the morning of the 28th April, '89, Lieutenant Bligh, Mr. Fryer (the Master), the Acting Surgeon, botanist, gunner, boatswain, carpenter, a Master's-mate, two Midshipmen (Messrs. Hayward and Hallet), and nine other subordinate officers and men, found themselves expelled from the *Bounty* in the immediate neighbourhood of Tofoa, and cast adrift in the launch—which was only 23 feet in length, 6 feet 9 inches in breadth, and 2 feet 9 inches in depth; and whose means of navigation, and stock of provisions, consisted of a quadrant, compass and sails, &c., 150 ℔s. of bread, 16 pieces of pork (each weighing 2 ℔s.), 6 quarts of rum, 6 bottles of wine, with 28 gallons of water (or not more than a full ration for 5 days, had there been no necessity for husbanding their stock), and 4 empty barrecoes. With these slender supplies, and its human freight, the boat was so heavily laden as to be scarcely 7 inches above the wave—

> "And just enough of water and of bread
> To keep, some days, the dying from the dead:
> Some cordage, canvas, sails, and lines, and twine,
> But treasures all to outcasts on the brine,
> Were added, after, to the earnest prayer
> Of those who saw no hope save sea and air;
> And last, that trembling vassal of the Pole,
> The feeling compass, Navigation's soul."

In the evening, the party reached Tofoa, and landed next morning; had great difficulty in procuring any water, and found nothing else to alleviate their distress, except a few cocoa nuts and plantains; subsisted on very scanty rations, met with some of the natives, and observed several neat plantations; remained on the island until the evening of 2nd May, when they were attacked by the natives with a shower of big stones, as they were in the act of embarking; had the quarter-master killed, were followed in canoes, and almost disabled by similar missiles (having no fire arms with which to defend themselves), until Mr. Bligh "adopted the expedient of throwing overboard some clothes, which the assailants stopped to pick up, gave over the attack, and returned to the shore—leaving the others to reflect on their unhappy condition."

It had been his intention, at first, to make for Tonga Taboo (the principal of the Friendly Islands), and seek assistance from its King, in equipping the boat, and procuring a sufficient supply of water, and provisions, to enable his party to reach the East Indies; but the treatment just experienced from the natives of Tofoa satisfied him there was little use in persevering in that intention. Even supposing the lives of the party would not be in danger, if they made the other island, the launch, and everything they had, would, most probably, be taken from them, and thus all prospect be precluded of their being able to return to their native country: Whilst, therefore, Mr. Bligh was considering what had best be done, as the boat (after getting away from the natives of Tofoa) sailed along its western side, he " was solicited by all hands to take them towards home; " and when he told them that no hope of relief remained (except they might find some sustenance on the northern coast of New Holland), till they came to Timor (a distance of full 1200 leagues), where there was a Dutch settlement, (but in what part of that island he knew not), they all desired to proceed thither, and agreed to live on one ounce of bread, and a quarter of a pint of water, per day. Accordingly, after examining their stock of provisions (now somewhat reduced from the original quantity), and recommending his people in the most solemn manner, not to depart from their promise, Mr. Bligh assented; and, on the evening of the 2nd May they bore away across a sea, where the navigation was but little known, in a small boat, deeply-laden with 19 men. *(a)*

I shall not harrow the reader with many details of the terrible voyage that ensued from Tofoa to the Great Barrier reef, and thence to Timor. But I may state, as showing its direction, and as some evidence of the difficulties, and almost unbearable hardships, that characterised it, as well as of the indomitable resolution of its Conductor (who brought it to a successful issue, notwithstanding), that its course at first lay W.N.W. from Tofoa, by some islands that were named "Bligh's," but are supposed to belong to the Fiji group; then N. of other islands, situate beyond the New Hebrides, and which I take to have been "Banks' Islands;" thence N.W. till (passing through the Great Barrier reef) these toilers of the sea found a little rest on islets close to, ran parallel with, and noted, other parts of, the north-eastern coasts of New Holland, and south-eastern shores of Torres Strait; landed on and named some islands there; pushed westward still; and, despite the greatest sufferings from tempest, famine, and thirst, in little under six weeks from their departure from Tofoa, they reached Timor—having thus traversed about 3,600 miles of ocean, in a crowded launch, with only a few days supply of food, even on starvation scale, and scarcely a drop of water remaining to the good, on their arrival there!

During the whole continuance of this protracted, arduous struggle, the "castaways" had to sit up, and lie stretched by turns, in the boat, as best they might—so cramped were they for want of space—though they had thrown away every rag of dress, and other article, they could possibly spare—while for the greater portion of the same period, or until they gained a smooth sea within the Barrier reef, they were exposed to the fury of many a storm; which forced them to take the course of the sea, run right before it, and watch their steering with the utmost care, as the least error in the helm would in a moment have been their destruction: and the clothes they had retained were wet with deluges from the

---

(a) Bligh had sailed from England within 7 months from the departure of the "First Occupation Fleet" for Botany Bay, and he knew nothing of the fate—success or failure—of that expedition. It was therefore (most probably), that he did not make for the southern coast of New Holland, but stood for the northern, of which something *was* known.

sky above, or the waves about, pouring upon, or breaking over the boat; they had 16 days of heavy and almost continuous rain; they were numbed with cold, as well, and could rarely procure warmth except by stripping, dipping their clothes in the sea (when saturated with rain), and then wringing them as dry as could be (*b*). They were worn out with bailing, at the same time; and at famine point (racked with gnawing hunger), almost from first to last; a morsel of biscuit, or of yam, bread-fruit, or cocoanut, a bullet's weight of pork, occasionally, or a scrap of the body and entrails, or a few drops of the blood, of a captured bird, with a teaspoonful of rum, their greatest allowance, till they reached the Australian shores; dreading to land on any of the islands they saw eastward of the reef (though some of them appeared to be inhabited and fertile), lest they should be destroyed by the natives; and chased by canoes on one occasion; now clamouring for the precious and daily diminishing store of food (which Bligh carefully guarded), that they might eat of it, and die; then, mournfully abandoning themselves to the meagre dole allowed by him, and upon their rigid adherence to which their preservation depended. Scarcity of fresh water at other times, and the dread of death from thirst, completed the measure of their trials.

Accordingly, the 10th day of the voyage showed a miserable set of beings, full of wants, and without anything to relieve them; some complained of prolonged constipation, and great pain in the bowels, and every one had almost lost the use of his limbs. . .
. . At the dawn of the 18th day, certain of them seemed half dead, their appearances were horrible; and their Commander could look no way without catching the eye of some one in distress. Extreme hunger was now too evident;. but none of them suffered from thirst, nor had anyone much inclination to drink; the desire that might otherwise have existed in that respect being, perhaps, satisfied through the skin. The sleep they each got was, at that time, in the midst of falling water; and they awoke with severe cramps and pains in their bodies, . . . All the afternoon they were so covered with rain and salt water, that they could scarcely see; they suffered extreme cold, and everyone dreaded the approach

---

(*b*) This process is said to have made them feel "more as if they had enjoyed a change of dry clothes than could well be imagined," and is recommended to others in a similar situation.

of night. Sleep, though they longed for it, afforded no comfort; and Bligh almost lived without it. . . . The night of the 21st day exceeded in misery that of any preceding it; the sea flew over them with great fury, and kept them bailing "in horror and anxiety. . . . . At daybreak, it was feared that another such night would put an end to the lives of several, who seemed no longer able to support their sufferings." But after this, the weather moderated; the sun broke through; bringing with it more cheerful countenances; and, "for the first time for 15 days, comfort was experienced from its warmth." It was thought, at the same time, that the cloudy and wet weather, to which they had been previously exposed, was a blessing rather than a calamity; as continued heat "would have caused them to die of thirst, and a spirit of resignation to God's will generally pervaded them." Nor was the bailing, however laborious, to be reckoned an evil—as it gave them exercise.

At one in the morning of 28th May (or 26th day of the struggle), the helmsman heard the sound of breakers; and Mr. Bligh no sooner "lifted up his head" than he saw them close under his lee, not more than a quarter of a mile distant; he immediately hauled on a wind to the N.N.E., and in ten minutes' time could neither see nor hear them. But now, being in lat. 13 S., and long. 144 W., the finding of a passage through the Barrier, and making for the coast of New Holland, were deemed desirable; the idea of getting into smooth water, and finding refreshments also, kept the peoples' spirits up; and, early next day, bearing away again, they soon saw the reef—at some 23 miles north of where the breakers were discovered the previous night. Still, the sea broke furiously over every part; and the boat had no sooner got near to it than the wind came at E., so that she could only lie along the line of the breakers; within which the waters rested so smooth that every person anticipated the satisfaction he would feel so soon as he could get within: But it was now perceived they were embayed; for they could not lie clear with the sails, the wind having backed against them; and the sea set in so heavily towards the reef, that their situation was become unsafe; while they could effect but little with their oars; having scarce strength to wield them; and it was beginning to be feared they would be obliged to attempt pushing over it; when a break in the reef, about a mile from them, was happily discovered; and at the same time an island of a moderate height within it, nearly in the same direction, bearing W. ½ N., presented itself; and was accordingly named the "Isle Direction." The boat entered the passage, with a strong stream running to the northward; it was about a quarter of a mile broad, with every appearance of depth; and they were soon within the reef in tranquil water.

The channel through which Bligh thus passed is situate in 12° 51' South latitude, or not far from " Providential Channel," through which Captain Cook had edged his way in the *Endeavor*, when re-entering smooth water from the outer sea, on the 16th Aug., '70—is nearly opposite to Cape Direction, on the north-eastern coast of Queensland—and is now known as *his* (Bligh's) " passage." When happily within the reef, he bore away N.W. (or as that coast trends); and, having promised to land on the first convenient spot he could find, all the past hardships of the enterprise seemed already to be forgotten; thanks were rendered to God for His gracious protection; and, "with much content, the party took their miserable allowance of the 25th part of a pound of bread, and a quarter of a pint of water per diem."

As they advanced within the reef, the main coast began to show itself very distinctly in a variety of high and low land; some parts of which were covered with wood; and, having found a suitable bay and sandy point, on an island (about a league in circuit), which lay a quarter of a mile from a projecting part of that main, the weary and almost exhausted voyagers landed there; stretched their limbs for the first time for six-and-twenty days; rested for two; during which they discovered and feasted upon oysters, berries, and fresh water procured by digging, and enjoyed refreshing sleep. One of those happy days being the anniversary of the restoration of Charles II., and the name not being inapplicable to their present situation—for they were here restored to fresh life and strength—the haven was called "Restoration Island." Here they also found some old native fire-places, a couple of ill-constructed huts (which had only one side loosely covered), and a pointed stick, three feet long, with a slit in the end of it, " to fling stones with—the same as the natives of Van Diemen's Land use ! " [much more probably to throw spears from.] The track of a kangaroo was also seen; " but whether these animals swim over from the main land, or are brought here by the natives to breed!" Mr. Bligh (who seems to have thought that the Australian aboriginal cultivated kangaroo stock-farming), " could not determine;" the latter, however, he considered " not improbable, as the marsupial might be taken with less difficulty in a confined space like this, than on the continent." He tried, too, some fern roots, as a substitute for bread; but in this he acknowledged himself " mistaken "; though he deemed these roots " very serviceable, in their natural state, to allay thirst," and accordingly had a quantity of them collected to take into the boat. Many pieces of cocoa-nut shells and husks were strewn about the shore; having been carried thither, most likely, from the New Hebrides, or some isle in Torres Strait; for there were no cocoa-nut trees seen on Restoration Island, or on the main. But on the nearest portion of the latter were several sandy bays, which at low water became an extensive flat; and the country had rather a barren appearance, except in a few places where it was covered with wood; a remarkable range of rocks lay a few miles to the S.W.; a high-peaked hill seemed to terminate the coast towards the sea, with islands to the southward; a tall " Fair Cape " showed the direction of the coast to the N.W., about seven leagues distant; and two small isles lay three or four leagues to the northward of Restoration Island.

Here the last of the pork (which had suffered from the pillage of some inconsiderate person) was consumed; then, a small quantity of oysters, and the fern roots, having been taken on board, and the water vessels re-filled, the boat put to sea again, after prayer (at which every one, now visibly improved in condition, was directed to attend), and the re-placing (with a large staple found in her) of one of the rudder gudgeons lost on the shore—which could not have been done had that loss occurred at sea. But as the party were embarking, 20 natives appeared, running and hallooing to them, on the opposite shore; they were each armed with a spear or lance, and short weapon [or throwing stick], which they carried in their left hands; and they made signs to the Englishmen to come to them: On the tops of the hills, the heads of many more aboriginals were perceived; whether these were the wives and children of those on the shore, or others waiting for the expected landing from the island, and hoping to prevent it, Mr. Bligh could not say; but, being himself " so discovered to be upon the coast, he thought it wise to make the best of his way, for fear of being pursued by canoes." He accordingly did so, 30th May—passing these people as near as he could with safety; and observing that they were naked, apparently black, "and their hair, or wool, bristly and short."

Fair Cape, with the neighbouring coast (high and woody), was soon passed, and the direction of the onward shores (leading W.N.W.) followed as far as practicable; but at day break on the 31st, Bligh " was exceedingly surprised to find the appearance of the country entirely changed, as if, in the course of the preceding night, he and his comrades had been transferred to another part of the world; for they had now a low sandy coast in view, with very little verdure, or anything to indicate that it was at all habitable to a human being, except a few patches of small trees or brushwood." Many small islands were in sight to the N.E., about six miles off. The channel was taken between the nearest island and the main land, which were about a mile apart; leaving all the islands on the starboard side. Some of these are described as "very pretty spots, covered with wood, and well situated for fishing"; large shoals of fish were about; but none could be caught. In passing this strait, seven other "Indians" were seen, running towards the boat, shouting, and making signs for its people to land; some waved green branches or bushes as a token of friendship; though other gestures were less friendly. A little further on, was observed a large gathering of natives, who also approached, but not within 200 yards; they were armed in the same manner, and were of like appearance, as those noticed from Restoration Island.

Soon afterwards, Mr. Bligh landed upon a rocky island, of good height, not far distant, and sent out parties to look for supplies. His account of the incident that followed is somewhat comic:—Fatigue and weakness so far got the better of their sense of duty, that some of those despatched expressed their discontent at having worked harder than their companions, and declared they would rather be without their dinner than go in search of it; one person in particular (Purcell, the carpenter) went so far as to tell the Commander, "with a mutinous look, that he was as good a man as himself." It was not possible for the former to judge where this might have an end, if not stopped in time; therefore, to prevent such disputes in future, he determined, either, " to preserve his command, or die in the attempt!" and, seizing a cutlass, ordered the fellow to take hold of another, and defend himself; on which the mutineer called out, that "the Captain was going to kill him, and immediately made concessions." Some fine oysters, and clams, a small dog-fish, and a full supply of rain-water (got from the rocks), were then procured on this island. There was also observed, in a sandy bay, an old canoe, about 33 feet long, lying bottom upwards, and half buried in the beach. It was made of three pieces; the bottom entire, to which the sides were sewed in the ordinary way; and it had a sharp projecting prow, rudely carved, in resemblance to the head of a fish; the extreme breadth was about three feet, and it was thought capable of carrying 20 men. The island was named "Sunday Island."

Upon the 1st June, the party reached, and landed upon, one of four small "keys," or sandy spits, about 4 leagues from the coast, and surrounded by a reef of rocks mostly connected by sand banks; the whole forming a lagoon island, into which the tide flowed. Recent tracks of turtle were discovered here; "and innumerable birds, of the noddy kind," made it their resting place. But a few clams, and beans, the backs of two turtles, twelve noddies, and the remains of an ancient wigwam, were all that could be got to gratify either the palate, or the eye; and many of the people, having eaten the beans raw, suffered considerably; while Nelson, the gardener, was only saved from the effects of over exposure to the sun by the administering of small quantities of the wine, which had been carefully saved until now. A common danger might also have arisen (by betraying the Englishmen's position, had any natives been in the neighbourhood), from the sudden blazing up of the whole island (occasioned by a seaman who, not content with sharing a fire that had been lighted for all, insisted on having one for himself, and allowed it to spread). And, had it not been for the obstinacy of a bird-seeker, who separated from the others, and disturbed the noddies, a much greater number than those taken would have been procured—a "defeating of his plans which so much provoked the Commander that he gave this offender a good beating"—a chastisement which was the more deserved, if it be true (as also stated), that the culprit afterwards acknowledged "he had eaten nine birds raw, after separating from his companions!" The noddies obtained "were half-dressed, that they might keep the better;" and some of the clams were cut up in slices to dry. These constituted the whole of the supply furnished by this island-lagoon; and Bligh seems to have thought that he made a sufficient return to the lords of the soil, by " tying up to a tree a few gilt buttons, and some pieces of iron, for any of the natives that might come after him." A night's rest, that most of the party enjoyed before quitting the place, and which brightened them up a good deal, was perhaps the greatest advantage it afforded.

By dawn of the 2nd, the launch was under way again; soon experienced a rough sea, which (not having been befòre met with since she came within the reef,) was supposed to be occasioned by an open channel to the ocean beyond; and fell in with two other sets of "keys"—some of the most northern of them producing small trees, and brush-wood. These formed a pleasing contrast with the mainland previously passed, which was " full of sand-hills." The country continued hilly, and the northernmost land appeared like downs sloping towards the sea. Nearly abreast, was a flat-topped hill, which, on account of its shape, was called " Pudding-pan Hill;" a little to the northward were two other hills, that were named the " Paps;" and here was a small tract of country without sand, the eastern part of which forms a Cape.

As the boat stood on, fresh "keys" were approached, and left behind; so was a large and fair inlet, into which (Bligh imagined) there was a safe and commodious entrance; it lies in lat. 11° S., and was probably the mouth of " Escape River;" and about three leagues to the northward of this is an island, at which he arrived about sunset, and under a sandy point of which shelter for the night was taken. " This being rather a wild situation, it was thought best to sleep in the boat;" still, a party was sent to see if anything could be got; but they returned without success, having only observed a great number of turtle bones, and shells, in spots where the natives had been feasting—and their last visit seemed to be recent. The *rendezvous* was named " Turtle Island." Abreast of it, the coast had the appearance of a sandy desert; though it improved about three leagues further to the northward, where " it terminated in a point near to which are many small islands; between these Bligh sailed, finding no bottom at 12 fathoms; and having a high mountainous island with a flat top, and four rocks to the S.E. of it, that he called the "Brothers," on his starboard. Soon afterwards, an extensive opening appeared in the mainland, in which were a number of high islands, and was therefore named the "Bay of Islands." He continued to steer to the N.W.; and several islands and "keys" were in sight to the northward; the most northerly island was mountainous, having on it a very high round hill; and a smaller one was remarkable for a single peaked hill.

It is difficult to follow this portion of the voyage, either on Bligh's chart, or from the verbal description of it in his "Narrative;" but it may be taken (though there is no express mention of the circumstance), that the launch had now rounded Cape York (probably the "point" that was observed), and had passed a good way up Torres Strait; for he "had little doubt that the 'opening' he had named the 'Bay of Islands,' was the 'Endeavor Strait' of Cook, and that his track was to the northward of Prince of Wales Isles"—both of which lie N.W. of that Cape, and well within Torres Strait. It is added, that the coast to the northward and westward of the Bay of Islands is high and woody, and has a broken appearance, with many islands close to it; "among which there are some fine bays and convenient places for shipping." The northernmost of these islands he called "Wednesday Island." Reference is then made to a large reef met with to the N.W. of that island; and other particulars are given of the onward course of the voyage, including an allusion to some large sand banks that run off from the coast, and were accordingly styled "Shoal Cape" —a projecting point, most probably either of "Hammond Island" or "Thursday Island"—and to a small island where tribes of that bird resort, whence it was called "Booby Island"—a term that Captain Cook had previously attached to it, and for the same reason. It is recorded lastly—"Here terminated the rocks and shoals of the N. part of New Holland; for, except Booby Island, no land was seen to the westward of S., after three o'clock of the afternoon of the 3rd June;" and Bligh could not, with certainty, reconcile the situation of some parts of the coast he had seen to Cook's survey from the *Endeavor*, which was ascribed to the various forms in which land appears when observed from the different heights of a ship and a boat.

On the evening of the 3rd of June, the "outcasts" once more launched into the open ocean; and, miserable as their situation still was, and deplorable objects as they still were, the Commander was secretly surprised to see that the circumstances did not appear to affect anyone so strongly as himself; on the contrary, it seemed as if they had embarked on a voyage to Timor, in a vessel sufficiently calculated for safety and convenience; and to that cause (he thought) their preservation was chiefly to be attributed. The relief experienced from the fatigue of being constantly in the boat, the enjoyment of good rest at night, and the oysters, clams, birds, and water (though small in quantity), which they had procured since they gained the coast of New Holland, had inspired new hopes, and contributed to preserve their lives. He adds, that "for his own part, incredible as it may appear, he neither felt extreme hunger nor thirst: His allowance contented him, knowing he could have no more."

As the continued progress of the boat, day by day, left the Australian coast further to the eastward, I need not dwell upon its incidents, except to mention that a morsel of bread, and half a mouthful of water, were still the usual rations; that a booby was caught upon the 5th, the blood divided amongst three of the men who were the weakest, and the flesh reserved for dinner next day; that on the 7th, the sea was very high, and kept breaking over the boat; the Acting Surgeon and an old seaman giving way very fast, and could only be assisted by a tea-spoonful of wine; and that on the 9th, a small dolphin was taken, which, on being broken into bits, gave the principal sustenance for a couple of days. So that, on the morning of the 10th, after a very comfortless night, there was a marked alteration for the worse in many of the people, which gave Bligh great apprehension. An extreme weakness, swelled legs, hollow and ghastly countenances, a more than common inclination to sleep, "with an apparent debility of understanding," seemed the melancholy presages of approaching death; the Surgeon and the ancient mariner being in the saddest plight of all: But on the next day, the meridian of the eastern part of Timor had been passed, "which suffused universal joy and satisfaction;" and at dawn of the 12th, "with an excess of delight," they sighted the eastern shores of that island; though it then appeared scarcely credible to themselves that, in an open boat, and so poorly provided, they should have been able to reach it in 41 days from leaving Tofoa; having, in that period, run, by log, 3,618 miles; and that, notwithstanding their extreme distress, no one should have perished. Then, standing S.W. they reached Coupang, the capital of the Dutch settlement, on the 15th, where they landed " among a crowd of Indians;" and to come on shore was as much as some of the boat's company could do, being scarcely able to walk: But they were received with the utmost kindness, treated with the greatest care, and everything done that possibly could be done to restore them to strength and health, by William Adrian Van Este, the Governor of the settlement (though himself in a dying state), by Timotheus Wanjon, his son-in-law, and the next in command, and by Captain Spikeman, an Englishman who resided at Coupang.

The abilities of a painter (as has been well observed) could scarcely have been taxed to more advantage than in delineating the two groups of figures that, at the time of the landing, presented themselves to each other: And an indifferent spectator would have been at a loss which to wonder at the more—the eyes of famine sparkling at immediate relief, in the preserved; or the consternation of their preservers at the sight of so many spectres— whose death-like features, if the cause had been unknown, would rather have excited terror than pity; their bodies nothing more than skin and bones; their limbs full of sores; and rags their only clothing. In such condition, with tears of joy and gratitude flowing from the cheeks of their visitors, the inhabitants of Timor beheld them with a mixture of dread, surprise, and commiseration.

But in a short time, the party, with the exception of Nelson, the gardener, who died at Coupang, were sufficiently recruited to admit of their leaving this friendly settlement; which they did in a small vessel, purchased by Mr. Bligh for the purpose, that was named his Majesty's schooner " *Resource*," and " took in tow the launch which had so much contributed to their preservation:" They reached Batavia on 1st Oct., '89. There the launch (which he felt a natural reluctance to part with, and would have taken to England if possible), was disposed of; so was the schooner—and two seamen (Lenkletter and Hall), with Mr. Elphinstone, Master's Mate, died; " the hardships they had experienced having rendered them unequal to cope with the unhealthy climate of Batavia." Soon afterwards, Mr. Bligh and his people (save the Acting-Surgeon, who remained), sailed for England, in two detachments. Most of them arrived in safety— (the Commander touching at the Cape of Good Hope, whence "the gallant, good Riou" had taken departure a few days previously, in H.M.S. *Guardian,* bound for Sydney—which he never reached; his vessel having been disabled by the way, and himself reserved for another "deck," that was alike his death-scene "and field of fame." But the butcher of the *Bounty* died on the homeward passage; and the Surgeon had not been heard of when Bligh's "Narrative" closed. Thus, of the 19 persons who were forced by the mutineers into the launch, "it pleased God" (as he writes), "that 12 should surmount the difficulties and dangers of the voyage, and live to revisit their native country."

On his arrival in England (March, '90), Mr. Bligh published his account of that portion, and that portion only, of the voyage of the *Bounty* which related to the Mutiny, "for the purpose" (as he states) "of communicating *early information* concerning an event which had attracted the public attention!"—alleging, at the same time, "it was his intention that the *preceding* part of the voyage should be presented in a *separate* account"—which it never was. Nor did it appear in any form, until the eve of the trial by Court Martial of the 10 "mutineers," whom Captain Edwards brought to England, as afterwards related; when it was published *together* with another edition or copy of the Mutiny-part of his "Narrative"—that was thus *re*-published. And in each publication, Mr. Bligh made the most of his own achievements, tenderness, and sufferings; and he villified the mutineers, or alleged mutineers, to the utmost of his power, as ungrateful wretches, and cowardly conspirators: He made himself almost a paragon of perfection; and they were considerably blacker than devils. His efforts told. "Secure and hang the scoundrels!" was the shout that ran through England; and their innocent, badly used victim was made a Commander, and then (without any further service) a Post Captain, in the Navy. His own account of the Mutiny depicted him as a martyr, whose kindness and forbearance had met with a base return from a worthless ship's company. For the time being he was a hero; and little cared for the anguish endured by the families of the absent officers, and men, whom he aspersed, and many of whom (as he knew) had taken no real part in the Mutiny.

Floating, then, on the tide of popular favor which his "Narrative" had evoked, he was appointed, in the summer of '91, to H.M.S. *Providence* (with which the armed tender, *Assistant*, was also fitted out—to protect his person, perhaps, in the event of a second Mutiny on board the vessel he was immediately to command); and he was instructed to accomplish the baffled object for which the *Bounty* had been despatched, three years and a-half previously. Having succeeded in that mission, he returned to England in August, '93; when he obtained a gold medal from the Society of Arts, in acknowledgment of the services he had thus rendered. *(a)* Afterwards (that the story of his chequered career may be here completed), he distinguished himself by intrepid mediation at the Mutiny of the Nore, and at the battles of Cape St. Vincent, Camperdown, and Copenhagen (in 1797 and 1801), by coolness and daring—receiving the special thanks of Lord Nelson at the close of the last named; was appointed by the Crown Governor General of New South Wales in 1805; arrived there in Aug., 1806; was deposed and placed under arrest, in Jan., 1808, by Military Officers serving under him, for arbitrary, oppressive, and illegal conduct—which was followed by great duplicity, up to his departure for England—was made, subsequently, a Vice-Admiral of the Blue; and died peacefully in London, Dec., 1817: He was therefore both deserving and undeserving, fortunate and unfortunate, amongst men; as brave as he was unscrupulous; as daring as he was false; and could be as calm and collected in danger, as he was ferocious and tyrannical in uncontrolled authority.

Let us now return to the mutineers, and learn what became of them.

(*a*) He conveyed the bread-fruit to the West Indies (as his instructions were); leaving choice plants at St. Vincent, Jamaica, &c. But the importation has not been found to fully answer the expectation that had been reasonably entertained in its favor. The latitude of several of the West Indian Islands is nearly the same as that of Otaheite; but there would appear to be some difference in the situation in other respects, or in the nature of the soil, that prevents the bread-fruit plant thriving in the former so well as in the latter (Mutiny of the *Bounty*, p. 47).

CHAPTER III.—The Mutineers; and their Wanderings

April, 1789—March, 1791: Mr. Christian, and the 24 mutineers who remained in the *Bounty*, proceed to Isle Toubouai—Repelled from landing—Visit Otaheite, and procure live stock—All return to Toubouai, accompanied by Otaheitans, and form a settlement—Occurrences at Toubouai; occasioning another visit to Otaheite; where mutineers separate; Mr. Stewart, Mr. Heywood, with 14 others, remaining there; and Mr. Christian, with Mr. Young, the remaining 7, and some Otaheitans, &c., put to sea again, in *Bounty*—Fate of 2, and occupations of the rest, of former band, during residence at Otaheite; till the *Pandora* appears—and her mission.

WHEN Lieutenant Bligh, and his companions in the launch, had been turned adrift from the *Bounty*, on the 28th April, '89, the command of that vessel naturally devolved upon Mr. Christian, as having been next in rank (amongst the mutineers) to that outcast officer, and as originator and leader of the Mutiny itself. But as the launch bore away, and he stood gazing at it, with folded arms, and clouded brow, passion cooled, resentment waned, and his true position was brought home to his mind. The rash act had reduced him to a level with the lowest of his four and twenty comrades, and doomed him to a life of exile from civilized society. Some secluded isle must now be his abode and home, or a felon's death, the certain result of capture. "Alas for him that there had not been some friend at hand, on the dawn of that fatal day, to have pointed out the sure consequences of such a crime both to himself and others; the wide-spread anguish to so many families; the misery and disgrace to his own; and thus have saved him from the abyss of ruin into which he had so recklessly plunged, and in which all concerned in the Mutiny were more or less involved." *(a)* Let us remember, at the same time (in common justice), how long and how grossly he had been outraged by Bligh; and that the temptation to which he at last yielded was both immediate and great.

(a) "The Mutineers of the *Bounty*, and their descendants in Pitcairn and Norfolk Islands," by Lady Belcher, London, 1870.—A book of which I have largely availed myself, and that is full of interesting matter.

But the die was cast; what had been done was irrevocable; and it was essential for the weal of all who now stood with him on the *Bounty's* deck, that Christian should take the direction of affairs, and maintain discipline; and he did so. Mr. Bligh represents, that when the launch was cut adrift, there went up a cry from the ship of "Hurrah for Otaheite!" but no one save himself seems to have heard anything of the kind; and it is stated, on the other hand, that his own vows of vengeance, as he left the ship, reached the ears of those on board; and many were his indiscriminate accusations involving the innocent and the guilty. *(b)* At any rate, so far from proceeding to Otaheite, or seeking to do so, Christian directed the *Bounty* to be steered for the small island of Toubouai, or Toobonai, which is about four days sail to the south-westward of (or about 450 miles distant from) Otaheite, and which Captain Cook had seen in Aug., 1777. It lies in 20° 13' S. lat., and 149° 35' W. long.; it is one of the "Society" Group; and the mutineers arrived off it on the 28th May, 1789. It appeared a very fertile, and populous island, wooded almost to the water's edge, and surrounded by coral reefs. Amongst these, there was but one opening through which a vessel might be warped, and moored close to the shore. But the natives of the place assembled in great numbers, armed with clubs and spears, as the *Bounty* approached, and "vehemently blew their conch shells." Their aspect was so savage, and they seemed so determined to oppose a landing, that Christian thought it better, for the time being, to defer a project he had previously formed of establishing a settlement there; and he gave orders to change the vessel's course to Otaheite—where he could collect live stock to transport to Toubouai, when he returned thither (as he meant to do speedily), in the hope of then meeting with less opposition from its people. He also directed that all the young bread-fruit trees, with which the *Bounty* was laden, should be thrown overboard, (observing most probably that Toubouai possessed similar plants). The clothes left by the officers and men who accompanied Bligh in the launch, with the curiosities that had been gathered, and the articles of iron, and other objects of barter, that remained in the ship, he caused to be divided by lot among his people, to make what use of they

---

(b) Ibid.

pleased; and to the last he commanded their respect by his consideration and justice.

The *Bounty* reached Matavai Bay on the 6th June, '89, and the Otaheitans soon flocked on board—delighted to see their old friends, particularly Christian, to whom they were as partial as they had been to Captain Cook; while we are told, that Lieutenant Bligh was held by them in contempt, and detestation, on account of the meanness he had evinced in his trading, and other dealings with them. *(c)* Yet the quick return of the ship, with a portion only of her former inmates, and none of the bread-fruit plants, was a matter of much surprise; for the natives knew that she could not have been to England, and come back again, as they had previously heard of its great distance: Christian therefore stooped to avail himself of one of Bligh's artifices (in representing that he was the son of Captain Cook), by replying to their inquiries on the subject, that the *Bounty* had met Cook at sea; that *he* had taken the missing people and cargo, to assist in forming a settlement on an island he had just discovered (called Whytootakee); and that he had sent the vessel back to Matavai, in charge of Christian, to procure live stock and other provisions. The Otaheitans gave full credit to the story, and were willing to barter with Christian to any extent; as he had always treated them with kindness, and given full value for what he required of them.

Accordingly, by the 16th June, numerous hogs, goats, and fowls, some dogs and cats—even the bull and one of the cows which Captain Cook had left at Matavai during his third voyage, and upon which the natives put no value—were collected, and placed at Christian's disposal. *(d)* With these, and a quantity of fruit for present use, he set sail for Toubouai; being accompanied thither by every one of the mutineers who had gone to Otaheite with him, ten days before—(an answer to Bligh's pretence, that the Mutiny had been occasioned by a desire to secure a residence there).(*) But when the *Bounty* had proceeded a considerable

---

(c) Lady Belcher's "Mutineers," &c.

(d) Ibid.

(*) It may be mentioned, at the same time, that Mr. Heywood afterwards stated to Captain Edwards, that while he went away with the others from Otaheite on this occasion, it was impossible for him to separate from Christian, "who would not permit any of the party to leave him at that time, lest, by giving intelligence,

distance from Matavai, it was found that 8 men, 9 women, and 7 boys, belonging to that place, were stowed away in her, in addition to her proper crew. It is said, that most of the former had secreted themselves about the ship, and only made their appearance when she was out at sea; but their being on board could scarcely have happened without the previous knowledge of some at least of the hands; and as they were urgent to remain, and Christian was unwilling to return to Otaheite, he yielded to their entreaties, and permitted them to share the fortunes that might await the party at Toubouai—where they arrived on the 23rd June, after a very rough passage, in which several of the live stock (the bull included) were lost.

On this occasion, the natives of that island evinced a more friendly spirit than on the former visit (though the sudden change in their demeanor seemed unaccountable); they even aided in the long and laborious task of warping the *Bounty* through the narrow opening in the reef; and as the Otaheitans spoke a similar dialect to that of the inhabitants of Toubouai, they were of much general assistance; so that for a time a tolerable understanding prevailed. Landing the surviving animals and stores occupied several days; a spot four miles to the eastward of the opening in the reef was procured for the site of a settlement, a trench dug, a hut erected, and the armament of the *Bounty* placed upon its parapet. It was at this time, if ever, there may have been grounds for the poet's flight :—

> "How pleasant were the songs of Toubouai,
> When summer's sun went down the coral bay;
> When 'let us to the islet's softest glade,
> And hear the warbling birds,'! the damsels said . . . . .
> Or plunge and revel in the rolling surf;
> Then lay our limbs along the tender turf,
> And, wet and shining from the sportive toil,
> Anoint our bodies with the fragrant oil."!

But all this did not take place without some opposition from the male portion of the native race. Indifference arose, and deepened into resistance; for they soon began to dread the white

---

the others might have been discovered [at Toubouai], whenever a ship should arrive." There is a similar statement in a letter, of Nov., '91, from Heywood to his mother. But to reach England, and not to settle at Otaheite, was the object of those who might otherwise have then severed themselves from Christian.

man's presence; collisions—battles between the two parties—
ensued, in one of which Christian, and another Englishman, were
severely wounded, and a number of the natives slain. Frequent
misunderstandings sprung, too, from the trespasses of the live stock,
which were turned adrift on landing, and found their way to the
yam and taro plantations, of which the Toubouaians were careful
cultivators.

A further obstacle to Christian's plans of settlement soon followed. Those of his present associates who had in truth taken no
part, or who had been passive rather than active participators, in
the Mutiny, declared their intention not to pass their lives at
Toubouai. Indeed, Mr. Stewart, Mr. Heywood, and Morrison,
seem to have thought of escaping in the cutter (still attached to
the vessel)—conscious of their innocence of any real share in the
outbreak, and anxious to avail themselves of any possible chance
of vindication. There were mumurings and discontents on the
part of others, arising principally from difficulties with the
islanders,—towards whom Christian would not countenance any
violence, except for self-protection. He had to deal, however,
with several ignorant and reckless seamen (portion of his little
band), who considered that the inhabitants of the island, being
men of colour, had no rights, and that whatever they possessed
might be taken by force, without scruple or recompense. And,
finding at length it would be impossible to maintain the settlement in the disorganized state of affairs then existing, Christian
assembled his comrades, on the 10th Sept., to ascertain their
feelings as to future proceedings. A desire to return to Otaheite,
and there separate, was expressed by some; and though, after much
discussion, the proposal was then overruled; yet, when the question
was re-opened next day, and a show of hands called for, sixteen
declared in its favour, and nine against.

A majority having thus determined upon that step, it was
agreed (writes Morrison) " that those who preferred Otaheite
should have arms, ammunition, and part of everything on board
the *Bounty;* but that the ship was to be left in possession of Christian, and his eight adherents, in a proper condition to go to sea,
after landing the others," and to search for a new place of refuge,
as it was felt that Toubouai was no longer fitted for that purpose;
"and, everything being settled, we began " (Morrison adds) " to

get ready for the expedition; filling the water casks, and mending the sails."

"A party was now sent to collect stock, and search for the cow, which had not been seen since she was landed; but the natives set upon them, beat them severely, and drove them back to the fort. Christian therefore ordered some of his followers to go in quest of the stock, and to punish the offenders—taking with them the eight Otahetian men, and the boys—one of whom always carried the Union Jack. About a mile from the landing place, they were surrounded by 700 of the natives, who had formed an ambush into which they fell. The islanders all bore clubs, spears, and stones, and fought with more fury than judgment; otherwise, the whole of the assailed party must have fallen into their hands. After many obstinate and furious efforts the natives, giving ground, retired with great loss, and the stock was collected without further trouble. On the 14th, we killed the cow, which proved excellent eating; and, this evening, came on board the young chief, Taroa-Meina, with two of his friends, who informed us that 60 natives had been killed in the fight, and 6 women (supplying them with missiles). Among the men, several of note, one the brother of a chief, had been shot by Christian. Our visitor said that he himself had been so much our leader's friend that, if he staid on shore, he should be killed; on which the other told him he was going to Otaheite—whereat the Toubouain seemed rejoiced, and asked if he and his two companions might accompany. Christian agreed, and much satisfaction was expressed.

"Having filled sufficient fresh water, we weighed our anchor on the 17th Sept., and dropped down readily to the opening, the ship being much lighter than before.(*) When clear of the reef we lay by, and filled salt water to keep her on her legs, and at noon made sail; leaving Toubouai never to return to it, but well stocked with hogs, goats, fowls, dogs and cats. When we first met its natives, we judged, from their appearance, that they were cannibals; but we soon found that, although they had no animals on the island, and lived only on fruit, vegetables, and fish, they detested the idea of eating human flesh. We now stood to the

---

(*) I infer that the 24 Otaheitans who had accompanied the Europeans to Toubouai now returned to their own island; though, most probably, some of these were amongst those who again left it with Christian and his party, as shall be seen.

THE MUTINEERS; AND THEIR WANDERINGS. 49

N.N.E. with a favourable breeze and fine weather; and during the passage the armorer was employed in making iron-work for barter. On the 20th, we reached the island of Mytea, under which we hove to, and divided the trade, ammunition, arms, wine, slops, &c., into lots—which were put into the cabin for safety till the ship should come to anchor. On the 21st we bore away, and anchored on the 22nd in Matavai Bay—where, everything being settled, the following persons prepared to go on shore (as they did), and trust to it for their future:—

WENT ON SHORE.

Mr. Stewart ...... Midshipman	John Sumner	Able-bodied seaman
Mr. Heywood ..... Midshipman	Michael Byrne ...	do.	do.
Joseph Colman .... Armorer	Thomas Ellison ..	do.	do.
Chas. Churchill ... Master-at-arms	R. Skinner	do.	do.
James Morrison ... Boatswain's mate	M. Thompson	do.	do.
Charles Norman .. Carpenter's mate	W. Muspratt	do.	do.
Henry Hildebrandt Cooper	T. M'Intosh......	do.	do.
Thomas Birkett .. Able-bodied seaman	T. Millward......	do.	do.

THOSE WHO REMAINED IN THE "BOUNTY," WERE—

Mr. Fletcher Christian.. Master's mate	William M'Kay ..	Able-bodied seaman
Mr. Young .... Midshipman	John Williams ...	do.	do.
John Mills .... Gunner's mate	Matthew Quintall	do.	do.
William Brown .... Gardener	Alex. Smith, *alias*		
Isaac Martin...... Able-bodied seaman	John Adams ...	do.	do.

and with them the young Toubouain Chief, and his two friends, who had become so fond of Christian that they would not leave him. Three Otaheitan men, with their wives, also joined the party, and one of the women took with her an infant daughter, 10 months old—who in after years married a son of Christian, and became the mother of the future Mrs. Nobbs, wife to a worthy Chaplain, of whom proper mention will be subsequently made. In all, there determined to follow the fortunes of Christian 28 persons—a number which must therefore have included, in addition to the men, wives, and child specially enumerated, 10 other souls—women, from whom are sprung the dauntless whalers and dark-eyed Junoes of Pitcairn and Norfolk Islands.

"So as soon," continues Morrison, "as the ship came to anchor at Matavai, those for the shore began to land their chests, hammocks, &c.; but, having only one boat that could swim, and a tolerable high surf going, it was night before we all got off; being afraid to venture many at a time in the canoes of the natives —though they made a much better hand of the surf than we could do in the boat; being, however, apprehensive of the canoes, we were forced to wait for the boat's returning to carry the ammunition, &c. Having at last landed everything, we found the Otaheitans again ready to receive us with every mark of hospitality; each striving to outdo others in civility and kindness towards us; and all were glad when we said that we had come to stay with them. Among the things we carried on shore were carpenters' tools, and part of those belonging to the armorer, a pig of iron for an anvil, a grindstone, some bar-iron, a suit of clothes, some iron pots, a copper kettle, and about 3 gallons of wine, per man. Each (except Byrne, who was blind) had also a musket, pistol, cutlass, bayonet, cartridge-box, 17 charges of powder, a quantity of lead whereof to make bullets, and some spare belts. Having a musquetoon and two muskets to spare, the former was kept under my care, and the muskets fell by lot to Norman and Birkett. We asked for the saws, of which there were a 'ships' and 'cross' in the vessel; but, as Mr. Christian wanted them himself, he gave some trade in lieu—also two spy-glasses, and an old azimuth compass. He wished us to take the swivels on shore, but we declined, as they could be of no use. The canvas and sails, which he said we should not want, were however divided amongst us; and two Toubouain images, brought from the island, were put into my hands, as a present for the young King. Mr. Christian told us he would stay a day or two, and hoped we would assist him to fill some water, as he intended cruising about in search of some uninhabited island, where he would land his stock (pigs, goats, and poultry, of which a large number were on board, together with some plants), and where he hoped to spend the remainder of his days, without seeing the face of any European, except those who accompanied him. Having, meanwhile, made Poeno (one of the Chiefs of Matavai Bay) our friend, I and Millward went to live with him, and were treated as members of his family, but with more attention and respect. The others of our party also went to the houses of *their* friends, where they were entertained in like manner.

"At daylight on the 23rd Sept., we found the *Bounty* under weigh, and standing out of the bay; but, it proving calm, she was not out of sight until noon, at which time she stood away to the northward on a wind. Christian had said he intended staying a day or two; but we thought he did not care to remain at Otaheite any longer than could be helped." He had, however, (before sailing) landed on the island, and spent some hours with Stewart and Heywood, at the house of Tippaoo, a Chief who had been their friend on the two preceding visits, whose property was situate on the bay, near the landing place, and whose daughter Stewart married. It was the last time the three young men were to meet on earth; and its sad solemnity may well be imagined, as they thought or spoke of other days, their hopes, fears, and settled resolve. "As the day began to dawn, Christian prepared for departure; and Stewart and Heywood accompanied him to the beach, when a conversation took place to the following effect: Christian observed, that in the event of Mr. Bligh reaching England in safety, and upon his making known to the authorities what had happened, a ship of war would certainly be sent out in search of the *Bounty*, and those who had remained in her. Even if no intelligence of the expedition were received at the Admiralty, within a reasonable period, search would be made: And he earnestly advised Stewart and Heywood to go off at once to any ship of war that might appear, and give themselves up to the Commander: 'You are both innocent' he said; 'no harm can come to you, for you took no part in the Mutiny.' Then turning to Heywood he recapitulated all the events connected with that 'unfortunate disaster,' as he termed it; and again declared that when Stewart came to call him to relieve the watch, on the morning of the Mutiny, and he went on deck, his brain seemed on fire; and, finding Hayward asleep, and Hallet not yet up on duty, the idea of taking the ship first entered his mind: He added emphatically, that *he alone was responsible for the act, and exonerated all, even his adherents, from so much as suggesting it.*" Christian also related other circumstances in relation to the Mutiny, which Heywood was to communicate to his (Christian's) family, when he returned to England—circumstances, he thought, that might extenuate, though they could not justify, the crime he had committed against the laws of his country.

"Then Christian took a final leave of his friends, and stepped into the boat that awaited him:" Soon the *Bounty* was under weigh; "with many a long, lingering look," her progress was watched by every seaman she had left; and gentle hearts did throb, and lustrous eyes grew dim, when it was learned "that they should see his face no more"; for both he and Mr. Young bore with them the love of many—and the memory of that may have solaced many a lone, sad hour in their after lives.

While Christian thus bade farewell to Otaheite, the officers and seamen who remained there separated into small parties, and resided in different districts of the island; some of them (including Stewart and Heywood) prepared to await, as patiently as they could, the arrival of a ship from England, in search of the *Bounty*, and her people. But Morrison was not inclined to do so; and he thought it might be possible to build a small vessel in which to reach Batavia, and thence find a passage home. His comrade, Millward, and eight others, including the armorer, cooper, and carpenter's mate, entered into the design. Thus, out of the 16 "mutineers" who had landed on Otaheite, at least twelve had done so as a means, simply, of reaching England; and there is no evidence that any of the remaining four entertained any such thoughts of settlement at the former, as Mr. Bligh was pleased to attribute to them all. On the 12th Nov., '89, the keel of the vessel was laid; and, after contending with numerous difficulties, and exercising much ingenuity, in her construction, by the 5th Aug., '90, a schooner of 30 feet in length, 9 feet 6 inches in breadth of beam, and 5 feet in depth of hold, was launched by the artificers, with due ceremony, and christened the *Resolution*. During the building of this little craft, Morrison acted both as director, and Chaplain, to the hands employed; distinguishing the Sabbath day by reading to them the English Liturgy, and hoisting the British colours on a flagstaff erected near the scene of their operations. She was then fitted up with masts, and all requisites, except proper material for sails, which could not be had; but at length some matting was procured, and applied to the purpose: The first trial trip answered well in all other respects; but the matting-sails proved unequal to their object; and Morrison and his assistants felt they must abandon the proposed voyage to Batavia, with the prospect of proceeding thence to England—a great disappointment, as hope to the contrary had stimulated them to exertion, and cheered their labors,—the incessancy of which was an unfailing wonder to the simple islanders amongst whom they toiled,—and it was found that the craft could only be used for pleasure excursions round the island.

Meanwhile, Thompson had insulted a member of one of the principal families of the district in which he lived; and for this offence was knocked down, but not otherwise injured, by an incensed relative. He vowed vengeance for the affront; and, soon afterwards, in the most wanton, cowardly manner, shot a native and his child. The widow of the former, and mother of the latter, received the utmost consideration and sympathy from the other Englishmen; and Thompson was shunned by all of them, except Churchill; with whom he moved into the interior, and soon quarrelled. Their feuds ended in his shooting Churchill, "for which, and for his prior misdeeds, he *himself* met with just retribution at the hands of the natives. Thus closed the career of two of the most violent of the mutineers.

All this time, Mr. Stewart employed himself in the formation and cultivation of a garden; and enjoyed much happiness with his young wife: And Mr. Heywood devoted himself to the study, and in writing a vocabulary, of the Tahitian language, which afterwards proved of great value to the Missionaries. But when twelve months had elapsed since their last arrival at Otaheite (in Sep., '89), and no tidings of home, or relatives, reached them, he suffered much —now from dejection, then from restless longing: So did most of his brethren in exile. Nor could the loveliness of the isle, the softness of its clime, or the regard of its people, cheer the one, or allay the other feeling. And a yet further probation of six months had to be endured ere suspense was terminated, and the means of returning to their native land presented themselves. But on the morning of 23rd March, '91, a vessel was observed standing in, and rounding the point of Matavai Bay, which proved to be H.M.S. *Pandora*, commanded by Captain Edward Edwards, and "come in search of all the conspirators."

For, no sooner was the British Government made acquainted with the fact of the Mutiny, and Mr. Bligh's version of the circumstances disseminated, than it was determined that every possible effort should be made to apprehend the perpetrators of it, and bring them to the scaffold. Bligh's concealment of his own gross behaviour, which had induced the Mutiny, the false account he gave of most of the important features that marked it, and the calumnies which he heaped upon nearly everyone that remained in the *Bounty* (whether willingly or unwillingly), after he had been ejected from it, had done their work. "Down with the mutineers! Down with the whole lot of them"! was the answering cry of excited England; and the incensed Admiralty, assuming that everyone who continued, or was detained, on board that vessel, must have been an active participator in the *Mutiny*, was prepared to hang each of them; though, when some of the real facts became known, and prejudice and passion had run their course, of the ten men and youths who were brought to trial as mutineers—as the "atrocious villains" whom Bligh described — four of them were acquitted, as absolutely innocent, others were recommended to mercy, and only a small number were considered deserving of extreme punishment.

But while the howl against all of them was both loud and fierce, the *Pandora* frigate, of 24 guns, and 160 men, was despatched in pursuit of them, under Captain Edwards—who proved himself a still greater savage than Bligh, and more fitted for the custody of the "black hole of Calcutta," than the command of British seamen, or the guardianship of English prisoners. Mr. Hayward who had been one of the Midshipmen of the *Bounty*, asleep at his post—and Mr. Hallet another of her Midshipmen, who had been almost as neglectful—on the morning of the Mutiny, and accompanied Bligh in the launch, were now 3rd and 4th Lieutenants in the avenging vessel—whose orders were, to proceed, in the first instance, to Otaheite, and (if the mutineers were not found there) to visit the different groups of the Society and Friendly Islands; and use the utmost exertions to secure, and bring to England in close confinement (but with due regard to the preservation of their lives), all or such of the delinquents as might be discovered—" to undergo there the punishment due to their demerits." The ordinary maxim of law was reversed, and they were deemed guilty before they were either convicted, or tried. There is no country in the world in which love of justice is stronger than in England; but they are unfortunate, there as elsewhere, against whom a proper shout or sensational cry is raised. "Stone them," first, and "try them," afterwards!, is then the "watchword and reply." The "mutineers" of the *Bounty* were no exception to the rule; and the fury of the storm having now reached Otaheite, the most innocent of the band were in the grip of the remorseless Edwards.

CHAPTER IV.—" Pandora's Box ;" and Wreck.

March, '91—June, '92 : Surrender or capture of the 14 " mutineers," who had staid, and survived, at Otaheite, and of the schooner they built—" *Pandora's* box ;" and other agonies inflicted by Captain Edwards, and Lieutenant Larkin—The story of Peggy Stewart—Fruitless search for Mr. Christian, and his eight companions—Wreck of the *Pandora*, drowning of four of the prisoners (some of them in chains), and other loss of life, in or near to " Endeavor Passage "—On the reef! and further inhumanities of Captain Edwards—Expedition of the saved, in ship's boats, to Timor—Trials of all, and fresh brutalities of Edwards to his captives, during it—Arrival at Coupang—Miseries there; and Mr. Larkin again !—Wretched voyage to Batavia; where they find gallant William Bryant, and his mates—The schooner is sold, and the ragged are clothed—To the Cape of Good Hope, and England !—Fate of Bryant, and party.

THE *Pandora* had now reached Matavai Bay, upon her errand of capture; and before the anchor was down, Mr. Stewart, Mr. Heywood, and Colman, went on board, and gave themselves up to her officers; two others of the 14 surviving "mutineers," then in the neighbourhood, quickly followed their example; and they were all put in irons, manacled, and taken below, immediately they appeared.

Morrison, Ellison, and Norman, had sailed in their schooner (*Resolution*), the day before, to the north west part of the island. Mr. Corner, the *Pandora's* 2nd Lieutenant, and Mr. Hayward (the 3rd), were therefore despatched in the launch, and pinnace, to endeavor to intercept her, and capture them—together with the remaining six " mutineers," who were believed to be on the other side of the island. The Lieutenants caught sight of the *Resolution*, and chased her out to sea; but she gained upon them, and, night coming on, they were obliged to give up the pursuit, and return to the ship. It was soon learned, however, that the schooner had returned to the shore; on which the same officers were again sent in search; and the party in the launch now succeeded in taking her, as she lay at anchor in a small bay. But the three "mutineers" who had manned her during the previous chase had now quitted her (a friendly intimation had reached them of the arrival of the *Pandora*, and of the intention to arrest them); and, having made a fatiguing journey for the purpose, they came and surrendered to Mr. Corner before he found their craft: He received them courteously, but placed them under custody; at the same time ordering them refreshments, which they much needed: Soon afterwards the pinnace joined; and Mr. Corner, having placed the three prisoners in charge of Mr. Hayward (to take them on board the *Pandora*), proceeded in the launch to seize the *Resolution*, and the "mutineers" still at large—which was done, ere long.

Meanwhile, Morrison, Ellison, and Norman found themselves in guard of their former shipmate, Mr. Hayward (whom Bligh had kept in confinement for 11 weeks, and threatened to flog, at Otaheite); but his then trials had made no impression upon him, and he took little notice of his present captives, beyond inquiring about the *Bounty*, and those who had remained in her; though he informed his prisoners of the reception which Stewart, Heywood, and their three companions, had met in the *Pandora*, and of the treatment *they* also might expect—and, as preparation, he directed their ankles to be fettered, in order to prevent escape. It was therefore with much difficulty they mounted the side of the ship; and, on gaining the deck, Captain Edwards ordered them below, to be heavily chained, as Stewart, Heywood, Colman, and the other two who first surrendered, had been. Sentinels were placed over the eight, with directions to shoot the first man who should speak —especially if they addressed each other in the Otaheitan language, or spoke to the natives who crowded on board. They were allowed plenty of provisions, however; and their friends on shore were permitted to supply them daily with fresh cocoa-nuts: They were kept between decks for several days; and some dirty hammocks were given them to lie upon; but as these were full of vermin, they had them removed, as they preferred the bare boards. They were also unable to make use of the change of linen ordered for them by Captain Edwards; their irons being clinched so tight that it was impossible for them to raise or use their arms. The heat, too, between decks was excessive: Still their position was thought preferable to being in the "round-house" which (they had heard) was preparing on the quarter-deck for their reception; and the boards of which were so roughly put together, as scarcely to afford any shelter from sun or rain.

But when the *Resolution* reached the ship, and the remaining six " mutineers " were brought on board, and had been duly ironed and manacled, *all* of them were huddled into that " house " (or " *Pandora's* box," as it was termed), " through the scuttle at the top, about 18 inches square." This " box " was fastened by bolts through the coamings of the hatchway. There were two other scuttles, of nine inches square, in the bulk-head of the box, to admit air to the prisoners; these apertures were secured against escape by iron gratings; and even the stern ports of the ship were barred inside and out. The length of the " box " was 11 feet at the deck, and the width 18 feet at the bulk-head. In this contracted space, 14 prisoners were confined for upwards of four months! Two sentries were stationed on the top of it; and a Midshipman paced up and down across the bulk-head. No one was allowed to hold any communication with the captives, except the master-at-arms, and he only on the subject of their provisions. Their condition in this dreadful confinement became daily more pitiable, owing to the extreme heat; and Morrison quaintly records, that " their prison-house was only washed out once a week; they were washed with it; and this was the only ablution allowed them." . . . . Each officer of the ship, as he was relieved from his watch of this foul crib, examined the state of the shackles; M'Intosh's limbs being slight, he contrived to liberate one leg at night, which was a great relief; till the circumstance being observed, and reported to Captain Edwards, the 1st Lieutenant, Mr. Larkin, was instructed to make a general inspection of the irons. The leg-irons were immediately reduced in size to fit close; and (writes Morrison) " Mr. Larkin, in trying the handcuffs, placed his foot against our breasts, and, hauling at them with all his strength, in several cases took off the skin with them!! Those that could be hauled off in this manner were reduced, and fitted so close that there was no possibility of turning the hands in them; and when our wrists began to swell, he told us ' the handcuffs were not intended to fit like gloves.' Sickness soon appeared among the prisoners, and their limbs became galled from the tightness of their irons. One or two of the greatest sufferers were released from their handcuffs; but their legs were still kept fastened to the two iron bars which ran across the deck. (*a*)" And all this was done by the order of British officers!

During the whole period of her stay at Otaheite, the ship was daily surrounded by canoes bearing not only supplies, but numerous friends of the prisoners, full of sorrow and lamentations for their misfortunes. Few, however, were allowed to come on board to see them; but among the few was a young girl, the Chief's daughter, whom Stewart had married, and named "Peggy." She came with their infant in her arms; and, seeing her husband lying within the den, among the other prisoners, heavily ironed, her grief knew no bounds. Even the hard hearted Captain and 1st Lieutenant were touched at her sorrow; and she was admitted into the "box." Rushing forward, she embraced, and with reiterated cries she clung to, him; till the scene becoming too painful, she had to be removed by force. So completely unnerved by the interview was poor Stewart, that he prayed, for both their sakes, she should not be allowed to see him again. But she could not be deterred from remaining on the beach, from early morn to midnight; for there she could, at all events, see the vessel that held him. Her father and friends were often observed endeavoring to persuade her to take food and rest; but in vain; she was daily at her post; and within a few weeks of the departure of the *Pandora*, she sank, broken hearted, into an early grave; leaving her infant to the care of a sister, who took a mother's interest in the little orphan, and had her educated by the Missionaries, who afterwards settled on the island. To my mind, the barbarities that occasioned the death of that hapless girl constituted a far greater crime than the Mutiny of the *Bounty;* and the selection of such men as Bligh and Edwards, by the Lords of the Admiralty, for the command of that vessel, and of the *Pandora,* was also a much graver offence against decency and humanity than the latter was against Naval discipline. Yet the Mutiny is branded; and the girl's death, with the Admiralty's nomination, and subsequent advancement of

---

(*a*) Mutineers of the *Bounty*, &c., pp. 79, 80, 81 : In the letter to his mother, of Nov. 1791, Mr Heywood thus writes :—"There was a sort of prison built on the after part of the quarter-deck, into which the 14 of us were put in close confinement, with both legs and both hands in irons; and we were treated with great rigor; not being allowed ever to get out of this den, and being obliged to eat, drink, sleep, and obey the calls of nature, there."!

the men who were the cause of both, is ignored, by the unreflecting and sycophantic.

Captain Edwards appears to have been absolutely indifferent to the terrible sufferings he was imposing upon Mr. Stewart, and the other 13 manacled men, whom he had chained like wild beasts in the fearful " box " he had constructed for their custody. And, the necessary supply of water and provisions having been obtained, the *Pandora* sailed from Otaheite on 19th May, 1791, accompanied by the *Resolution*—which had been fitted with proper sails, manned by a Midshipman and four seamen, and instructed to keep the ship in sight : They stood to the north-west (somewhat in the direction Christian had taken when last leaving the island) ; and for three months they prosecuted a diligent search amongst the Society and Friendly Isles for him and the mutineers who had adhered to him—a service in which the schooner proved very useful, as her light draught enabled her to lie close to the extensive reefs encountered during the investigation. But after a time the *Resolution* became separated from the *Pandora* (as was also a jolly-boat, having a Midshipman and four seamen on board, that were never again heard of) ; and eventually, about the middle of Aug., the search had to be relinquished as fruitless : The ship's course was then laid for Timor. Christian and his comrades lay too close to be discovered in the little isle they had selected for their final refuge ; "the quarry" was safe from the hawk ; and for seventeen years the place of their retreat remained unknown to the world. (*b*)

Meanwhile, the *Pandora* held her course N.W. and W., intending to pass through the Great Barrier reef, not far from where Captain Cook had gained the open sea from the shoals within, in Aug., 1770 : And, all along, the tortures endured by the prisoners in her hellish " box " had been well nigh intolerable, or incredible. Huddled together, bound, and helpless, they had no means of steadying themselves when the ship lurched ; and, being thrown one upon the other, they unavoidably bruised and wounded both themselves, and each other, with their irons and manacles ; till, at

---

(*b*) The only trace of the *Bounty* which the *Pandora* could discover, consisted in a yard and some spars, having the broad arrow upon them, and marked with the name of the former ship, that were found by Lieutenant Corner, upon one of the Palmerston group. How they got there is not known.

the solicitation of Mr. Corner (who always evinced much kindness and consideration towards them), Captain Edwards allowed short pieces of plank to be secured to the deck, to remedy the frequent collisions—but from their cramped cell they were not once permitted to move, no matter how stifling the heat, or drenching the rain, that beat upon them; and to the transverse bars they still remained chained, as if they had been dogs—while Edwards ate, drank, and slept composedly! O heart of man! whose pulsations God has given, what are thou not capable of? Blurred by sin and passion, it grows at times as hard as granite, and as cruel as vultures' claws; and His compassion can alone excuse its savagery.

Let us now revert to Morrison's Journal : On the 22nd Aug., '91 (he writes), " we approached Endeavor opening," or about 15° 40′ S. lat., " and narrowly escaped striking on a reef; obliging us to work to windward, for some days, without finding any other opening." The *Pandora* appears, however, to have made considerable northing at the same time; for, by Sunday, the 28th, she had attained the latitude of 11° 20′ S., or nearly opposite to the projection on the mainland which is known as " False Orford Ness;" and upon the morning of that day, the 2nd Lieutenant was sent with the yawl to make a closer examination, while the ship was hove to; " but the current running strongly on the reef, she was forced upon it, in the midst of a heavy surf, at the moment the returning boat had come within hail, and was warning her people of the danger—but in vain. The ship was driven further upon the reef, with violent and repeated shocks; and we expected every surge that the masts would go by the board. Seeing her in this situation, we judged she would not hold long together. As we were in danger, at every shock, of killing each other with our irons, we broke them, that we might be ready to assist ourselves; and informed the officers of what we had done. When Mr. Corner was acquainted with the circumstance, he came aft, and we told him we should attempt nothing beyond an effort for the saving of our lives—a chance which he promised we should have; telling us not to fear.

" In the meantime, the ship had lost her rudder, and with it part of the stern post; and, having beat over the reef, between 11 and 12 p.m., she was brought up in 15 fathoms water with both anchors; and the first news was 'Nine feet of water in the hold!'

Colman, Norman, and McIntosh, were then ordered from the 'box' to the pumps; and the boats were got out. But so soon as Captain Edwards learned that we had broken our irons, he *caused the rest of us to be hand-cuffed, and leg-ironed, again, with all the irons that could be mustered;* though we begged for mercy, and all desired leave to go to the pumps—but to no purpose!! His orders were put into execution, though the water in the hold had increased to 11 feet, and one of the chain pumps was broken! The master-at-arms, and corporal were now armed with a brace of pistols each, and placed as additional sentinels over us, with orders to fire upon us if we made any movement; and the master told us that the Captain had said, he would either shoot, or hang to the yard arm, those who might make any second attempt to break the irons. There was no remedy, and no consolation but prayer, as we expected never to see daylight; and, having recommended ourselves to Almighty protection, we lay down, and seemed for awhile, by the stillness we preserved, to forget our miserable situation. But we could hear the officers getting their things into the boats, which were hauled under the stern for that purpose; and some of the men on deck said, '*they* shall not go without us.' This made some of us start; and hearing the gratings the master-at-arms cried, 'Fire on the rascals!' As he was just then over the scuttle, I spoke to him, and said: 'For God's sake, don't fire; what is the matter? what is the matter?; there is no one here stirring.' In a few minutes after, one of the boats broke adrift, and, having but two men in her, she could not reach the ship again, till another was sent with hands to bring her back. And now we began to think they would set off together, as it was natural to suppose that every one in them would first think of saving his own life. However, the boats returned, and were secured with better warps.

"We learnt next, that the boom having been cut loose for the purpose of making a raft, one of the top-masts fell into the waist, and killed a man, who was heaving the guns overboard; and everything seemed to be in great confusion. At daylight, August 29th, the boats were hauled up, and most of the officers being aft on the top of the 'box,' we observed that they were armed, and preparing to go into the boats by the stern ladders. We begged that we might not be forgotten; when, by Captain Edwards' order, Hodges, the armorer's mate, was sent down to take the irons off Muspratt and Skinner, and send them up, along with Bryne (who was then out of irons); but Skinner, being too eager to get out, was hauled up with his handcuffs on, and the other two following him close the scuttle was shut and barred before Hodges could get to it; and he, in the meantime, knocked off my hand-irons, and Mr. Stewart's. I begged of the master-at-arms to leave the scuttle open, when he answered, 'Never fear, my boys! we will all go over together.' Scarcely were the words out of his mouth, when the ship took a sally, and a general cry of 'there she goes!' was heard. The master-at-arms and corporal, with the sentinels, rolled overboard; and at the same instant we saw, through the stern-port, Captain Edwards swimming to the pinnace, which was some distance astern—as were all the boats which had pushed off on the first appearance of motion in the ship. Birkett and Hildebrandt were yet hand-cuffed, and the ship under water as far as the main-mast. It was now beginning to flow in upon us, when Divine Providence directed James Moulter (boatswain's mate) to the place. He was scrambling up upon the 'box'—and hearing our cries said, 'he would either set us free, or go to the bottom with us;' at same time, he took out the bolts, throwing them and the scuttle overboard—such was his presence of mind; though he was forced to follow instantly, as he was nearly drowning.

"So we all got up except Hildebrandt, and were rejoiced, even in this trying scene, to think that we had escaped from our prison; though it was as much as I could do to clear myself of the driver-boom before the ship sank. The boats were now so far off that we could not distinguish one from the other; however, observing one of the gangways come up, I swam to it, and had scarcely reached it, before I perceived Muspratt on the other end, whom it had brought up; but, having fallen on the heads of several others, it had sent them to the bottom. Here I began to get ready for swimming; and, the top of our prison having floated, I observed on it Mr. Heywood (who had been the last but three to jump overboard), Birkett, Colman, and the 1st Lieutenant: Seeing, at same time, Mr. Heywood take a short plank, and set off to one of the boats (bearing between his teeth his mother's last gift, a Prayer-book), I resolved to follow him; which I did by means of another short plank. After having been about an hour and a half in the water, I reached the blue yawl, and was taken up by Mr. Bowling,

Master's mate, who had also taken up Mr. Heywood. After rescuing several others, we were landed on a small sandy islet on the reef, about two and a half or three miles from the ship. Here we soon found that four of our fellow prisoners were drowned— Skinner and Hildebrandt, *who had their handcuffs on*, and Mr. Stewart and Sumner, who were struck by the gangway." Thus, those of the "mutineers" who had given themselves up to Captain Edwards, or been captured by his officers, were now reduced to 10 in number; and Stewart, one of the missing dead, had gone, it is hoped, to the poor girl whose heart that Edwards had broken. " But Birkett, *being landed with his handcuffs on*, the Captain ordered them to be taken off. We also heard that 35 of the *Pandora's* ship's company were lost—among whom were the master-at-arms, and ship's corporal; but all the officers were saved."

In that portion of *his* Narrative submitted to the Court Martial by Captain Edwards, which relates to the loss of the *Pandora*, scarcely any mention is made of the mutineers; still less is it disclosed that 11 of them were kept handcuffed, and in irons, by his express orders, whilst the ship was breaking up, and would therefore, most probably, have been all drowned, except for the courage and humanity of the armorer's and boatswain's mates, who, at the risk of their own lives, freed 10 out of the 11 of their irons, and eight of their manacles; and the only allusion Edwards makes to the fate of those who *were* drowned is, that " four of the mutineers were lost with the ship." But the following statement, believed to have been drawn up by one of the principal officers (Lieutenant Corner), fully confirms Morrison's account of the business, and proves (as Sir John Barrow justly observes) that the representation given by Morrison of the " brutal and unfeeling behaviour of Captain Edwards is but too true."

After stating that three of the *Bounty's* men had been let out of irons, and set to work at the pumps (as previously mentioned), it is added, " the others offered their assistance, and begged to be allowed a chance of saving their lives; instead of which two additional sentinels were placed over them, with orders to shoot any one who should attempt to get rid of his fetters. Seeing no prospect of escape, they betook themselves to prayer, and prepared to meet their fate; everyone expecting that the ship would soon go to pieces—her rudder and part of the stern-post being already beat away." When the *Pandora* was actually sinking, and every effort making for the preservation of the crew, "no notice" (continues the statement) "was taken of the prisoners, although Captain Edwards was entreated by Mr. Heywood to have mercy upon them, when he passed over their prison, to make his own escape; the ship then lying on her broadside, with the larboard bow completely under water. Fortunately, the master-at-arms, either by accident or by design, when slipping from the roof of the 'box' into the sea, let the keys of the irons fall through the scuttle or entrance, which he had just before opened, and thus enabled them to commence their own liberation, in which they were generously assisted by a boatswain's mate, who clung to the coamings, and pulled the long bars through the shackles; saying he would set them free, or go to the bottom with them. Scarcely was this effected, when the ship went down, leaving nothing visible but the top-mast cross-trees. The master-at-arms, and all the sentinels, sank to rise no more. The cries of them, and the other drowning men, were awful in the extreme; and more than half an hour had elapsed before the survivors could be taken up by the boats. Among the former were Mr. Stewart, John Sumner, Richard Skinner, and Henry Hildebrandt, two of whom perished with their hands [and one of them having his feet] still in manacles;" while Birkett, a third manacled man, managed in some way to reach a boat, or was picked up by it.

In his "Voyage round the World, in H.M.S. *Pandora*," Mr. Hamilton (her Surgeon) adds, "When the vessel foundered, the crew had just time to leap overboard, accompanying the act with a most dreadful yell. The cries of the men drowning in the water were at first awful in the extreme; but as they sank, or became faint, their shrieks died away."—

> " She gave a heel, and then a lurch to port,
> And going down head-foremost, sunk. . . . .
> Then rose from sea to sky the wild farewell!
> Then shriek'd the timid, and silent stood the brave;
> Then some leaped overboard with dreadful yell,
> As eager to anticipate their grave;
> And the sea yawn'd around her like a hell,
> And down she suck'd with her the whirling wave,

> Like one who grapples with his enemy,
> And strives to strangle him before he die.
> And first one universal shriek there rush'd,
> Louder than the loud ocean, like a crash
> Of echoing thunder ; and then all was hush'd,
> Save the wild wind, and the remorseless dash
> Of billows ; but at intervals there gush'd,
> Accompanied with a convulsive splash,
> A solitary shriek—the bubbling cry
> Of some strong swimmer in his agony."

When the survivors from the wreck had been collected on the sandy islet, a tent (resumes Morrison) " was erected for the officers and another for the seamen ; but the prisoners were not suffered to come near either. The Captain had told us, we should be treated as well as the ship's company ; but, on our requesting him to give us a spare boat's sail to shelter us from the sun, as we had but scanty clothing, it was refused—though we were in lat. 11° 20′ S., nor was any use made of it—and we were ordered to keep on a part of the islet by ourselves, to windward of the tents, not being suffered to speak to any person but each other. The provisions saved being very scanty, the day's allowance was only two musket-balls weight of bread, and a glass of wine ; of the water, being but a small quantity, none could be afforded us. We staid here till the 31st Aug., fitting the boats, during which time the sun took such an effect on us — as we had been cooped up for four months — *that we had our skin flayed off from head to foot,*" [as if "we had been dipped" (wrote Mr. Heywood, July '92) " in large cauldrons of boiling water !"]   " We kept ourselves," resumes Morrison, " covered in the sand during the heat of the day ; this being all the shelter the islet afforded ; for it was only a small bank washed up on the reef, scarcely 150 yards in circuit, and not more than six feet above the level of high water. During the night, as we found the air very chilly, and having no covering, we threw up a bank of sand, to sleep under its lee—that proved but an indifferent barrier, as we had frequent showers of rain, sufficient to make our lodging very miserable, though not sufficient to save any with which to allay our thirst, which was very great. We tried for water, but found none ; and Mr. Corner, kindling a fire, got a copper kettle, which he filled with salt water, made it boil, and attended to it all night—preserving the drops of steam condensed in the cover, till a teaspoonful was mustered." (*a*)

The boats—pinnace, launch, and two yawls—being (continues Morrison) ready on the 31st, ninety-nine souls, officers and surviving people of the *Pandora*, with the 10 prisoners, were distributed amongst and embarked in them; having about 1,000

(*a*) The preceding account of the place (about 11° 20′ S. lat.) at which, and the circumstances under which, the *Pandora* was lost, have been taken from Morrison's Journal; and it has been seen he was on board at the time; though a prisoner in irons, almost up to the last moment: He was also one of the survivors who gained the "sandy islet," immediately after the wreck; and he remained there for 3 days in comparative freedom, though otherwise, in a wretched plight. He shared, too, in the boat voyage thence to Timor: And the most recent Government Map of Queensland marks the "*Pandora Entrance*" at about the spot on the Great Barrier reef where Morrison represents the calamity to have occurred.

But the same Map gives a "*Pandora Passage*," as well, at about 9° 54′ S. lat.; and Captain Flinders, in the Introduction to his own Voyage, Ch. XVI-II.; citing "Voyage round the World, in H.M.S. *Pandora*, by Geo. Hamilton, Surgeon," describes the wreck as if it had taken place in the immediate neighbourhood of the Murray Islands; and mentions subsequent incidents, to which Morrison makes no allusion, tending to show that the vessel had passed through the Great Barrier reef before the wreck occurred. He writes, that Captain Edwards "made the reef of Torres Strait," on 25th Aug., 91, in about the lat. of 10 S. and two degrees of long. to the east of Cape York. Steering thence westward he fell in with the Murray Islands, lying in lat. 9° 57′ S. and long. 143° 42′ E. Some canoes with two masts were seen running within side of the reef which lay between these islands and the ship. The reef was of considerable extent; and, during the entire of next day, Edwards ran along it to the southward, without finding any passage through. On the 27th, unsuccessful search was continued; but on the 28th a boat was despatched to examine an opening in the reef; and the ship stood off and on, waiting the result. At five in the evening, the boat made a signal of a passage being found; but fearing to venture through, so near sunset, without more particular information, he called the boat on board. In the meantime, a current or tide set the *Pandora* upon the reef; and, after beating there, till 10 o'clock, she went over into deep water, and sunk in 15 fathoms, at daylight on the 29th.

A dry sand bank was perceived within the opening at a distance of four miles; and thither the boats repaired, with the remaining officers and people; 39 men having lost their lives in the melancholy disaster. Not being able to save anything from the wreck, Captain Edwards, almost destitute of provisions and water, set sail on 30th Aug., with his squadron of four boats, and steered for the north-east part of Terra Australis. No reef or other danger seems to have been encountered in the way to the coast; but in the course along it some islands and reefs were seen. From one part of the coast, two canoes, with three black men in each, paddled hard after the boats; but though they waved and made many signs, it was not thought prudent to wait for them. At one of the York Isles, the natives, for some trifling presents, filled a keg of water for the party; but refused to bring any more, and soon afterwards let fly a shower of arrows amongst the unfortunate sufferers. Happily, no one was wounded, and the aggressors were put to flight by

miles to run before they could reach the Dutch settlement, at Timor; and with the scanty allowance of two musket-balls weight of bread, and hardly a gill of water and wine together, per man, to serve for each twenty four hours that must be spent under a scorching sun ere Coupang could be gained. This slender dole was served out daily, at noon; and, on account of their intense thirst, few of the party could partake of the bread. (*b*) At various places on the coast of New Holland, they tried in vain to find water; where small supplies might have been obtained, the natives opposed their landing so fiercely that they were obliged to keep off, being too weak to contend with them; and though at a small uninhabited island, in the vicinity of the shore, an ample quantity was found by digging, they had nothing to carry it in except their boots, and some tarpaulin bags, which contained but 200 gallons—a poor supply for 99 men, during 14 days—the earliest date at which they could make Timor.

---

a volley of musketry. At the Prince of Wales Islands good water was found; which much alleviated the prevailing distress. Here the howling of "wolves" (probably wild dogs) was heard, and a *morai*, or heap of bones was discovered, amongst which were two human skulls, the bones of some large animals, and some little bones: These were heaped together in the form of a grave; and a long paddle, supported at each end by a bifurcated branch of a tree, was laid horizontally along it. Near to this were the marks of a fire having been recently made; and the ground about was much footed and worn. But a few small oysters, a harsh austere fruit, resembling a plum, and a small berry of a similar taste, were all that could be found for food. "There is a large Sound formed here, which (says Mr. Hamilton) we named *Sandwich Sound*, and commodious anchorage for shipping in the bay, to which the title of *Wolf's Bay* was assigned; and in which there were from 5 to 7 fathoms all round. Near the centre of the Sound is a small dark coloured rocky island."

In the afternoon of 2nd Sep., Captain Edwards passed out to the northward, with his little squadron, from amongst the Prince of Wales Islands; and the same evening, by steering westward, he cleared all the islands and reefs of Torres Strait; reaching Timor on the 14th.

Perhaps the *Pandora Passage*, which is marked on the Queensland map as in lat. 9° 54′ S., may relate to the course of some other vessel than that of Captain Edwards, though of the same name.

(*b*) One of the men in the launch, with Mr. Heywood, had tied round his waist, when he left the *Pandora*, a bag of dollars—his small savings. He suffered from intense thirst more than the rest, and offered the dollars to the companion seated next to him, on condition that *he* would give up the glassful of wine and water about to be served out to him. The tempted one looked at the dollars, then at the glass, which the owner of them was ready to seize, and, throwing the bag back to him, exclaimed, "They are not worth to me this draught of water."

But the ruffianism of Captain Edwards towards his wretched captives knew of no mitigation on that or any other account:— " On the 9th Sep.," (writes Morrison), " as I was lying on the oars of the pinnace, talking to M'Intosh, the Captain " (with whom they were) " ordered me aft, and, without assigning any cause, directed me to be pinioned with a cord, and lashed down in the bottom of the boat; and Ellison, who was asleep there, was ordered the same punishment. I attempted to reason with him, and inquired what I had now done to be thus cruelly treated? urging the distressed condition of all; but received for answer, ' Silence, you villain! are you not a prisoner? You piratical dog! what do you expect?' I then told him it was a disgrace to a man-of-war Captain to treat a prisoner in such an inhuman manner; upon which he started up in a violent rage; and, snatching a pistol that lay in the stern sheets, threatened to shoot me. I still attempted to speak; upon which he swore, ' If you say another word I'll heave the log at you!' and, finding that he would not listen to any reason, and my mouth being so parched that I could scarcely move my tongue, I was forced to be silent and submit; and I was tied down so that I could not move. In this miserable situation, Ellison and I remained for the rest of the voyage." British seamen bound hand and foot; thrust to the bottom of a frail boat (the only hope of life during the perilous voyage in which they were then engaged); and held there for six long days and longer nights! Thank God, no Naval officer can now indulge in any such outrages; and the present race are perhaps the last men in the Queen's service who would countenance them in any way. (*a*)

On 15th Sep. the boats sighted Timor; and their inmates were all landed at Coupang by the 19th; when it was found that the other prisoners (borne thither in the launch and yawls) had been better treated than those in the pinnace; but their fare had been the same. Weak as they all were, they were put in stocks,

---

(*a*) A Captain of a ship of war cannot at present place a seaman in irons, or punish him with any severity, from mere caprice or ill humour. A warrant must be drawn up previous to any such punishment; 24 hours must elapse between the committal of the offence and infliction of the punishment; and the particulars of the former, with the amount of the latter, must be stated in writing, signed by the Captain, and transmitted to the Admiralty.

in the guard-room of the Castle; and in that filthy cell they remained a week; at the end of which the Dutch Military Surgeon paid them a visit; but he was unable to enter until the slaves had washed it! He directed that their irons should be taken off, and their legs only linked together. "We continued here" (says the Journal) "till the 5th Oct., when we were removed on board the *Remhang*, a Dutch vessel then in the roads—and Mr. Larkin, coming previously to the prison, with cords for the purpose, pinioned us with his own hands; setting his foot against our backs, and bracing our arms together so as almost to haul them out of their sockets! We were tied two and two by the elbows; and, having our leg irons knocked off, were conducted to the beach, and put on board a long boat, to proceed to the ship. Before we reached her, some of us fainted, circulation being stopped by the arm-lashings; and when we got on board, we had both legs put in irons, and the lashings taken off." A fitting Lieutenant was Mr. Larkin to Captain Edwards; and their names shall live in a common infamy.

At Timor, they found gallant William Bryant (an ex-convict from Port Jackson), his devoted wife, and five brave mates (still liable to sentence there), with two little children of the Bryants—who, flying from want and savage punishments, had slipped fetters, and "leave tickets,'"—had escaped through Sydney Heads, on the night of the 28th March, 1791, in a frail boat, of one and twenty feet, and had made that island, after the most daring voyage ever performed on any coast; toiling, striving, hoping, fearing, as they struggled along the entire of the eastern shores of Australia, and either through Torres Strait, or round by New Guinea (*which*, no one can now tell), and at last reached the green shores of Timor—the very place they meant to make, when they left Sydney six months before they were discovered at Coupang!—and whose subsequent story is as interesting as it is sad.

The *Remhang* was bound for Batavia, terribly leaky, and only kept from foundering by the pumps going night and day. At first, this hard work was performed by the prisoners in turn; but, in their exhausted condition, it had to be remitted; and they were again put in irons. The ship having arrived at Samarang, the previously missing schooner *(Resolution)* was found at anchor; she had been there for some weeks; and her crew had suffered almost similar privations as those who were shipwrecked in the *Pandora*. The *Resolution* was now refitted, furnished, and ordered to accompany the *Remhang* to Batavia; which both reached on 7th Nov. Mr. Heywood, and his companions, were now placed on board an old hulk, and allowed to come on deck one at a time, to shave and wash—an indulgence they had been denied for many months; and here the schooner was sold by Captain Edwards, who distributed the price she brought between the Dutch Governor of the place, and the *Pandora's* people. (*a*) Their share of the money enabled the latter to purchase some nankeen cloth; and they employed certain of the prisoners to make up suits of clothes; paying them for the work: The latter were thus enabled to buy clothes for themselves; and Heywood, who was an expert plaiter, earned a little cash by making straw hats; "till Captain Edwards forbade these occupations—which had not only yielded that assistance, but were of use in relieving the tedium of captivity—and again ordered on the dreadful manacles." But the Dutch Governor, touched by sufferings and privations to which the British Commander was insensible, did his best to alleviate them in so far as he could.

Three Dutch vessels were hired at Batavia to carry the *Pandora's* company, and their prisoners, to the Cape of Good Hope, which they attained on 15th Jan., '92. During the voyage, those unfortunates were confined between decks, had to sleep on bare planks, once more, and were half starved. The upper deck, too, being very leaky, "they were alternately drenched with rain and salt water, as the vessel rolled terribly." But on reaching the Cape, they were transferred to H.M.S. *Gorgon*, and in the absence of Captain Parker, her Commander, they were received with much kindness by Mr. Gardner, the 1st Lieutenant. They were only chained by one leg; and Morrison remarks, "Mr. Gardner very humanely gave us a sail to lie upon—a luxury we had not enjoyed for twelve months." They were also permitted to sit on deck for

---

(*a*) Though constructed under the difficulties alluded to at page 52, the schooner had proved a remarkably quick sailer; and, being afterwards employed in the sea otter trade, is said to have made one of the quickest passages ever known from China to the Sandwich Islands. Subsequently, the little vessel was purchased at Canton by Captain Broughton, R.N., to assist him in surveying the coast of Tartary, and was the means of preserving 112 men of H.M.S. *Providence*, when wrecked to the eastward of Formosa, in 1797.

six or eight hours a day, to enjoy the fresh air. They remained at the Cape until 5th April, when the *Gorgon* was ordered to England; and Captain Edwards took his passage in her, with some of the *Pandora's* crew, and the prisoners—who were thus carried to Spithead, which they made on 19th June, '92 : There the captives were transferred to H.M.S. *Hector*, commanded by Captain (afterwards Sir George) Montague—a gallant officer and gentleman, by whom they were treated very considerately; every indulgence compatible with their position and safe custody being allowed them.

Four years and four months had elapsed since these unhappy men (returned in manacles) had left England in the *Bounty*, with cheerful prospects and light hearts; and " during 15 months of that time they had been principally in irons "—enduring many privations, and much needless sufferings and barbarities; yet the health of several, notwithstanding the weakness, misery, and agony, felt by all, continued tolerably good throughout, and none of their number died from sickness; while of the *Pandora's* people many suffered from fever, and several died—though Mr. Heywood tells us (and we can well imagine his comrades were not better off), that " he was without a friend; and had only a shirt, and a pair of trousers to put on, and carry him homeward."

I should have mentioned, that Captain Edwards (with the instinct of an ocean policeman) had demanded and obtained from the Governor of Timor the surrender of poor Bryant, and his party, as prisoners of the Crown illegally at large; and carried them to Batavia, in the *Remhang*, along with his other captives : How the former fared, on the passage thither, is not recorded; and we know not : Nearly all of them were, or had been, " wretched convicts ! "—and if they were deemed unworthy of Mr. Larkin's delicate attentions, so much the better for them : But we do know, that Bryant, one of the children, and two of his grown companions, died at Batavia; another of them was drowned in the Strait of Sunda (between Java and Sumatra); and Mary Bryant, with her surviving child, and remainder of the party, having been borne by Edwards to England, where—though the courage and determination, fidelity, and sufferings they had evinced in their desperate boat voyage from Sydney to Timor, excited much compassion—they were brought up at the 'Old Bailey,' in Aug., '92, and ordered by the Court to remain in Newgate, "till the periods of their original sentences of transportation" (which were for life as to some of them) " should expire!"

Would the world have fared the worse, or the cause of peace and order have suffered in any way, had these poor fugitives been pardoned? And may it not be that many of the punishments which *Society* now demands of the fallen will be deemed in after years to have been somewhat unnecessary? At any rate, theirs was a gallant struggle for life and liberty; and the memory of it should live in Australian history, while manly courage and devotion, tender faith, and motherly love, find a place in the hearts of our people.

Chapter V.—The Court Martial.

1792—Sep., Nov.: The trial by Court Martial, in England, of the 10 "mutineers" brought there by Captain Edwards—The Court; "Hamlet" and his "Uncle" —The charges, evidence, and defences—The verdict; and proceedings under it —After career of the chief witnesses, and parties, to the trial.

ON the 12th Sep., '92, the survivors of the *Bounty's* men, brought from Otaheite by Captain Edwards, were placed upon their trial at Portsmouth, by Court Martial, on board H.M.S. *Duke*, under the presidency of Vice-Admiral Lord Hood. They were Mr. Heywood, Morrison, Norman, Colman, Ellison, McIntosh, Birkett, Millward, Muspratt, and Byrne: And the members of the Court were, Lord Hood (President), Captain Sir H. S. Hammond, Bart., John Colpoys, Sir George Montague, Sir R. Curtis, and seven other Naval officers.

One of the witnesses for the Crown was Captain Edwards, who ought to have been dismissed from the Service for his barbarities to the prisoners, and have been tried for his own life, as well, for having kept Hildebrandt in irons, foot and hand, and Skinner and Birkett in manacles, when the *Pandora* was going to pieces; thus causing the death by drowning of two of those seamen: And for the survivors to have disclosed at their trial, by *his* cross-examination, or that of other witnesses, the inhuman tortures to which they were subjected by Edwards, from the time of their surrender, or arrest, up to that of their arrival at the Cape of Good Hope—tortures that might fairly have atoned for the share any of them had taken in the Mutiny, nearly three and a half years previously—would have placed them in a pretty position by the honoured Crown witness who had imposed them, and whose testimony was reserved almost as the *last* piece of evidence for the prosecution: With bated breath, therefore, and only as some of them addressed the Court, towards the close of the proceedings, could *allusion* be made to Edwards' inhumanities: While Captain

Bligh, who should have been the principal witness for the Crown (but whose cross-examination would have proved that his own coarseness of nature, tyrannous conduct, and base outrages upon Christian, and others, were the occasion of the Mutiny), was not called at all as a witness for the prosecution; and the prisoners (against whom, and nearly every other person on board the *Bounty*, his mendacious "Narrative" had raised a bitter prejudice throughout England), were prevented calling him, by the Admiralty having, in the summer of '91, sent him to the South Seas, on his second bread-fruit expedition. Indeed, it is almost impossible to imagine a more pitiable or censurable parody upon the administration of justice, than was involved in the absence of Bligh, and the calling of Edwards, on the trial of the mutineers (*a*). It should be observed, however, that the evidence actually given by Captain Edwards, as a witness on that occasion, was correct in itself, and moderate in tone. He was more truthful, and, perhaps, less passionate, and foul in language, than Mr. Bligh—but more cruel, and more reckless of the sufferings and lives of others.

During the trial, Mr. Heywood had the benefit of the presence, and (in so far as the course of procedure at Courts Martial admitted,) of the assistance, of an experienced Naval friend (Mr. A. Graham), as well as of a Legal gentleman (Mr. Const); but at whose retainer, worthy Commodore Pasley, expressed his regret, as sea-officers (he said) "had a great aversion to Lawyers." None of the other prisoners appear to have had any such aid, though their lives were at stake, and most of them illiterate seamen (unable therefore to defend themselves with any ability, or properly understand the passing proceedings). (*b*) And they were arraigned on the following charges—that Fletcher Christian, Master's mate of the *Bounty*, assisted by others of the inferior officers and crew, armed with muskets and bayonets, had violently

---

(*a*) None of the prisoners surrendered to, or were taken by, Captain Edwards, personally; they gave themselves up to his officers, or were captured by them; and Lieutenants Corner and Hayward gave the necessary proofs of all that.

(*b*) Notwithstanding the Commodore's prejudices, it was unfortunate for all the prisoners—but most fortunate for Bligh and Edwards—that the Heywoods abandoned their original intention of retaining *Mr. Erskine* for the defence of the boy Peter: It is stated, that the King's Attorney-General, and Judge Ashurst, attended the trial.

and forcibly taken that ship; and that Mr. Bligh, together with the Master, boatswain, gunner, and other persons (numbering 19 in all), were forced into the launch, and cast adrift; that Captain Edwards, in the *Pandora*, was directed to proceed to Otaheite, and other islands in the South Seas, and to use his best endeavors to recover the said vessel, and to carry in confinement to England the said Fletcher Christian, and his associates, or as many of them as he might be able to apprehend, so that they might suffer condign punishment, &c.; and that the prisoners (by name) had been brought to England, &c., and were now put on their trial. (c)

Mr. Fryer, the Master of the *Bounty*, deposed that, having, been relieved of the watch, on the night of 27th April, '89, and having retired, leaving all quiet, he was alarmed, at dawn of next day, by an unusual noise; and that, on attempting to jump up, Skinner (afterwards struck by the gangway, and drowned, during the wreck of the *Pandora*), and Quintall (who was now with Christian in their island refuge), laid their hands upon his breast, and desired him to lie still, saying he was their prisoner; that on expostulating with them, the answer was, "Hold your tongue, or you are a dead man! but if you remain quiet, there is none on board will hurt a hair of your head;" that, on raising himself on the locker, he saw Mr. Bligh, in his shirt, going on deck by the ladder; and Christian holding him by a cord, with which he was bound; that Churchill, the master-at-arms (whom Thompson subsequently shot at Otaheite), then came to his cabin, and seized a brace of pistols and a hanger, saying, " I will take care of these, Mr. Fryer;" that he inquired, on observing Mr. Bligh bound, what they were going to do with the Captain; that Sumner replied, "Put him into the boat, and let him see if he can live on ¾th's of a pound of yams a day!" that he remonstrated at such conduct, but in vain; that one of the three men added, 'Mr. Bligh must go in the small cutter ;" on which he (Mr. Fryer) exclaimed, "The small cutter! Why, her bottom is almost out, and very much eaten by the worms!"—to which Sumner and

---

(c) Such is the statement of the charges as set out both in the "Mutiny and Piratical Seizure of the *Bounty*," and in the "Mutineers of the *Bounty*;" &c. ; but in charity to Naval Courts Martial, we must assume, there was a further allegation, that the *prisoners* were amongst "the inferior officers and crew" who participated with Christian in the Mutiny; otherwise, *they* would not have been touched by the charges.

THE COURT MARTIAL.

Quintall both rejoined, 'the boat is too good for him." After much entreaty, he prevailed on them to ask Mr. Christian if he might go on deck, which, after some hesitation, was granted. And, "when I came on deck" (continued the Master), "Mr. Bligh was standing by the mizzen-mast, with his hands tied behind him; Mr. Christian holding the cord in one hand, and a bayonet in the other. I said, 'Christian, consider what you are about!' 'Keep silent, sir!' he rejoined, 'I have been in hell for weeks past; Captain Bligh has brought all this on himself;' I told him that Mr. Bligh and he not agreeing was no reason for his taking the ship. He again directed me to be silent; but I urged—'You and I, Mr. Christian, have been on friendly terms during the voyage; therefore, give me leave to speak. Let Mr. Bligh go down to his cabin, and I make no doubt we shall all be friends again.' Once more he replied, 'Hold your tongue, sir!; it is too late;' theatening me if I did anything more: and on my asking him to give a better boat than the cutter; he said, 'No, that boat is good enough'; [but he afterwards substituted the launch, a larger and stouter boat, on the entreaty of Mr. Bligh—] who now whispered to the Master, that the man behind the hen-coops (Isaac Martin) was his friend, and desired the other to knock Christian down—" which Christian must have heard, but took no notice of." Mr. Fryer then attempted to get past Christian to speak to Martin; but he put his bayonet to the Master's heart, saying, "Sir, if you advance an inch further, I will run you through,"! and directed two armed men to take him down to his cabin, which was done. Shortly afterwards, he was desired to go on deck again, when Christian ordered him into the launch. On which, Mr. Fryer observed, "I will stay, if you give me leave;" "No, sir,"! he replied, "Go directly into the boat."! Then Bligh, on the gangway, said, "Mr. Fryer, stay in the ship."! "No," rejoined Christian, "go into the boat, or I will run you through.' The Master further stated, that during all this time very opprobrious language was used by the people towards Mr. Bligh; that with great difficulty they prevailed on Christian to suffer a few articles to be placed in the launch; that after Bligh and 18 other persons had been put in her, several of those remaining on the ship called out "shoot him!;" and that Cole, the boatswain, advised the former to cast off the boat, and take their chance, as the mutineers would certainly do them some mischief, if they staid much longer. Lastly, Mr. Fryer, gave the names of those who were under arms during the Mutiny; and added that Colman, M'Intosh, Norman, and Byrne wished, but were not allowed, to go into the boat, declaring that they had nothing to do in the business; and that he did not perceive Mr. Heywood on deck at the seizure of the ship [he was asleep in his hammock when the Mutiny broke out:] The Master also stated, that he would have staid in the ship, in preference to going in the boat, if permitted to do so; and that if he had so staid (in expectation of re-taking her), he would not have hesitated a moment (such was his confidence in him) in entrusting Mr. Heywood with the design, and asking him to assist in it, at the first opportunity. Mr. Fryer expressed similar confidence in Morrison, whom he did not see armed, and who was a steady man.

Cole, the boatswain, deposed that, being awakened out of his sleep by the commotion on the morning in question, he went up the hatchway, having seen Mr. Heywood and Mr. Young in the opposite berths (below); that coming on deck he saw Captain Bligh with his hands tied behind him, and four sentinels (including Ellison and Birkett) standing over him. Cole asked Mr. Christian what he meant to do, and was answered by his being ordered to hoist the boat out [I think the launch is here referred to]; that he saw Heywood "lending a hand to get the fore-stay-fall along," and, when the boat was hooked on, "speak something to him," but what it was does not remember, "as Christian was threatening him at the time;" that Heywood then went below, and does not recall seeing him afterwards. (*a*) Cole added, that Colman, Norman, M'Intosh, and Byrne were crying (the three first at the gangway, and the fourth in the cutter, which was alongside), because they could not get into the launch; and that he had reason to believe Mr. Heywood, also, was detained in the *Bounty*, contrary to his inclinations; that he thought, all along, that Gentleman was intending to come away; he had no arms; and he assisted to get the boat out, and went below; that he

---

(*a*) The poor boy's "lending a hand" to get out the launch, evidently occurred under the same coercion as affected both the boatswain and the carpenter (Crown witnesses at the trial), when they rendered like assistance; and Mr. Bligh had entreated that the launch, rather than the cutter, should be allowed him.

heard Churchill call out 'keep them below,'! meaning, doubtlessly, Heywood" [and Stewart]; and that he saw Muspratt with a musket in his hand, but not until the latter part of the business.

The evidence given by Peckover, the gunner, was similar to that of the boatswain; and the carpenter's (Purcell's) corroborated, generally, that of the three preceding witnesses; the last named person adding, "I looked upon Heywood as confused, and that he went below on his own account, in order to collect some of his things to go in the boat; while he was assisting me in getting her out, he did not, in any degree, whatever, manifest a disposition to aid in the Mutiny; nor did I, by any means, consider either him, or Morrison, concerned in it."

Lieutenant Hayward (whom Mr. Christian states he found asleep on his watch, when he went to relieve him, and that then, for the first time, the idea of taking the ship occurred to him,) deposed, that Christian, having come upon deck, and soon afterwards gone down to "lash his hammock up," speedily returned, accompanied by Birkett, and a number of other armed men, but quickly went below again to Mr. Bligh's cabin; that Ellison then quitted the wheel, and armed himself with a bayonet; that other armed men appeared on the deck; that Mr. Heywood, Mr. Stewart, and Morrison were unarmed upon the booms; that a cry of "Murder!" was heard from below; and Churchill called out for a rope; "on which Mills, contrary to all orders and entreaties, cut the deep sea line, and carried a piece of it to their assistance" (What was Hayward, himself, doing all this time, except perhaps indulging in those useless "orders and entreaties?")—that Mr. Bligh was now brought upon the quarter-deck, with his hands bound behind his back, and was surrounded by most of those who came last on deck. On this witness adding that, when he went below to collect some clothes, he saw Heywood in his berth, and told him to go into the boat, he was asked by the Court, If Heywood was prevented by any force from going upon deck; and he answered, "No." And when the Court inquired, "Did you, from his behavior, consider him as attached to his duty, or to the party of the mutineers?" his reply was, "I should rather suppose, after my having told him to go into the boat, and he not joining us, that he was on the side of the mutineers; but that must be understood only as an *opinion*, for he did not in the least take any active part; and I observed in his countenance marks of sorrow." This "opinion" of Hayward, however consistent it may have been with what *he himself* knew of the facts—and however much it may have told against Heywood with the Court Martial—is entirely displaced, and refuted, by the facts known to other persons, to which reference has been already made—namely, that when Stewart and Heywood (after collecting "the things" they meant to have taken with them into the boat) were returning to the deck, Thompson, by Churchill's command, presented a pistol at Stewart's breast, ordering him to remain below; that Stewart then hailed Churchill, and said, "If you will not let us go, I desire you will inform the Captain that we are detained by force." The reply was, "Aye, aye, sir!" but the message does not appear to have been delivered; and when, at last, on Stewart and Heywood being allowed to gain the deck, the former demanded of Christian the reason of their detention—though the latter denied having given any orders to that effect, Churchill said, "*he* had kept Stewart and Heywood below, *to prevent their going with Captain Bligh in the launch;* and added, "If anything should happen to you, Mr. Christian; there would be no one else to depend upon for navigating the ship."

Mr. Hayward also alleged, that he saw Muspratt among the armed men. And he, with Mr. Corner, proved the surrender of some, and the capture of others, of the prisoners, as has been already shown. But the spirit in which the former gave his evidence throughout may be inferred from this portion of it— Upon being re-called, he said that Morrison appeared joyful during the Mutiny; and, on being asked by him, If he could declare before God and the Court, that what he stated was not the result of private pique, replied—"Not the result of any private pique, but an opinion formed *after quitting* the ship, through your not going with us in the launch; *there being more boats than one: but I cannot say you could have had the cutter!*" This witness (remarks Sir John Barrow) "was pleased to remember nothing that was in favor of the prisoners;" and though he was promoted soon after his return to England with Bligh, there is no reason to doubt the truth of Christian's statement, that he found him asleep upon his watch, and that circumstance immediately prompted the seizure of the ship. It is not strange, then (as shall be seen), that Mr. Hayward's evidence was not considered "satisfactory" by the Admiralty.

Lieutenant Hallet, late a Midshipman of the *Bounty*, and who had also received promotion (notwithstanding the circumstances, or inducements to the Mutiny, that have been previously mentioned, was asked whether he saw Mr. Heywood on the day of it? and said—"I saw him once on the platform, standing still, and looking attentively towards Captain Bligh; never saw him under arms, nor spoke to him; did not know if he offered to go in the boat; when standing on the platform, Captain Bligh said something to Heywood, but what it was witness did not hear—on which Heywood *laughed, turned round, and walked away.*" The last six words of this testimony weighed heavily against Heywood in the minds of his Judges. But Cole deposed that Bligh could not (having regard to the distance between them) have spoken to Heywood, when on the booms, loud enough to be heard by him; that he (Cole) did not observe anything of levity, or apparent merriment, on Heywood's part; that, on the contrary, he was alarmed; so was Hallet; and that Mr. Bligh himself had begged "that no more people should go in the launch," as she was overloaded.

There is a letter, too, written 29th March, '92, or about six months prior to the Court Martial, by Hallet, to Miss Nessy Heywood, in which he says, "I cannot (as you may readily conceive it was a time of *great confusion* among us), declare *positively* the part your brother acted in the Mutiny," (*a*)—

(*a*) As to the portion of Mr. Hallet's evidence at the Court Martial under comment, Miss Nessy Heywood thus writes to her sister Mary, in the Isle of Man—"With respect to that little *wretch*, Hallet, his intrepidity in Court was astonishing; and after every witness had spoken highly in Peter's favor, and given testimony of his innocence so strong that not a doubt was entertained of his acquittal, the other declared, unasked, that while Bligh was upon deck, he looked at and spoke to Peter. What he said to him, Hallet could not hear (being at the distance of 20 feet from Bligh, and Peter was 20 feet further off, consequently a distance of 40 feet separated Mr. Bligh and my brother); but Hallet added, that Peter, on *hearing* what Mr. Bligh said to him, laughed, and turned contemptuously away! No other witness than Hallet pretended he saw Peter laugh; on the contrary, all agreed he wore a countenance on that day remarkably sorrowful; yet the effect of his cruel evidence was wonderful on the minds of the Court." And it will be seen that Mr. Hallet, himself, afterwards admitted that it could not be relied upon; and expressed his deep sorrow at having given it.

G

also a letter (dated in the *end* of October, '92, when, therefore, there was no possible object to be gained by misrepresentation), which was sent to a friend of the Heywoods, by Mr. Graham (already alluded to, and a man of high character), in which it is stated, "it will be a gratification to Mr. Heywood's family to learn, that the declaration of some of the other prisoners, since the trial, have put it past all doubt that the evidence" (Mr. Hallet's) "upon which he was convicted, must have been (to say nothing worse of it) an unfortunate belief on the part of the witness, as to circumstances which either never had existence, or were applicable to one of the other Gentlemen who remained in the ship, and not to Mr. Peter Heywood." And when, not long afterwards, Mr. Hallet (then a Lieutenant in H.M.S. *Penelope*) lay upon his death bed, he expressed his contrition for the evidence he had given against Heywood; and said he had since felt convinced he had spoken too positively of facts concerning which he could not be certain; for that, in the confusion of the fatal morning, he was quite bewildered: He added, that on the voyage to England, with Mr. Bligh, he had been much influenced by that officer, who had taken a prejudice against Heywood; and he earnestly entreated the Captain of the *Penelope* (on board of which he was dying), that this information might be communicated to his former shipmate, and his family, as the only reparation in his power to make for the injury he had inflicted on them.

"Against the prisoners Ellison, Birkett, and Millward" (it is stated) "the testimony of all the witnesses clearly and distinctly proves that they were under arms the whole time of the Mutiny, and actively employed against Captain Bligh." But in so far as the evidence is set out, either in the "Mutiny of the *Bounty*," &c., or in the "Mutineers of the *Bounty*," &c., it does not *disclose* anything that affected Millward. Perhaps, however, he was one of the "armed men" referred to by Mr. Hayward; though it may be remembered that Morrison stated, he had agreed with the Master, *and Millward*, in an attempt to re-take the ship from the mutineers, until they were detected and prevented by Churchill and Smith.

Lastly, Captain Edwards mentioned (as his officers had previously proved), that Mr. Stewart, Mr. Heywood, Colman,

Morrison, Norman, and McIntosh, voluntarily surrendered themselves, on the arrival of the *Pandora* at Otaheite.

Such was the evidence given on this remarkable trial—in which "the part of Hamlet was omitted" (or Captain Bligh was allowed to absent himself), and "Hamlet's uncle" (or Captain Edwards, of the "*Pandora's* box,") was placed in the witness box: The actual facts, too, whether they contradicted or supported, explained or added to, that evidence, have been stated in this and preceding Chapters. And Mr. Heywood, being called upon by the Court for his defence, denied, generally, that he had taken any part in the Mutiny, and said he never imagined that, by remaining in the ship (as Mr. Fryer wished, and Mr. Bligh told him to do), he would lay himself open to a charge of complicity in the proceedings, which, from first to last, he condemned; that it was quite out of the power of a young boy, surrounded by armed men, to make any diversion in favor of Mr. Bligh (*); and that he could scarcely have been blamed had he hesitated about entering a boat which was already within eight inches of the water's edge, so over-crowded was it (and into which Mr. Bligh had entreated that no one else should be permitted to come); but that he had, nevertheless, determined to risk his life with those who accompanied his Commander; and went below, with Stewart, to collect some necessaries, before doing so, but was prevented by Churchill and Thompson from returning

---

(*) The nearest approach to any effort by Mr. Bligh, himself, to regain the *Bounty*, when he was still on board her (though in the hands of the mutineers), was, as we have seen, to desire the unarmed Master "to knock down Christian," who had a bayonet and pistol! And although Bligh—with the eighteen scantily armed men, who were put into the launch—could scarcely have been expected to make any struggle to retake the vessel from the twenty-five men who remained in her, and had a sufficiency of arms, if they desired to use them; he might have allowed that part of his case to rest there, instead of representing (as he did) upon his return to England, that young Heywood should have aided him in regaining possession of her! This pretence, its impudence, and exposure, are best stated in the terms of a letter written to Heywood by his noble hearted sister ("Nessy"), in July, '92, when he was awaiting his trial:—
"Captain Bligh told Mr. Wilson, in conversation, that his greatest hope of assistance in suppressing the Mutiny was from his dependence on *your* joining a party in his favor. . . . I must observe, in answer, that his confidence in his other officers must have been very small, when (without making any effort himself, except by *words*, even when he was in the boat, and his hands at liberty), he depended upon a boy of *fifteen* to be his defender!"

on deck! that Hayward and Hallet had been mistaken as to portions of their evidence, as they were much confused at the time, and nearly four years had since elapsed; that no doubt, also, the hardships to which they were exposed in the launch naturally tended to embitter their feelings against those who remained in the *Bounty*; that he had taken the earliest opportunity of surrendering himself on the arrival of the *Pandora* at Otaheite; and that some regard should be had to the sufferings he had endured at Otaheite, and on the homeward voyage; that Captain Edwards had chained and punished him with terrible severity—so much that when the *Pandora* was threatened with instant destruction—when fear and trembling came on every man on board—in vain, for a long time, were his repeated cries, that the galling irons might not, in that moment of consternation, be allowed to prevent his hands from being lifted up to Heaven for mercy.

And had Mr. Heywood then known that such entries existed, he might have informed the Court, that, in his original Journal, Mr. Bligh not only states, that *none of his officers were suffered to come near him while held a prisoner by Christian;* but adds, " as for those whose cabins were in the cockpit, there was no relief for them; *they endeavoured to come to my assistance, but were not allowed to put their hands above the hatchway:*" Yet he suppressed the one admission, as well as the other, from his published " Narrative;" and his conduct in so doing has, indeed (as Sir John Barrow suggests), " the appearance of a deliberate act of malice, by which two innocent men (Stewart and Heywood) might have been condemned to suffer an ignominious death " —one of whom was actually brought into that predicament; and the other only escaped it by a premature grave. (*d*)

Morrison's defence was very similar to that of Mr. Heywood; except that he mentioned he had agreed to join with Mr. Fryer, and Millward in an attempt to retake the ship from the muti-

---

(*d*) Bluff Colonel Howell puts the common sense view of young Heywood's case very fairly, when he wrote to him, about a fortnight before the trial—"I would as soon believe the Archbishop of Canterbury set fire to the city of London, as suppose you, then a boy of 15, and of irreproachable antecedents, could, directly or indirectly, join in any such d—— piece of business as this Mutiny was." And the placing of the lad upon his trial at all, on a charge of *Mutiny* at sea, alleged to have been committed when he was little more than a child, was simply shocking.

neers; but that they were detected, and prevented by Churchill, and Alexander Smith. "Mr. Hayward," he added, "dropped a hint to me, that he intended to knock Churchill down: I told him I would second him; pointing to some of the Friendly Island clubs, sticking in the booms, and saying 'There were tools enough'; but I was suddenly checked by finding that he went into the boat, without making the attempt he proposed."

In his defence, Muspratt said, that he took up the musket which was observed in his hands, when he understood that the Master intended to rescue the ship, and for the purpose of aiding him in that design; that he quitted the musket the moment he saw Mr. Bligh's people get into the launch; and that "Mr. Hayward's evidence must stand so impeached before the Court as to disentitle it to the least attention."

Byrne's speech was very brief and very good—"It has pleased God almost to deprive me of my sight, which often puts it out of my power to carry the intentions of my mind into execution; but I make no doubt it appears to the Court, that, on the morning of the Mutiny, my desire was to quit the *Bounty*, with the officers and men who went away in the launch: I do not know whether I may be able to repeat the exact words of those who detained me; but some said 'we must not part with our fiddler;' and Charles Churchill threatened to send me 'to the shades,' if I attempted to quit the cutter, into which I had gone for the purpose of attending Lieutenant Bligh."

I cannot find any record of the defence offered by any other of the prisoners; and some of them were absolutely dumb, from the beginning to the end of the trial—unable to apply themselves to, or deal in any way either with, the evidence, or the facts of the case; and no one was at liberty to speak for them (such being the enlightened rule observed in Court Martial proceedings),

When the trial was concluded, the Court justly acquitted Colman, Norman, McIntosh, and Byrne of the charges preferred; but declared that those charges had been proved against Mr. Heywood, and Morrison—(a finding that was utterly opposed to the weight of evidence, and to every fact affecting them), as well as against Ellison, and Birkett (who were shown to have participated in the Mutiny), and also against Muspratt and Millward; though (in so far at least as is revealed by the reports), there was only a tittle of evidence affecting the former, and none whatever touching the latter, unless he was one of Mr. Hayward's "armed men": And the Court accordingly adjudged, that each of the six last named prisoners should suffer death, by being hanged by the neck on board one of his Majesty's ships of war. At the same time, that august Tribunal was pleased "humbly and most earnestly to recommend Heywood and Morrison to the King's mercy, in consideration of various circumstances," as one of those reports puts it; and on the express ground, according to the other, that, "if not opposing the Mutiny, it was clear they were not actively concerned!" Yet they were found "Guilty," and sentenced to be hanged!—One of them, too, a boy of 15 at the time of the occurrence!! And it was not strange that Heywood, writing to Dr. Scott, after his conviction, should have observed, "Could most of the witnesses who appeared for the prosecution, be tried, they would suffer for the same and only crime of which I have been declared guilty." It was in the same letter that he besought that Gentleman "to endeavor to mitigate his distressed mother's sorrow; to give my everlasting duty to her, and my unabated love to my disconsolate brothers and sisters; and to encourage them, by my example, to bear with fortitude and resignation to the Divine will, their load of misfortunes, though almost too great to support."

But there was little doubt on the mind of any one who had seen the minutes of the Court Martial, that both Heywood and Morrison had been wrongfully convicted. And, though smothered to a large extent, by his absence, "yet, here and there, in course of the trial, so much was disclosed of oppression, and unjustifiable treatment of both officers and men, by Mr. Bligh, that the tide of public opinion and favour greatly changed." They, and not he, began to be considered as victims: warm and true friends, therefore, interested themselves on behalf of Morrison and Heywood; and, after five weeks of torturing suspense and anxiety, on the morning of the 27th Oct., '92, the King's Warrant for their free and unconditional pardon was received by Captain Montague, on board the *Hector*. On the same day, Lord Hood, who had been President of the Court Martial, wrote to his uncle, Captain Pasley, offering to take the latter as a Midshipman on board the *Victory;* but the offer was declined; and he was received, in like capacity, on his uncle's own ship, the *Bellerophon*. And Morrison was soon afterwards promoted to the rank of gunner, on his appointment to a vessel (as already noticed). At the last moment, too (or immediately before the time fixed for Muspratt's execution), the Lords Commissioners of the Admiralty arrived at the conclusion, that the evidence given by Mr. Hayward was not "satisfactory;" and as it was chiefly upon his testimony that the other had been condemned, a respite during his Majesty's pleasure (subsequently enlarged to a pardon) was extended to Muspratt. But Ellison (a lad of 17 at the time of the Mutiny!), Millward, and Birkett, were executed on board H.M.S. *Brunswick*, in Portsmouth harbour, two days after the discharge of Heywood and Morrison, or three years and seven months from the committal of their offence—to which (however unjustifiable in itself) they had been partly goaded by the ruffianism of Mr. Bligh, and during fifteen months of which period they had been treated like savage beasts by Captain Edwards.

It might have been thought that the inflictions they had endured in "*Pandora's* box," for that long period, and the supreme agony of the last dreadful hour, when they were still kept in chains, though the ship was going to pieces about them, and it was feared they must all go down in manacles to the yawning depths beneath (as others did), unable "to lift their hands to heaven for mercy," had been sufficient punishment for their offence. It was considered necessary, however, by the Admiralty (which had appointed such men as Bligh and Edwards to be their Commander, and gaoler), that they should again undergo the bitterness of death, or last penalty of the law, as "a warning to others never to be led into acts of insubordination and violence against constituted authority"—however revolting had been the abuse of its position and powers. Mercy is the first attribute of God, and last of man, who too often ignores the causes of his brother's fall, strikes at the result alone, and calls vengeance "justice."! Yet it is remarkable that, while a *Naval* officer and five seamen were condemned to death for Mutiny, and three of the latter were executed accordingly, under sentence of a Naval Court Martial, Major Johnstone, of the New South Wales *Military* Corps, having risen in rebellion against the same Mr. Bligh, in Jan., 1808, and having arrested and forcibly de-

posed him from his then office of Governor-General of that
Colony (on account of far more excusable acts than those of
which the mutineers of the *Bounty* complained), was merely
"cashiered," when convicted of that offence, on *his* trial by a
Military Court Martial, at Chelsea Hospital, in May, 1811;
and that the two officers next in command to Johnstone, who
both countenanced and availed themselves of the revolt of their
Major, received promotion from the Home authorities! The
humble sailors were hanged, as a warning to the Navy against
Mutiny; and the Commissioned soldiers were lightly dealt with,
or rewarded, as an encouragement to the Army in insurrection.

The history of Captain Bligh, from the time of his return to
England, after the Mutiny, up to his death, 27 years later, has
been summarized at page 42.

Captain Edwards speedily became an Admiral; and had
there been a second New South Wales, to be honoured by his
Government of it, more than probable it would have been so
favored; there was only one, however, and Captain Bligh was
considered the more *deserving*.

Of his 1st Lieutenant, the *gentle* Mr. Larkin's, after doings,
I cannot find any trace; and it is perhaps as well.

Mr. Hayward was, in due course, appointed to the command
of the "*Swift*," sloop of war; which, with himself, was lost in a
typhoon in the China Sea.

Of Mr. Hallet, his appointment to the *Penelope* frigate, his
recantation, and death, mention has been already made.

And with respect to their principal surviving victim—after
Mr. Heywood's liberation, he served in the Navy for many years
(until July, 1816), in every part of the world, in conflict with the
enemy, surveying expeditions, and diplomatic missions; and rose
through all its grades till he became a Post Captain—ever
proving himself a skilful sailor, loved Commander, and loyal
Gentleman: He subsequently declined still higher recognition of
his claims; and died in Feb., 1831.

Morrison's fate has been disclosed in p. 17.

PART II.

Story of the Pitcairn Islanders.

Chapter VI.—Pitcairn; and its Refugees.

1789, September—March, 1829: Pitcairn Island, and settlement there of Mr. Christian, the eight mutineers remaining with him, and Otaheitans, &c, who joined them—The dismemberment and sinking of the *Bounty*—Discovery of the survivors, and descendants of the party, in 1808, by the *Topaz*; and what her "log book" said about them—Visit, in 1814, of the *Briton* and *Tagus*, reports by their Commanders on the island and islanders; their appearance, manners, pursuits and customs; the climate, products, and village of Pitcairn—John Adams' account of occurrences in the island from 1789 to 1814, and comments thereon—Christian and his " cave ;" oppression and misconduct of the Englishmen towards the men of color; jealousies, plots, and strife; five of former, and all of latter, slain; violent end of two others of the mutineers—Conversion of Adams; its happy effect on the islanders and place; and death of Mr. Young—Accessions to the community (of Buffitt and Evans in 1823)—Arrival of the *Blossom* in 1825; and Captain Beechy's picture of the happiness and comfort, simplicity of life, peace and purity of the islanders—A fresh accession (of Mr. George H. Nobbs) in 1828; and sketch of his life—The death of " Father Adams," in 1829.

WE shall now revert to the story of Christian, and the eight comrades who, adhering to his fortunes, sailed with him from Matavai Bay, in the *Bounty*, on the morning of 23rd Sep., 1789—as well as with the three Toubouaians, three Otaheitan men, one child, and 13 women, already referred to—(the other "mutineers" remaining behind, and undergoing the vicissitudes described in the two preceding Chapters).

As the *Bounty* cleared the bay she stood to the northward; but this was probably a "blind;" for her real destination lay to the south-east. There happened to be a book on board, prior and subsequent to the Mutiny, which described a voyage made by Captain Philip Carteret, in H.M. Sloop, *Swallow*, when on a mission of discovery in the South Pacific, in 1766-7-8-9; and Christian had read in this book that, on the morning of 2nd July, 1767, a "young Gentleman," named Pitcairn, being on the look-out at the mast-head, observed a spot in the horizon which, on approaching it next day, appeared to rise like a great pyramid out of the sea. (a) It proved to be an island a mile and a half in length, and four and a half miles in circumference; its summit attaining a height of 1008 feet; itself almost surrounded by a coral reef, and covered with trees. The coast was formed, for the most part, of rocky projections, off which lay numerous fragments of stone; while a small stream of fresh water trickled down at one end of the island. The surf, which broke upon the shore with great violence, rendered landing impossible then; though in fine weather there would be no great difficulty in the way. The place seemed to be uninhabited; a great number of sea-birds hovered around; and the waters almost swarmed with fish. It lay in lat. 25° 4' S., and (according to Carteret) in long. 133° 30' W. [but in reality its longitude is 130° 24' W.], or about 1200 miles S.E. of Otaheite: and it was then named "Pitcairn," after the young discoverer. (b)

The "lone isle of the ocean" thus pictured—

"Where over the reef the surge rolls free,
Like a circlet of pearls round an emerald stone"—

presented to Christian's mind a fitting place of refuge for himself, and others, whom the Mutiny of the *Bounty* had made outcasts from *home*, and outlaws from England. Here they would be safe from pursuit, and could rest in quietude; conscience their only law, and God their only Judge. It would be suitable, also, to to those islanders (Otaheitans and Toubouaians) who had joined their lot with his, and belonged to the same sea as that from which *it* sprang. He therefore steered for Pitcairn Island, soon after leaving Otaheite; but, owing to the incorrectness of the longitude assigned to it by Carteret, the cruise now made in search of it occupied several weeks; till the wanderers began to fear "it was not." At length, towards the end of Oct., or begin-

---

(a) It was visible at a distance of more than 15 leagues.
(b) But circumstances will be referred to in Chapter VIII., which show that this island *was* inhabited in years gone by.

ning of Nov., '89, a far distant rock, rising high in the midst of the ocean, came in sight; and as it was neared they observed with delight the lofty precipices which bound the isle on every side—precipices that forbade facility of landing—and a depth of water right up to its very shores, which seemed to preclude the possibility of ships anchoring off it. Here (for the place was Pitcairn) lay the shelter the mutineers had longed for, where they might live in peace—"no man making them afraid"—and die in peace, when their time came. And in truth the spot was well chosen—far from the haunts of ships and men. "What a little speck it looks in the vast Pacific!" (wrote Mr. Fortescue Moresby, who visited it in the *Portland*, in Aug., 1852) "a mere rock, apparently incapable of resisting the mighty waves of so vast an ocean. Easily, indeed, would a vessel, not knowing its exact position, miss it. The mutineers might well deem themselves secure on so small an island, so remotely situate from their country. At that time, also, these seas were but little frequented. Even now, that numerous vessels trade on them, *we* have seen only one, over a track of 4500 miles— so immense is the extent of those waters." And Christian's party, though earnestly desiring the rest and safety which Pitcairn should bring, could scarcely have been prepared for the natural products—cocoa-nut trees, bananas, plantains, and bread-fruit trees—which they found on some of the ridges; and they were still more impressed by the pervading beauty of its interior; forests of fig-trees and palms clothing the mountain sides; lovely valleys, shaded by precipices; and exquisite vines forming endless canopies of sylvan network; with many a clustering

> "Fig-tree ; not that kind for fruit renown'd
> But such as, at this day to India known,
> In Malabar, or Deccan, spreads her arms—
> Branching so broad and long, that in the ground
> The bended twig takes root, and daughters grow
> About the mother tree—a pillar'd shade,
> High over-arch'd, and echoing walks between."

Round the friendly shores so offered to them, the course of the *Bounty* was now directed; and her boat, having been "twice pulled round the island" (says Mr. Brodie), whilst engaged in the necessary search, came at length to a bend in the coast, where the wanderers effected a landing. That nook was destined to be her last resting place, and has ever since borne the name of "Bounty Bay": For here the vessel was taken alongside; and, after the stock had been landed, nearly every available article of which she was composed, or that was found in her—even to the planks that covered her ribs, the copper, nails, bolts, &c., masts and sails—were stripped, and removed; then, that no trace of her remains might be left which could lead to a discovery, and the last link between the mutineers and Otaheite, home, or Europe, be destroyed, her hull was set on fire; and, when that was burnt to the water's edge, the rest was sunk in 25 fathoms, on the 23rd Jan., 1790. The guns she had carried were consigned to the deep at same time. (*a*) But the *Bounty's* name has survived many a great three-decker; and will outlive many another still unlaunched; since, be the crime of the daring men who seized and bore her to Pitcairn what it may—and in the eyes of Naval authority there could hardly be a graver one—it was a sudden, perilous, deed, induced by insult and oppression, visited for many a month and year, by suffering and torture, by hope deferred, anguish, and death; and while it shocked all sense of discipline, it did much to rid a noble Profession of such savages as Bligh and Edwards.

No doubt, if the victims of Bligh's outrages had waited patiently until they returned to England, and then preferred formal charges against him, for his treatment of them, they *might* have had the satisfaction of obtaining his dismissal from the Service; but such an expectation, however it might affect calm and disinterested minds, was not likely to weigh with men defrauded of their daily food by their Commanding officer; denounced by him, without a particle of justification, as "wretches," "liars," "d——d villains," and "thieves;" all of them threatened with, and some of them subjected to, lengthened imprisonment and the lash, for comparatively trivial causes, or no cause whatever—treatment such as British sailors could not now be exposed to for an hour. And

---

(*a*) Yet, in Aug., 1841, Captain Jenkin Jones, of H.M.S. *Curacoa*, having ascertained the spot where the *Bounty* had been sunk, succeeded, with some difficulty, in raising the charred hull, and found (such had been the solidity of her timbers) that her "heart of oak" had survived the power of fire and water, and the effects of submersion for more than half a century. And in Jan., 1845, two of her guns, which had then lain for 55 years on a bed of coral, fathoms deep in the sea, were fished up: "One of them was thenceforth used for belching forth fire and smoke on great occasions;" the other was condemned to silence, having been spiked.

it is a little strange that, *when* the barbarities both of Bligh and Edwards became perfectly well known to the Admiralty, so far from those Gentlemen being visited either with punishment or censure, each of them received honor and promotion.

From the time of their landing on Pitcairn Island—or more correctly, from that of their sailing from Otaheite—a long period elapsed before any tidings reached Europe of Christian, or his associates. The interval was one of war, and of great enterprises; and, however some of them may have been mourned as dead, or worse than dead, by relatives or friends, the surviving mutineers of the *Bounty* (if any of them did survive) had passed from the public mind. But there came a gleam of light in Sept. 1808, or 19 years from the events last referred to which revived the memory of them: That glimpse was perceived by, and transferred to the log-book of, an American trading vessel, the *Topaz*, commanded by Matthew Folger, then in the South Seas; and a copy of the entry in his log reached the British Admiralty in May, 1809. The *Topaz* was short of water, and approaching a rocky island, found to be in lat. 25° 4′ S., and long. 130° 24′ W., when the Master's attention was attracted by seeing smoke rising from it, besides other signs of habitation. The shore, on which a tremendous surf was breaking, appeared inaccessible; but a canoe was presently seen darting from it; and soon, to the astonishment of all on board, they were hailed by its occupants, in good English, with offers of assistance, if any of the ship's people desired to land. Mr. Folger declined doing so; but one of his sailors, an Englishman, volunteered to go in the canoe, if the *Topaz* stood in sufficiently to admit of his swimming back to her, in case of his being attacked. He reached the shore in safety; and the first person by whom he was accosted on landing, was a man calling himself "Alexander Smith;" adding, he was one of the crew of the *Bounty*, and the only survivor of the party of nine Englishmen who had left Otaheite in her [Sept., '89]; that some of the children of the mutineers, by the Otaheitan women who had accompanied them, were now grown up; and that, including himself, the population of the island—Pitcairn Island—(since such it was) amounted to 35 persons, of whom he had been for a long while the guardian and instructor. With this unexpected intelligence, the sailor returned to the ship; and the Master immediately landed. Smith supplied him with a short account of feuds that had broken out among his former comrades, himself, and the colored people who came with them, terminating in the violent end of 13 out of the 15 men; that only Mr. Young had died a natural death; and that he, himself, alone remained of the 15. In return for these tidings, Smith eagerly inquired as to the events that had occurred in Europe during his long seclusion on the island. Mr. Folger told him of the French Revolution, of the war between Great Britain and France, and of the Naval victories —the Nile, Trafalgar, &c.,—achieved by the former; on hearing of which, the recluse, unable to restrain his enthusiasm, threw up his hat, and gave a loud "hurrah"! exclaiming, "Old England for ever"! Smith also gave to Mr. Folger the chronometer, and azimuth compass of the *Bounty*. (a) And in the beginning of 1814, Rear-Admiral Hotham, then cruising off the American coast, transmitted to the Admiralty a letter received from Mr. Folger, to the same effect as the entry in the log of the *Topaz*, but dated March, 1813, and containing many encomiums on Smith, for his excellent moral and religious training of the little community over which he presided.

The intelligence thus conveyed to England in 1809 and 1814 —especially the first intimation of the discovery of the retreat and fortunes of Christian and his party—" re-awakened public curiosity; and the newspapers and periodicals teemed with their story," and that of the *Bounty*, for a year or two from the former date. But the war still prevailed; and public interest again subsided in the matter. No steps were taken to communicate with the newly discovered Colony. Our ships of war were fully occupied in convoying fleets of merchantmen, cruising in search of the enemy, and blockading his ports; and the proceedings of Major Johnstone's Court Martial had taught men even more than

---

(a) This chronometer had been twice used by Captain Cook on his voyages of discovery: It was supplied to Mr. Bligh when fitting out the *Bounty*: and the mutineers carried it with them to Pitcairn Island. Mr. Folger stated, that shortly subsequent to his recovering it from Smith, it was taken from him by the Governor of Juan Fernandez. But, after a series of "adventures," it reached England in 1843; and now reposes in the United Service Museum, Great Scotland Yard, London; having been presented by Sir Thomas Herbert, who had purchased it at Valparaiso: It was exhibited in the Royal Institution, Albemarle Street, in 1844.

was previously known of Captain Bligh—of whose victims in Pitcairn Island, Smith now appeared to be the sole survivor. (b) But towards the close of 1814, two English frigates, the *Briton* (commanded by Captain Sir Thomas Staines), and the *Tagus* (under Captain Pipon), being in search of an American ship, the *Essex*, which had been seizing English whalers in the Southern Pacific, made the further discovery, and revealed the additional facts, disclosed in the following letter received at the Admiralty, and addressed to its authorities, from the first-mentioned officer, early in 1815:—

"'*Briton,*' *Valparaiso,* 18*th October,* 1814.

"*I have the honour to inform you, that, on my passage from the Marquesas Islands to this port, on the morning of the* 17*th Sep., I fell in with an island where none is laid down in the Admiralty or other charts, according to the several chronometers of the '* Briton *' and '* Tagus.*' I therefore hove to until daylight, and then closed to ascertain whether it was inhabited—which I soon discovered it to be, and, to my great astonishment, found that every individual on the island (forty in number) spoke very good English, as well as Otaheitan. They proved to be descendants of the deluded crew of the '* Bounty,*' who* [*when they last quitted Otaheite*] *proceeded to the above-mentioned island, where the ship was burnt.*

"*Christian appears to have been the leader and sole cause of the Mutiny in that ship. A venerable old man*" [*whatever may have been the effects of exposure and care, he was only* 50 *years of age at this time*], "*named John Adams*" [*his real patronymic of '* Alexander Smith,*' had been changed to this, for some reason, since the visit of the '* Topaz *'*], "*is the only surviving Englishman of those who then left Otaheite in the '* Bounty,*' and whose exemplary conduct and fatherly care of the whole of the little Colony cannot but command admiration. The pious manner in which all those born on the island have been reared, and the correct sense*

(b) Between the visit of Folger's vessel and that of the *Briton* and *Tagus*, next mentioned, none other anchored at the island to the knowledge of the inhabitants; but a boat party must have landed unperceived in search of cocoa-nuts, from one of two vessels that were one evening observed in the interval, standing in for the island, very much to the general alarm; for one of the Quintalls found a strange clasp-knife lying on the beach, next morning, among a number of broken cocoa-nut shells. The islanders "lay close," and their visitors were probably unaware that the place was inhabited. Quintall rushed to the village on making the discovery— "feeling, like Robinson Crusoe, when he saw the print of a human foot on the sand;" but the two vessels were gone.

of religion which has been instilled into their young minds, by the old man, have given him pre-eminence over all of them; they look up to him as the father of one and the whole family.

"A son of Christian was the first born on the island [in 1790, or], about 24 years ago: he was named 'Thursday October Christian:' the elder Christian fell a sacrifice to the jealousy of an Otaheitan man, within 3 or 4 years after their arrival on the island. The mutineers were accompanied thither by 6 Otaheitan [and Toubouain] men, 13 women [and a child]; the first were all swept away by desperate contentions between them and the Englishmen; and 5 of the women died at different periods" [all the mutineers also died, or were killed, with the exception of Adams]; "leaving at present only him and 8 women of the original settlers. [Their children constituted the remainder of the population.]

"The island must, undoubtedly, be that called 'Pitcairn,' though erroneously laid down in the charts. It produces in abundance yams, plantains, hogs, goats, and fowls; but [at most points] the coast affords no shelter for a ship or vessel of any description; neither could a ship water there without great difficulty. Since Christian and his companions landed upon it, only one ship has ever communicated with the place; this occurred about 6 years since, and that was the 'Topaz,' of Boston, Matthew Folger, Master. The island is completely iron-bound with rocky shores, and the landing in boats must be at all times difficult; though it may be safely approached within a short distance by a ship.

"*(Signed)* T. STAINES."

This third account of the lost mutineers, and their descendants, fanned the smouldering flame of English interest; and, as further particulars were sought for, Captain Pipon of the *Tagus*, being applied to, drew up a narrative, of which the following is a summary:—The curiosity of the people of the *Briton* and *Tagus*, aroused by meeting with an island in a position not marked on their ships' charts, was still more excited (when they ran in for the land,) on perceiving a few huts, neatly built, amidst plantations laid out with some order and regularity; and these appearances confirmed the first impression that the island was not "Pitcairn's," because that had been described by navigators as being *un*inhabited.

Presently, a number of persons, who had assembled on the rocks to watch the proceedings, were observed; and two men were seen rapidly descending to the shore, with canoes on their shoulders. One of these canoes was boldly launched on the breakers, and then dexterously paddled through the reef, alongside of the *Briton*. "Won't you heave us a rope, now?" was the startling request that followed, in good English; and, on its being complied with, a fine young man sprang actively on the deck. His athletic figure was quaintly attired in a vest without sleeves, and trousers to the knee only; and his hat was jauntily decked with black cocks' feathers. To the question, "Who are you?" he answered with ingenuous frankness, "I am Thursday October Christian, son of the mutineer, by a Tahitian mother, and the first born on this island." (He had been so named from the day and month of his birth). His age was 24; and he was accompanied by a handsome youth of 18—George Young, eldest son of Mr. Midshipman Young, who was now dead. But as girls of T. O. Christian's own age seem to have been then rather scarce in the island, *he* was married to the widow of that Mr. Young, and was therefore step-father to his present companion, who was only six years his junior. (a)

The robust appearance and height of the two young men, and especially of Christian, were very striking. Jet black hair fell down to his shoulders; and though his complexion was dark, and much tanned from exposure, there was nothing of that red tinge of skin so common amongst the Pacific islanders. George Young was also free from it; and their deportment, whole bearing, and natural, easy manner, were as much removed from undue familiarity as from conventional shyness and restraint. Sir Thomas Staines, himself, showed them over the ship—whose size, the guns, and every object around them, were new and wonderful in their estimation. The sight of a cow not only astonished, but alarmed them—they seemed to think her a very large goat, or horned sow; while a little black terrier excited their warm admiration—"I know that is a dog,"! exclaimed Young—"I have read of such things." Although strangers to mechanical contrivances, and to most of the useful arts of civilized life, they displayed an intelligent appreciation of everything they saw, and were eager for information on all objects connected with the ship. At the close of their visit, Sir Thomas

---

(a) This Mrs. Christian was one of the survivors of the Otaheitan women who had sailed to Pitcairn Island in the *Bounty*; and (being then the last of the original party) died in 1850.

ordered refreshments to be provided for them in his own cabin; but, before sitting down, they devoutly folded their hands, and repeated a short prayer of thankfulness for the food they were about to partake; and at the conclusion of the repast, they offered another, which, they said, had been taught them by their revered pastor and teacher, John Adams.

As Christian and Young entreated their host to accompany them on shore, to see Adams, both Sir Thomas, and Captain Pipon, placed themselves under their guidance; and their skill bore them safely through the surf, and past the rocks to the landing place. "It required, however, no small exertion to get on shore, and up the steep ascent to the village—where Adams, his blind wife, and the whole community, were ready to receive them;" and, having ascertained that the strangers intended no harm to their "beloved father," as the islanders termed Adams, they willingly assented to his conducting the Captains to his house. Here they were entertained on eggs, fowl, yams, plantains, and bread fruit; found Adams' family to consist of his wife, three daughters, from fifteen to eighteen years of age, a boy of 11, a daughter of his wife by a former husband, with a son-in-law; and received his version of what had occurred on the island since he, and his now dead mates, had landed there 25 years before. Though little more than 50, and healthy and robust in form, Adams' countenance looked aged and worn, betraying marks of anxious thought; and as he stood hat in hand, while conversing with his guests, he smoothed his scanty locks, according to the fashion of sailors of the olden time. He frankly disclosed, it is said, all the circumstances which had happened during the Mutiny; though he "denied being accessory to, or having any previous knowledge of it."

This—joined to the fact, that when, in 1825, Captain Beechy, in H.M.S. *Blossom*, touched at Pitcairn, Adams again "denied all complicity in the Mutiny," and said he was sick in his cot when it broke out, and that he was afterwards compelled to take a musket in his hand—would lead to the inference that he meant to represent, either, he had taken no part whatever, or at least no active part, in that proceeding, when it did arise. But, unless a large portion of the evidence given at the Court Martial was strangely mistaken, he was the most prominent, and extreme of all the mutineers, next to Christian; was the third armed man who came upon deck; and stood sentry over Bligh with a loaded musket, and fixed bayonet. His allegations to the contrary, in 1814, and 1825, may perhaps be palliated, in some degree, by the circumstances of the case; wishing to stand as fair as possible in the estimation of his guests, the British officers, whose presence (as they sat by his table), may have recalled many an early dream, or saddened memory. But he proceeded to inform Captain Beechy, that Mr. Stewart had advised Christian to take possession of the *Bounty*, and that that advice led to the Mutiny —a representation in support of which he did not adduce a particle of evidence, and which (we have seen) was wholly inconsistent with the real occurrences, as well as with the solemn asseveration of Christian, himself, on that night when he parted for ever with Stewart and Heywood, on the beach of Matavai Bay. Let us hope, then, that at least that misrepresentation by Adams (who played such a noble part in Pitcairn Island during the last 30 years of his life), was the result of misconception merely. Yet, his contradictory accounts of the habits, death, and burial of Christian (to be more fully noticed by and by), will scarcely admit of that charitable construction. It should be noted, meanwhile, that he expressed to Captains Staines and Pipon "great disapprobation of the conduct of Captain Bligh, not only towards the men, but also towards the officers, of the *Bounty*." And it is remarkable that while, after the lapse of 25 years from the date of the Mutiny, a common seaman, who took a leading share in it, censured the Commander under whom it arose, in the presence of other Naval Captains, who held his liberty—perhaps his life—in their hands, not a word of blame is attached to Christian, who planned that Mutiny—nay, he is rather excused —a circumstance that speaks volumes in *his* favour, and against Bligh. Nor did any one of the prisoners tried at the Court Martial seek to justify or defend himself, at the expense of Christian, in any way. There was no stone cast at him by them.

"I asked Adams," resumed Captain Pipon, "if he had any desire to return to England; and I must confess his replying in the affirmative caused me much surprise: He told me, he was perfectly aware how deeply he was involved; that, by following the fortunes of Christian, he had not only sacrificed every claim on his country, but that his life was a necessary forfeit for such an act, which he supposed would be exacted from him were he ever to return. Notwithstanding all this, 'nothing,' (he said), 'would give him so much gratification as to see, once more before he died, the country which gave him birth, and from which he had been so long estranged.'" In another person, this would have had the appearance of so much "acting;" and it seems singular that any man would desire to leave what was undoubtedly a happy island home, and his wife and children resident there, for the mere gratification of again seeing a land which he had left 26 years previously, where his "life was forfeit," and would, he thought, be "exacted" from him on his visiting it. "There was a sincerity in his speech, however," (continues Captain Pipon), "which I can hardly describe, but it had a powerful influence in persuading me these were his real sentiments. My interest was excited to so great a degree that I offered him a passage for himself, with any of his family who chose to accompany him. He appeared pleased at the proposal; and, as no third person was then present, he sent for his wife and children—while the rest of the community surrounded the door. He communicated his desire to them, and requested their acquiescence. Appalled at such a proposal, no less sudden than opposed to their wishes, they were all at a loss for a reply: One of his daughters, although overwhelmed with tears, broke the silence: 'Oh, sirs!' (she cried), 'do not take from me my father; do not take away my best, my dearest friend!' Here her voice failed her; she was unable to proceed; leaned her head on her hand, and gave full vent to her grief. His wife, also, (a Tahitian woman) expressed the most lively sorrow." The wishes of Adams soon became known among the other islanders, who joined in pathetic solicitations for his stay amongst them: Not an eye was dry; tears even stood in those of the men, and the women wept bitterly.

Captain Pipon describes the isle of Pitcairn as being truly "a garden of Eden," its lofty mountains towering to a height of 1008 feet over the level of the ocean; above these craggy pinnacles, myriads of sea birds wheeled in mazy circles; and groves of palm and cocoa-nut trees, with the beautiful bread-fruit tree—the staff of life to the island—clothed the rocks down to the water's edge. In the deep valleys flourished in profusion most of the tropical fruits, with the Taro root, from which bread could be made, and other valuable edible productions. The climate, also, would admit, with care, of the successful cultivation of English fruit and vegetables: as the range of temperature was from 76 to 80 in summer; and seldom fell below 59 in winter. (a)

In the midst of beautiful scenery, and beneath the banana, the plantain, and the wide spreading banyan, stood the pretty village of Pitcairn, on an elevated platform of rock. The several houses surrounded a large grassy square, securely guarded by pallisading, to preserve it from the depredations of the poultry, hogs, and goats, which were otherwise allowed to roam at liberty about the island. On one side of the square stood the house of John Adams; on another, that of Thursday October Christian. These, and all the little dwellings which clustered around them, were formed of wood, had generally two stories, and were substantially constructed. Their internal arrangements bespoke great cleanliness and comfort; and the beds and bedding were remarkably neat.

European habits were visible in the farming arrangements, as each dwelling had attached a pen for fattening hogs, another for fowls, a bakery, and a building for the manufacture of cloth; and all their arrangements were obviously on a settled plan, unlike anything to be met with on other South Sea islands. In their houses they had a good deal of decent furniture, consisting of beds laid upon bunks, with neat coverings: they had also tables, and large chests to contain their clothing. Their agricultural implements were made by themselves from the iron supplied by the *Bounty*, which, with great labor, they had beaten out into spades, hatchets, &c. And Adams kept a regular Journal, in which were entered the nature and quantity of work performed by each family, what each had received, and what was due on account: It seemed, too, that besides private property, there was a sort of general stock out of which articles

---

(a) No feathered songster, however, enlivened the forests, with the exception of one small species of fly-catcher; but in after years this want was supplied by an importation of little warblers, taken there by Captain Prevost, in the *Virago*, from Valparaiso. He introduced, also, a variety of roses and myrtles, by the thoughtful direction of Lord Palmerston.

were served to the various members of the community; and, for mutual accommodation, exchanges of one kind of provision for another were very frequent — as salt for fresh; vegetables and fruit, for poultry, fish, &c.—also, when the stores of one family were low, or wholly expended, a fresh supply was raised from another, or out of the general stock, to be repaid when circumstances were more favorable.* Their clothing and linen (adds Mr. Brodie) were made of the bark of the paper mulberry tree, macerated in water, and then beaten out to the desired thickness by large pieces of wood. This manufacture formed the employment of the elder women; the younger working with their fathers and brothers in the plantations, cultivating yams and sweet potatoes.

"And if" (says Captain Pipon) "we remarked with much admiration the fine athletic young men around us, the appearance of the women was equally pleasing; some of them really handsome, and one and all well grown and finely formed, owing, most probably, to the mountainous nature of the island, and the habit from infancy of ascending and descending the rocks, with great weights on their shoulders." The women's dress was composed of a loose bodice, with a drapery reaching to the ankles, and so disposed as to show the symmetry of their persons, not unlike the robes of Hindostanee women; and they wore their long black hair neatly braided into a knot at the back of the head, without pin or fastening of any kind; while a wreath, ingeniously worked, of the sweet scented pono tree, sometimes intertwined with another of a brighter hue, completed their toilet.

But far beyond the personal grace of these simple islanders, were their modesty and gentle behavior; and Adams assured his visitors of their excellent conduct. Each person considered whatever he possessed was for the general good; so that there was no difficulty in settling disputes. Whenever hasty words happened to be uttered, the offender was ready to make ample amends to the injured party; and such was their strict sense of truth, that any statement involved in a sarcasm, or joke, which was not in accordance with actual fact, was deemed censurable.

---

* See *Quarterly Review*, Vol. III., p. 378, &c.

When at length the Commanders of the frigates had to say farewell to these interesting people, they promised to represent to the British Government the admirable state of their community; and that they might rest satisfied no attempt would be made to remove Adams from amongst them. The officers once more entrusted themselves to the guidance of T. O. Christian, and George Young, whose canoe bore them through the surf to the ships—at which a liberal supply of articles conducive to the comfort of the islanders was placed at their disposal; and, with warm adieus on all sides, the youths returned to their expectant friends, and the ships proceeded on their voyage to Valparaiso.

The story which Adams told Captains Staines and Pipon, of the occurrences on the island, after Fletcher Christian, and his associates, had landed there, in the close of Oct., or early in Nov., '89, may be thus abridged : Having surveyed their new Kingdom, Christian divided it into nine portions; retaining one for himself, and distributing the remaining eight among his European companions —to whom (I infer) the Toubouains and Otaheitans attached themselves in little parties; and they began to erect habitations, and commence settlement. But Christian (according to Adams' then representation) " seemed uneasy, and would spend whole days in a cave, opening from a high ridge of almost inaccessible rocks at the furthest extremity of the island." Here, he secured a supply of water (the " trickling stream " was in this neighbourhood), with a stock of provisions; and thither, possibly, he meant to retreat in the event of discovery, await his pursuers, and defend his life to the last. (*b*) Or, he may have reserved this secluded spot as one to which he might retire, when sad and bitter reflections pressed upon him. As he gazed across that wide expanse of ocean which his position commanded, a sail on the horizon could be no welcome sight; neither was there, amid the great wilderness of waters which surrounded him, a single person of whom he could inquire for tidings—nor, with the exception of Mr. Young, even speak—of home, and distant friends—of his mother, and lone sister—for he had both; though there was a

---

(*b*) "So difficult," says Captain Beechy, "was the approach to this cave that, even if a pursuing party were successful in crossing the ridge, Christian might have bid defiance to any force, so long as his ammunition lasted."

friend (and the surest of all), whose Holy Word (as well as the English Church's Book of Prayer), "he constantly read." It is as probable, therefore, that his "cave" may have served as a place of devotion, as that it was intended for a retreat, where a desperate man could sell his life most dearly; and that the softening influence of that blessed Word, and exquisite Liturgy, may have there lightened his heart, rather than wrongful thoughts have steeled his arm. And to Captain Beechy, in 1825, Adams stated, that Christian "was always cheerful;" that his example was of the greatest service in inciting his companions to labor; that he was naturally of a happy, ingenuous disposition, and won the good opinion and respect of all who served under him—which cannot be better exemplified (he said) "than by the fact of his maintaining, under circumstances of great perplexity, the regard of all who were immediately associated with him, up to the time of his death."

This respect and regard did not, and could not, however, long extend amongst the Toubouain and Otaheitan men; for there is evidence that some at least of the Europeans soon forgot, after landing at Pitcairn, what was due not only to the brotherhood, but to that special trust and friendship on the part, of those colored dependents, which had brought them together. The sense of superiority over all darker races which is so deeply rooted in the white man's heart, quickly evinced itself; and both the Toubouains and Otaheitans were made "hewers of wood, and drawers of water," to their English allies. A spirit of still graver injustice characterized the proceedings of one of the latter, at any rate: For, Williams' wife having been killed by a fall from the cliffs, he persisted (in spite of remonstrances) in taking to himself by force the wife of an Otaheitan. In vain did his comrades depict the cruelty and sinfulness of his conduct; he threatened to leave the island if they interfered; and, as he was their "armorer," and a skilful workman, whose services were considered indispensable, they weakly yielded to him—and that concession speedily led to his destruction, and that of five of themselves; and the consequence of this outrage was, that the island, where peaceful tranquility had reigned, became the abode of many an evil passion, and the scene of many a foul deed.

First, a plot was formed by the colored men, for the murdering of all the English; and, though that conspiracy was discovered in sufficient time to prevent its execution (the wives of the latter informing their husbands of it, by means of a song, concluding with the words—"Why black man sharpen axe?"—"To kill white man—"); another was quickly hatched. This one, according to Adams, was fatal to Christian: Indeed, if the following extract from the "Mutiny of the *Bounty*" be not based on a mistake, in confounding Christian with Williams, the former brought his fate upon himself—"The immediate cause of Christian's murder was, his having forcibly seized on the wife of one of the Otaheitan men, which so exasperated the rest that they not only sought the life of the offender, but of others also, who might (as they thought) be disposed to pursue the like course." . . . "He was shot dead while digging in his field, about *11 months* after the settlement on the island." This passage, however, exactly describes the case of Williams; and in the later and more accurate work, "Mutineers of the *Bounty*," it is merely stated, that Christian "was shot while cultivating his garden." Each of these two accounts (though the one goes considerably further than the other) is founded on statements made, or supposed to have been made, by Adams to the Commanders of the *Briton* and *Tagus*, in 1814: While the representation contained in Sir Thomas Staines' own letter to the Admiralty, and derived from the same source, bears (as we have seen) a somewhat intermediate complexion as to the motive that influenced Christian's fate, or occasioned his death (as alleged), and is altogether inconsistent with those statements as regards *time*—"Christian fell a sacrifice to the jealousy of an Otaheitan man, within 3 *or* 4 *years* after their arrival on the island:" It is possible, too, that Captains Staines and Pipon understood Adams to speak of Christian, when in reality he referred to Williams: And there is either no ground for the assertion in the entry about to be quoted, or some of the islanders gave to an officer of the *Topaz*, in 1808, a totally different account from any of the above as to the circumstances of Christian's death; since *this* is recorded in the log book of that vessel—"The Second Mate asserts that Christian, the ringleader of the Mutiny, *became insane* shortly after their arrival on the island, and *threw himself off the rocks into the sea.*" That, however, appears, by every other version of the story of the mutineers, to have been the end of McCoy; and, as it is not likely that two of them died by similar means, the presumption is, either, that the Mate, or the log-writer, confused Christian's name with McCoy's. Nor would Christian " have retained the respect" of all who knew him, and " no act of his, even to the close of his days, have diminished that respect " (as Adams himself declared), if he had committed the offence said to have been attributed to him by the same Adams, and had occasioned the massacres resulting from it. It will be remembered, also, that at Toubouai, at least, Christian would not countenance any oppression upon *its* natives, or colored race.

There remains the curious fact, that, from the commencement till towards the close of Captain Beechy's visit to Pitcairn Island, in 1825, as hereinafter mentioned, the old mutineer " invariably evaded all inquiries *as to the burial place* of Christian; alleging *his utter ignorance of the spot;* but, the question being at last put direct by the Commander as he was taking final leave, Adams answered, that 'Christian had been buried in his own garden.' " (*a*) Whether or not that reply has been ever verified, I do not know; though Mr. Nobbs declares, "Nor stone, nor sod, marks his *unknown* grave;" and the island " Register" represents that the bones of all the murdered white men were buried in one common grave, dug for the purpose, in Aug., '94. The circumstances mentioned in the annexed note may render the settlement of the question one of some interest. (*b*)

(*a*) The authority, or passage (in "Mutineers of the *Bounty*," p. 183) from which this fact is derived is somewhat obscurely expressed: It may mean that even from the prior visit of the *Topaz*, Adams had so "evaded," and "alleged." If so, the argument is the stronger.

(*b*) About 1809, a report prevailed in Cumberland, in the neighbourhood of his native place, and was current for several years, that Fletcher Christian had returned home, made frequent visits to a relative there, and that he was living in concealment in some part of England—an assumption considered improbable, though not impossible. In the same year, however, a singular incident occurred. Captain Heywood [our old friend Peter, then a Post-Captain], who was "fitting out" at Portsmouth, happened one day to be passing down Fore-street, when a man of unusual stature, very much muffled, and with his hat drawn close over his eyes, emerged suddenly from a small side street, and walked quickly past him. The height, athletic figure, and gait so impressed Heywood as being those of Christian, that, quickening his pace till he came up with the stranger, he said in a tone of voice only loud enough to be heard by him, "Fletcher Christian."! The man

Whatever was the fate of Christian, it is certain that four others of the mutineers—Williams, Martin, Mills, and Brown—were shot by the incensed Toubouains and Otaheitans, on the occasion of the second plot; the remaining four, Mr. Young, Adams, McCoy, and Quintall, narrowly escaping with their lives. Adams, indeed, was severely wounded by a ball, which passed through his neck, and was twice felled to the ground, but succeeded in getting down the rocks, and ultimately made peace with his assailants. Williams, the original transgressor, was the first man shot; Christian came next, if killed at all; Mills, confiding in the fidelity of an Otaheitan, who was by his side at the time, stood his ground, but was slain by him and another; Martin and Brown were separately attacked, and disposed of—one with a maul, the other with a musket. Mr. Young, who was very handsome, "and a great favorite with the women," was secreted by them during the attack; and McCoy and Quintall got away to the mountains. " Here " (writes Captain Beechy) " this day of bloodshed ended, leaving only four Englishmen alive out of nine. It was a day of emancipation to the blacks, who were now masters of the island, and of humilia-

---

turned quickly round, and faced his interrogator [but little of his countenance was visible; and, darting up one of the small streets, he vanished from the other's sight. Captain Heywood hesitated for a moment, but decided on giving up the pursuit, and on not instituting any inquiries. Recognition would have been painful, as well as dangerous to Christian, if this were he; and it seemed scarcely within the bounds of probability that he should be in England. Remarkable as was the occurrence, Captain Heywood attached no importance to it, simply considering it a singular coincidence]. Another account of the concluding portion of the occurrence substitutes the following for the clauses in brackets. " The face of the stranger was as much like Christian's as the back; and Heywood, exceedingly excited, ran also. Both ran as fast as they were able; but the former had the advantage; and, after making several short turns, disappeared. The circumstance frequently recalled itself to Heywood's memory during the remainder of his life." Note to the "Mutineers of the *Bounty*," p. 185; "Mutiny of the *Bounty*," pp. 338-9.

Had Christian before the arrival of the *Topaz*, in 1808, found some vessel that carried him to England, and been really seen at Portsmouth, by Captain Heywood, in 1809;? and does he now rest in some other place than the refuge which he chose in '89? Nearly all the evidence as to his death in that island rests on statements conflicting, or unwillingly made, by Adams, at different times; and he may have desired to preserve the secret, and to shelter a second retreat (wherever it was), of his old friend and leader. Nor is it likely Captain Heywood was mistaken in the man whom he believed, at the moment, to be Christian, whom he addressed as such, and who darted away immediately on hearing the name. Neither is the independent report which prevailed, and was current for several years, in his native county, and the neighbourhood of his birth place, that Christian *had* returned home, to be disregarded.

tion and retribution to the whites." But the former soon began to quarrel among themselves over choice of the women whose husbands had been disposed of; the result of which was the speedy destruction of all the men of color, with one exception, by those widows, and by some other of their country-women, it is said; and the last survivor of the male portion of that swarthy race, was shot, it is alleged, by Mr. Young, not long afterwards, at the instance of his wife. (*a*) All those events are stated to have happened so early as Oct., '93.

McCoy and Quintall returned from the mountains; and comparative tranquility prevailed on the island for a considerable period. But an unhappy discovery was then made, from which violent and sanguinary consequences ensued. McCoy, who in early life had been employed in a distillery in Scotland, made some experiments with the Ti-root (*Dracœa-terminalis*), by turning the copper kettle of the *Bounty* into a still; and unfortunately succeeded in extracting from the root an ardent spirit. (*b*) Henceforth both he and Quintall "were in a continual state of inebriety,— until the former, fastening a stone round his neck, threw himself from the rocks, and was either killed or drowned; while Quintall (who had lost his wife by a fall from the cliff, when in search of birds' eggs), became a morose and alarming companion to his two surviving countrymen. "There were no limits to his exactions, and he was constantly threatening to take their lives, should they not comply with his demands. He thus became so dangerous that Mr. Young and Adams felt compelled to destroy him, for

---

(*a*) The other Otaheitan women were so horror-stricken and grieved at the execution of the various deeds of violence they had witnessed, that, although they were treated with additional kindness by the surviving Englishmen, the greater number of them formed a plan, in 1794, to leave the island in one of the *Bounty's* boats. Fortunately for them, the boat proved leaky, and their intention was thus frustrated ("Mutineers of the *Bounty*," &c.). But the "Register" states, that the boat in which the poor women meant to leave was "built for the purpose, launched, and upset," and that that mishap prevented any further venture. It fairly adds, "had they launched out upon the ocean, whither could they have gone, or what would they have done by themselves, drifting upon the waves? They must have fallen a sacrifice to their folly;" "Oeno," the nearest island to Pitcairn, being about 90 miles distant (to the northward); a barren place, too, of coral formation, and most difficult of access: and the next nearest island ("Elizabeth," or "Henderson's"), which is more particularly referred to in Chapter VIII., being 120 miles from Pitcairn.

(*b*) The spirit made from the ti-root has been described by a Naval Captain, as "not unlike whisky, and very good."

their own preservation;" and thus terminated the last scene in the sanguinary tragedy of Pitcairn Island. This was early in '99. (c)

Mr. Young and Adams were then the sole survivors of the nine Englishmen, and six colored men, whom the *Bounty* had brought to Pitcairn Island, ten years previously; but there also survived eight of the women, and the child, who had accompanied them. It may be here observed, that Mr. Young's name was only once mentioned at the Court Martial (by Mr. Hayward), as having taken, or being supposed to have taken, any part whatever in the Mutiny; while Mr. Cole seems to have alluded to him as being in the same position as Mr. Heywood (detained on the *Bounty*, as Mr. Bligh was being cast adrift). But he was greatly attached to Mr. Christian; and, once committed to *his* fortunes, he never swerved from him, or them. Adams was a man of humble origin, and acquirements, but the sequel showed that he must have possessed great natural capacity. The son of a lighterman, and brother of a waterman, of London, he had picked up his slender stock of learning from printed papers collected in the streets of that city, and elsewhere: by the help of these he had taught himself to read and write; and that was the extent of his attainments when, at the age of 22, he joined the *Bounty* as an able-bodied seaman, in '87.

Happily, the minds of these two men had not been irreparably seared by the crimes they had witnessed, or shared in; and in them, solitude, reflection and saddened memories, had so wrought, that they desired to change the tenor of their past ways, " and to

---

(c) Mr. Brodie professes to give full details of the plots, feuds, and murders, which resulted in the violent end of all the men of color, and of all the Englishmen, except Mr. Young and Adams, and to do so on the authority, and *verbatim* recital, of Arthur Quintall, sen.: But *he* was born some time between 1794 and 1799; and the island "Register" shows that every one of those colored men, and most of the Englishmen, were killed in 1793, and the entire of the latter, with the above mentioned exceptions, by 1799: Therefore, Arthur Quintall could not have had any personal knowledge of the circumstances which he took upon himself to relate to Mr. Brodie; and as such circumstances, if founded on fact, would prove that every one of the parties to those quarrels and conspiracies (or, as Quintall represented, every grown man and woman on the island, whether white or black in natural complexion), was a fiend of the most treacherous, cruel, and ferocious character—and as the particulars thus served up are contradicted in numerous respects by the entries in that "Register"—it will be more satisfactory, as well as reasonable, to adopt Adams' version of the story of the island, and its people, between 1789 and 1799, than that of Quintall, as reported by Mr. Brodie. I have therefore done so.

return to those paths which lead to tranquility and peace." This is the Missionary account of the circumstances that then occurred; and, though somewhat dramatic, and over-colored, there is no reason to doubt its substantial accuracy:—Being under the influence of terrifying dreams, which had lately visited him—that the angel Gabriel came down from heaven, and warned him of his danger, arising from his wickedness—and that he had been carried away "to view the flames and torment of the bottomless pit"—Adams, towards the close of '99, was turning over what remained of the articles taken from the *Bounty,* when he came upon two dusty books that had been previously cast aside as useless. They were a Bible, and Prayer Book of the English Church. (*a*) He opened the former, and read amongst other passages—"As I live, saith the Lord, I have no pleasure in the death of the wicked; but that the wicked turn from his way, and live" . . . . . and, again, "Though your sins be as scarlet, they shall be as white as snow; though they be red like crimson, they shall be as wool." Tears began to flow; and he continued to read from the same great treasure-house, day by day, till his heart was touched; and "the wicked old sailor" (as the Missionaries put it) became "a new creature." At any rate, a sense of new duties now arose in his mind; a number of children (19—many of them between the ages of seven and nine) were growing up in the island "without care and instruction—they had nothing before them but an example of sin and crime, and were a wild race which united European vices with heathenish degradation; but henceforth, a new era dawned on Pitcairn. Adams looked round upon the young people, in their ignorance; and, feeling that he was in a measure responsible for it, determined he would do his utmost to teach them the value of the books he had so long neglected: He began to pray for them, and for himself—this, three times a day; and, one morning, as he was sitting under a tree with Bible on knee, and considering how best to begin the work of instruction, two youths came to receive his orders: He directed them to dig up a piece of ground, and plant it with yams; promising them a reward for their labour; but they remained standing before him, as if they had something

---

(*a*) Another account describes the books, as a "Bible and Prayer Book that Christian had constantly studied, but which had not been used since his death, and were now diligently sought for," by Mr. Young, and Adams.

to request, till one of them said, "You promise a reward; may *we* choose what it shall be?" and on Adams assenting, the other observed, "We have seen you constantly reading in that Book, and you talk much of the good that is in it: Will you teach *us* to read it, too?"

That was not bad for young savages, "who had nothing before them but an example of sin and crime," and "united European vices with heathenish degradation." To Adams, however, the request seemed an answer to his prayers; and, "in a few days, not only the two young men, but all the community, were learning to read." The Bible was the lesson-book; and, so great was the awakening thirst for knowledge, that he could scarcely do anything but answer questions. The island, "which of late had been the scene of nothing but wickedness and sanguinary quarrels," was now to experience the influence of that Holy Book; and great was the change in every respect. "All the blessings of civilization" followed in its train. Public worship was established according to the forms of the Church of England (the Prayer Book supplying the means); the Sabbath was rigidly observed—the utmost respect for truth inculcated, and the whole tone of morals raised; order and cleanliness became the characteristics of the people; dwellings were improved, the land was brought into better cultivation; and that happy, blissful condition of society created which was found to exist in Pitcairn Island, by the Commander of the *Topaz*, and the Captains of the *Briton* and *Tagus*, in 1808, and 1814. (*b*)

It may readily be believed, however, that all those blessings were not realized at once; though they were the growth of a very

---

(*b*) Mr. Brodie tells the story a little differently, and more circumstantially— Adams (he says) taught the islanders the Lord's Prayer, and Creed, immediately after his dream of Gabriel's appearance to him. Subsequently to that, requiring a piece of ground to be broken up, that he might plant yams in it, he engaged Edward Quintall and Robert Young, to do the work for him; and, as payment, a small phial of gunpowder was to be given. On the work being completed, the lads asked Adams whether he would prefer to give them the powder, or teach them some prayers out of his Prayer Book? He was much pleased with the question; consented at once to teach them; and offered them the powder as well; but they refused to take the latter. At same time, he told them if there were any more of the people who would like to be taught, he would teach them. The consequence was that the whole of them came to him, much to his delight.

In a sermon preached in London in Nov., 1852, the Rev. Mr. Nobbs stated, that the work for payment of which the lads took the scriptural exercises, rather than the powder, was, "making a mattock of iron from the wreck of the *Bounty*."

few years; and, first of all, morning and evening prayers were established in each family; two or three services were added to the duty of the Sabbath; and the children of each household were trained in piety and virtue. Nor were these the only aids to religion adopted by Adams, after Mr. Young's death, in 1800; for, on looking over the Prayer-book, one day, the former found that Ash Wednesday and Good Friday were fast days; and, conceiving that every Friday and every Wednesday were kept as fast days under the ritual of the English Church, he directed that it should be so at Pitcairn. They were kept accordingly until 1823, when Buffett arrived on the island, and told Adams of his error. Then, or about then, he remitted the ordinary Wednesdays as fast days —" at which the islanders " (Mr. Brodie tells us) " were very glad, as their hard labor, and two strict fast days a week, had not agreed with them. Many of them frequently fainted for want of food. But each Friday was observed as a fast day until Adams' death; by 1850, however, Good Friday was the only fast day recognized."

Meanwhile, or so long as Mr. Young was spared, after " the awakening" of himself, and Adams, the former took the leading part in extending its advantages to the islanders generally; though he was sedulously assisted by the latter, " who improved his own slender acquirements by associating with a man of superior education." But Mr. Young did not long survive his entering on those useful, noble, labors. An asthmatic complaint, with which he had been afflicted for a considerable period, proved fatal to him, at the age of 36. And thus (in the year 1800), John Adams became the sole surviving man on the island. He was then 36; and so faithfully and ably did he prosecute the mission upon which Mr. Young and he had embarked that, by the years 1808 and 1814, he had achieved the wonderful results described by the American Commander, and English Captains—" had succeeded in establishing a community such as has been the dream of poets, and aspiration of philosophers."

There were stages, too, in these good works, as in the prior ones. The loss of the last companion of his early days was a great affliction to Adams (Mr. Brodie adds), and was for some time most severely felt: It was a trial, however, that more than ever disposed him to repentance, and determined him to execute the pious resolution he had made. Still, he had an arduous task to perform. Besides the children to be educated, the Tahitian women were to be converted : and, as the example of the parents had a powerful influence over the children, he resolved to make them his first care. Fortunately, those Tahitians were naturally of a tractable disposition, and readily imbibed his precepts. The children also acquired such a thirst for scriptural truth, that Adams had soon to answer numerous inquiries by them, and to " exercise himself " by putting them in the right way ; and, as they grew up, they gained fixed habits of morality and piety. All the while, he eagerly devoted himself to the study of the Bible, and Prayer Book, and to imparting to others the knowledge thus procured. He was listened to with attention by all, as the sole survivor amongst them of the "*Bounty's* crew " (a talismanic term in Pitcairn at least), and was looked up to by the half-castes of the first generation, with patriarchal reverence. His efforts were crowned with success; the morals of the community became as strict as they had been lax; "religious observances were insisted upon even to severity of discipline ; and (when it came) the deathbed of the mutineer, and manslayer, was cheered by the consolating reflection that his labor had borne fruit—that the seed he had sown had taken deep root"— had brought some to repentance, and more to an acquaintance with God, and faith in a life to come. (*a*)

Whilst this reformation was progressing in that " far isle of the sea," as little attention was paid by the authorities in England

---

(*a*) Adams used to exhort the people before going a-fishing, or proceeding on any dangerous enterprise, to pray to God for His protection, and blessing. Upon one occasion he, and some of the Otaheitan women, were out fishing on the south side of the island. The surf became heavy, and broke their canoe. To ascend the precipice that rose above them was impossible. Their only alternative was (as he told them) to commit themselves by prayer to their Maker, and endeavor to swim to a rock some distance from the island, and thence to another part of it : This they did ; and at last they all reached the main shore in safety. (Mr. Murray's Pitcairn, &c.) And Mr. Nobbs wrote, in answer to a question put to him by persons in the United States :—" I have amongst the Pitcairn islanders not only many happy, but triumphant deaths : Herein, too, is the test of the Christian character ; for when we see one—who for a number of years has not only in word, but in deed, adorned the doctrine of God, our Saviour, in all things—brought by sickness, or casualty, to the confines of the eternal world, and about to enter the silent grave— proclaim his hope of glorious resurrection, with unabated energy and fervor—when we see one suffering the most acute agony, yet exhorting others to pursue the same path he had trod ; telling of the love of God to his soul, and of his desire to depart that he may enter into the presence of his Redeemer—can we hesitate to say, on the demise of such—' Let *me* die the death of the righteous, and let *my* last end be like his ? ' "—(*Ibid.*)

to the letter, and narrative, of the British officers last alluded to, as had been shown to the log-book and letter of Mr. Folger. War with France had ceased; but the Pitcairn islanders, their "father," and unexampled reformation, remained unnoticed by the British Government—to its shame be it said: And for 10 years from the receipt of Sir Thomas Staines' despatch, they were permitted to continue in that obscurity which such neglect, the many thousand miles that severed them from England, and the then almost unvisited expanse of waters that lay around them, had entailed.

In the interval, however, "Jenny," one of the Otaheitan women, who had come to Pitcairn in the *Bounty*, seems, for some reason, to have desired a change; for in 1817, she left the island, in the ship *Sultan*, of Boston; and her example was followed, in 1826, by Jane Quintall (daughter of Matthew), who departed in the *Lovely*, of London—vessels that had touched at their quiet home during those years. Whether these young ladies merely went to see the world, or whether the "old, old tale" had been whispered in their ears, by enamored sons of the *Sultan*, and the *Lovely*, beneath the stars, and amid the groves, of that home, does not appear; but they never returned to it. Between these dates, or in 1819, the Calcutta Diocesan Committee of the Society for Promoting Christian Knowledge, having learned that, while another Committee had forwarded a supply of Bibles to Pitcairn, there was a want of other publications, made a selection of such Prayer Books, and secular works, as appeared most suited to the situation of its people, and despatched them, to the care of John Adams, by the ship *Hercules* (Captain Henderson), bound for the South Pacific. They were gladly received, and much prized. And four years later, an accession was made to the population of the island, by the arrival and settlement upon it of two persons, altogether unconnected with the Mutiny: John Buffett and John Evans, seamen on board the ship, *Cyprus*, of London, which visited Pitcairn in 1823, were permitted to remain, and cast their lot with its people—the former officiating as schoolmaster to the children until the arrival of Mr. Nobbs, five years later; and marrying Dolly Young; and the latter espousing Rebecca Adams—grand-daughters of the mutineers, Mr. Edward Young, and John Adams.

In 1825, the *Blossom*, under command of Captain Beechy, R.N., which had been fitted out for a voyage of discovery, looked in at the island (as already noticed); and Adams, with 10 of his young subjects, put off in a boat to welcome another of his Majesty's ships. They did not venture at once "to lay hold," till they had first inquired if they might come on board?; but, on permission being granted, they sprang up the side, and shook every officer by the hand with marked satisfaction. Adams was now in his 60th year; he wore a sailor's shirt and trousers; he held a low-crowned hat in his hand, until desired to put it on; and he still retained his sailor's manners; doffing his hat, and smoothing down his bald head, whenever he was addressed by any of the officers of the *Blossom*. The young men were tall, robust, and healthy, with good natured countenances, and an engaging simplicity of manner. Their dresses were whimsical enough; some had long coats without trousers; others, trousers without coats; and others again waistcoats without either. None of them had shoes or stockings, and there were only two hats among them—"neither of which," says Captain Beechy, "seemed likely to hang long together."

With two of his boats, he accompanied them on shore, where they were cordially received by the inhabitants. Their stay at the island, of three weeks, confirmed the statements of former visitors; and, as the party were entertained in turn at the different houses, the Commander had ample opportunity for gaining information, and noticing the habits of the inmates. Sunday was observed with remarkable strictness, and there were altogether five services in the day! All preparation for their meals was made on the Saturday, that there might be no undue work on the Sabbath. Their fare was simple and wholesome, consisting of pork or fowl, vegetables, and bread, or pudding made from the Taro-root, and abundance of bread-fruit, and bananas. Their drink was water, or tea drawn from a mild infusion of Ti-root, flavoured with ginger, and sweetened by sugar-cane. Attention to their visitors was unremitting. On the latter landing (in the afternoon), and expressing a desire to get to the village before dark, and to pitch their Observatory, every article and instrument found a bearer along a steep path, concealed by groups of cocoa-nut trees; the females bearing their burdens over the most difficult parts without inconvenience. The village consisted of five houses, which stood on a cleared piece of ground sloping towards the sea. As the men assisted in pitching the tent, the women employed themselves in preparing supper. The mode of cooking was precisely that of Otaheite, by heated stones ranged in a hole made in the ground. At young Christian's, the table was spread with plates, knives, and forks. The general South Sea Island custom, that women shall not eat in the presence of their husbands, prevailed in Pitcairn—"especially as there was a deficiency of seats"—though the female part of the society was highly respected. Far, however, from considering themselves neglected by a usage "that deprived us" (remarks Captain Beechy) "of their company at table, during the whole of our stay on the island, the women very good-naturedly chatted with us behind our seats, flapped away the flies, and by a gentle tap, accidentally or playfully delivered, reminded us occasionally of the honor that was done us." When the men had finished their repast, the women sat down to what remained. Their meals consisted almost always of baked pig, yams, and taro, with sweet potatoes, sometimes.

In the evening, beds were prepared. A mattress, composed of palm-leaves, was covered with native cloth, made of the paper mulberry-tree; the sheets were of the same material, and it appeared by their crackling that they were quite new from the loom, or rather the beater; but the whole arrangement was comfortable, and inviting to repose. The first sleep of the guests at each house was broken, however, by the melody of the evening hymn, which, after the lights were put out, was chanted by the whole family, in the middle of the common room—

> "Father! let our supplications
> Find acceptance in thy sight;
> Free from Satan's foul temptations,
> From the perils of the night,
> Oh, preserve us,
> Till return of morning light."

At early dawn, the sailors were also awakened by the morning hymn, and family devotion; after which the islanders all set out to their several occupations. Some of the women had taken the linen of their visitors to wash; or were preparing for the coming meal; and others were employed in the manufacture of cloth. The primitiveness, simplicity, and innocence of these women are strongly exemplified in the following description:—" By our bedsides had already been placed some ripe fruit; and our hats were crowned with chaplets of the fresh blossoms of the *nono*, or flower-tree, which they had gathered in the early morning. On looking round the apartment in which we slept, though it contained several beds, we found no partition, curtain, or screens; these had not yet been considered necessary. So far, indeed, from concealment being thought of, when we were about to get up, the women, anxious to show their attention, assembled to wish us good morning, to inquire how they could best contribute to our comforts, and to present us with some little gifts which the produce of the island afforded. Many persons would have felt awkward at rising, and dressing, before so many pretty, dark-eyed, damsels, assembled in the centre of a spacious room; but by a little habit we overcame this embarrassment, and found the benefit of their services in fetching water as we required it, and in substituting clean linen for such as we took off."

Their cottages were spacious, and strongly built of wood, in an oblong form, and thatched with the leaves of the palm tree, bent round stems and branches of the same, and laced horizontally to rafters, so placed as to give a proper pitch to the roof. An upper storey was appropriated to sleeping, and had four beds; one in each angle, and large enough for three or four persons to rest on. In the lower was the eating room; having a broad table in the centre, with several stools set round it; and communicating with the upper by a stout ladder. Beyond the outbuildings, and enclosures, described by Captain Pipon, were the cultivated grounds producing the banana, plantain, melon, yam, taro, sweet potato, and cloth plant, with other useful roots, fruits, and a variety of shrubs. Goats were numerous on the island; but their flesh was not relished; and the milk of the cocoa-nut was preferred to theirs. Yams constituted the principal food, either baked, boiled, or mixed with cocoa-nut, made into cakes, and eaten with molasses extracted from the ti-root. Pork was seldom indulged in; the people lived on fruit and vegetables; and, with such simple diet, early rising and much exercise, they were subject to few diseases. Captain Beechy states, "they were certainly a finer and more athletic race, than is usually found among the families of mankind." (*a*) The young children

---

(*a*) It was asserted, on the island, that George Young and Edward Quintall had each carried, at one time, a kedge anchor, two sledge hammers, and an armorer's anvil, weighing together upwards of 600 lbs.; and that Quintall once carried a boat

were instructed by John Buffett (the seaman who had settled on the island, as an assistant to Adams, about 1823,) in reading, writing and arithmetic; to which were added precepts of religion and morality, drawn chiefly from the Bible and Prayer Book—" than which, fortunately, they possessed none others to mystify and perplex their minds on religious subjects." Their Church observances, on the Sabbath, were well conducted; the prayers were read by Adams; the lessons by Buffett; with hymns preceding and ending. The service was long; but the neat and clean appearance of the congregation, the devotion that animated every countenance, "and the innocence and simplicity of the little children, prevented the attendance from becoming wearisome." O favored community, and enviable retreat! where peace and plenty reigned; wants but few; and unbroken confidence the common tie. Up with the birds! and to rest with the gloaming; "labor light the daily portion; and the hymn of praise the morning and evening sacrifice"— and all this effected by the zeal and piety of an humble sailor, who, whatever his previous life may have been, or however puzzling some of his later utterances, presents a remarkable instance of the power and blessedness of the Divine Word, even for temporal purposes; since, by the light of its precepts, he realized from the children of outlaws, on a wild ocean rock, what Plato or More

---

28 feet in length. In the water, the islanders, generally, were about as much at home as on land, and they could remain almost a whole day in the sea. They frequently swam round their island, the circuit of which is about five miles; and the women were nearly as expert swimmers as the men ("Mutiny of the *Bounty*," p. 357). When the surf beat heavily on the island, the men have plunged into the breakers, and swam to sea beyond them. This they sometimes did, pushing a barrel of water in front of them, when it could be got off in no other way; and in this manner, a ship has procured several tons of water without a single cask being stove (Murray's Pitcairn, pp. 155-6). It is stated, too, in a letter written from Valparaiso, in Oct., 1849, to the Rev. Mr. Murray, by the Rev. Mr. Armstrong, then British Chaplain there, that Lieutenant Wood, Commander of H.M.S. *Pandora*, (who visited Pitcairn some months previously), had informed him, that a young girl (18 years of age) was accustomed to carry on her shoulders 100 lbs. weight of yams over hills and precipitous places, and for a considerable distance, where one unaccustomed to such exercise could scarcely scramble; that a man, 60 years old, bore with ease the Surgeon of that ship (a big fellow, six feet high), up a steep ascent from the landing place, where he himself had in vain attempted to mount; the path being very slippery from recent rains; and that Lieutenant Wood was hoisted aloft in the arms of a damsel, and borne up the hill, with the utmost facility. (Morrison, p. 156: And see Mr. Wood's own account of Pitcairn, and its people, as stated in Ch. VIII., post.)

could but conceive. Yet that man would have been hanged as high as Haman, had Captain Edwards caught him in 1791!

To the departure of the *Blossom*, there succeeded three years of tranquility, contentment, and happiness; during which the old mutineer still ruled the little settlement; whose members continued to reverence him, fear God, and love one another; having "most things in common;" and, if not redeeming, by the grace and purity of their lives, the horrors amid which many of them were born, at least casting a veil around them which the hand of charity will be loth to withdraw. It was during that period, or in 1828, there arrived on the island (as already noticed), Mr. George Hun Nobbs, who was allowed to settle on it; relieved Adams of some of his labours; and contributed largely to the good of its people, by precept and example.

He was born in Ireland, in 1799; in early life, he had served in the British Navy; and, having quitted it, he entered that of the Chilian Government, under Lord Cochrane, by whom he was made a Lieutenant. On leaving that service, he, in common with many others, was unable to recover his pay; and, weary of the toils and dangers to which he had been exposed for many years, he desired to seek a resting place, and sphere of quiet usefulness, at Pitcairn, accounts of which had reached him: But finding difficulty in obtaining funds for the voyage thither, he became (after other attempts) a Mate on board a vessel bound for the Cape of Good Hope; trusting to procure a passage thence to Pitcairn, by one of the whaling ships calling there for supplies; he was taken ill, however, and unable to move for some time. Afterwards (as no immediate opportunity offered of accomplishing his object), he crossed to Valparaiso, and went thence to Callao; where he became acquainted with one Bunker, who had been Master of a merchant barque, and was then owner of an 18 ton launch; but whose health was so impaired, and his circumstances so reduced, that he could not fit her out. Mr. Nobbs undertook the task, on the understanding that he was to become part-proprietor; that the tiny craft was to go to Pitcairn; and that Bunker should accompany him there. The little money that Mr. Nobbs had saved was expended in preparing her for sea; and the two men embarked on a voyage of 3,500 miles. Fortunately, they had a fine weather passage; and, accomplishing it in six weeks, made Pitcairn on

15th Nov., 1828. But from fatigue and want of sleep during the expedition, Mr. Bunker died a few weeks after his arrival; and the launch, having been hauled on shore, was taken to pieces: Her timbers and woodwork served for the construction of a house for Mr. Nobbs, who (like Buffett and Evans) became a permanent settler on the island, married a grand-daughter of Fletcher Christian; was the island schoolmaster (in succession to Buffett), acted as its Surgeon; and became, eventually, its ordained Chaplain. Naturally, then, the sons and grandsons sprung from such a resolute, sailorly stock, have shown themselves intrepid boatmen, and dauntless whalers; pulling a powerful oar; and oft burying a keen lance in the quivering side of the great leviathan. One of those sons is now the Chief Magistrate of Norfolk Island; and in May, '84, "the old man was yet alive," full of years and full of honor. (*a*)

(*a*) The following is a detailed account given by the Rev. Mr. Murray of Mr. Nobbs' earlier days, and adventures. In 1811 he was entered on the books of H.M.S. *Roebuck;* and through means of Rear-Admiral Murray, he was, in 1813, placed on board the *Indefatigable*, Naval store ship, under Captain Bowles: In this vessel, the young sailor visited New South Wales, and Van Diemen's Land; whence he proceeded to Cape Horn and Cape of Good Hope, and thence after a short stay at St. Helena he returned to England. He then left the British Navy: But after remaining a short time at home, he received a letter from his old Commander, offering to procure him a berth on board a ship of 18 guns, designed for the assistance of the patriots in South America. He accepted this offer; and left England early in 1816 for Valparaiso; but the Royalists having regained possession of that place, he could not enter it until 1817: He afterwards held a commission in the Chilian Service, under Lord Cochrane; and was made a Lieutenant in it, in consequence of his gallantry in the cutting out of the Spanish frigate *Esmeralda*, of 40 guns, from under the batteries of Callao; and during a severe conflict with a Spanish gun brig, near Arauco, a fortress in Chili. In the latter encounter, Mr. Nobbs was in command of a craft, which sustained a loss, in killed and wounded, of 48 men out of 64, and was taken prisoner with the survivors, by the troops of the adventurous robber, General Benevideis. The 16 captives were all shot with the exception of Lieutenant Nobbs, and three English seamen: These four saw their fellow prisoners led out from time to time, and heard the reports of the muskets that disposed of them. Ever afterwards, he retained a vivid memory of that dreadful *fusillade:* Having remained for three weeks under sentence of death, he and his countrymen were unexpectedly exchanged for four officers attached to Benevideis' army. Mr. Nobbs then left the Chilian Service; went to Naples in 1822; in his passage from that city to Messina, in a Neapolitan ship, she foundered off the Lipari Islands; and, with the loss of everything, he reached Messina in one of the ship's boats. In May, 1823, he returned to London, in the *Crescent;* and in the same year he sailed to Sierra Leone, as chief Mate of the *Gambia*—but of 19 persons who went out in that vessel none but the Captain, Mr. Nobbs, and two men of colour, lived to return. In June, 1824, he again went

But long prior to the ordination of Mr. Nobbs, "father Adams" died (29th March, 1829), aged 65; and "his end was peace." He had persevered to the last in the good cause he had undertaken nearly thirty years before; and his deeds live after him; having left a name that is cherished with a reverence far beyond the bounds of his tiny isle. And if in early life he broke the laws of his country (as he undoubtedly did), and was a participator in later and far graver offences than the Mutiny of the *Bounty*, he was spared to prove, by the community which he established on Pitcairn Island, that the germs of a God-like nature are still strong within the heart of man, and may quicken into beings as noble, and as pure, as sages can conjure, or bards depict.

---

to Sierra Leone (now as Commander of the same craft); and was six weeks on shore ill of fever; but it pleased God to restore him to health in time to return with her; and he resigned command on his reaching England. Meanwhile, the Captain of a vessel in which he had once sailed had "expatiated so frequently" on the happiness of the people at Pitcairn, where he had been, that Mr. Nobbs resolved to go thither, if his life should be spared; and with this object in view he set out, on the 12th Nov., 1825, in the *Circassian*, bound for Calcutta; but he was detained there until August, 1827; then, after a narrow escape from shipwreck; in the Strait of Sunda, he crossed the Pacific in a New York ship, called the *Ocean;* went to Valparaiso, and thence to Callao; where he met Mr. Bunker; expended £150 in refitting his launch; and made the voyage to Pitcairn, as above mentioned.—(Murray's Pitcairn, &c.)

CHAPTER VII.—The Otaheite business; and Queen's Deputy!

1830, March—Close of 1837—Visit to Pitcairn of the *Seringapatam*; and sketch of the islanders, by Captain Waldegrave—Their shipment, by British Government, from their own isle to Otaheite; how induced, and effected; the unhappy results; and return of the survivors to former (including incidents mentioned in reports of Captain Sandilands, of the *Comet*, and of Captain Freemantle, of the *Challenger*)—The usurpation of Mr. Joshua Hill; and subjection of the native islanders; his outrages upon "the three Englishmen"; and ultimate discomfiture.

ON 15th March, 1830, H.M.S. *Seringapatam* reached Pitcairn, bearing the islanders a present of clothing, and agricultural implements, from the British Government; and, two days later, her Commander, Captain Waldegrave, writes:— " I was hospitably received by George Nobbs, and all the inhabitants. My officers and men were most kindly treated at breakfast and dinner, and slept in their houses. My crew received a supply of cocoa-nuts and fruits. . . . .

. . . The Christian simplicity of these islanders is very remarkable. They appeared to have no guile. Their cottages were open to all; and all were welcome to their board; the pig and fowl were killed and dressed—the beds were ready—each native was willing to show any and every part of the island; and to a somewhat particular question put by myself, or Mr. Watson, as to the character and conduct of individuals, the reply was, ' If it could do any good to answer you, I would; but as it cannot, it is wrong to tell tales.' They informed me, there were 81 persons on the island; and when, after frequent counting, we only reckoned 79, one quietly gave the Christian names of two others, but declined saying who their parents were, as ' it would be wrong to tell my neighbour's shame.' Before they began a meal, all joined in the attitude of prayer, with eyes raised to heaven; and one recited a simple grace, grateful for present food, but beseeching spiritual nourishment: Each responded, 'Amen'; and, after a pause, the meal began; at the conclusion, another thanksgiving was offered up. Should anyone arrive during a repast, all cease to eat—the new guest says grace; to which each repeats 'Amen'; and then the meal is continued."

The following year was marked by a most extraordinary and insane proceeding on the part of the British Government; for, on the 6th March, 1831, all the inhabitants of Pitcairn (including the three Englishmen, and their families,) were embarked on board the *Lucy Anne*, of Sydney, and taken to Otaheite, where they arrived on the 21st. Mr. Nobbs wished to remain on the former island, with his wife and children; but the rest of the people so earnestly desired him to accompany them, that he consented to do so. The removal of the entire party was superintended by Captain Sandilands, of H.M. Sloop, *Comet*, which had arrived for that purpose in the preceding month, accompanied by the other vessel. The circumstance is next to incredible; but it is no less a fact, that the happy, contented, and pure minded Pitcairners were carried off from their own loved isle, and sought to be settled in licentious Otaheite! The ties that bound them to England were recklessly severed; and an attempt was made to convert them into subjects of an almost savage, and notoriously immoral, country—in which, too, the horrors of war were then pending. This outrage was occasioned by the officiousness of certain ignorant intermeddlers, who represented to the English Government, that there would not soon be sufficient accommodation for the islanders on Pitcairn; though eleven-twelfths of it remained uncultivated, even so late as 1856; and one-half of it was capable of cultivation. The simple people were either led, or allowed, to believe, when the vessels came for them, that a refusal to comply with its wishes would give offence to England, to which they had ever looked with filial reverence; and bitter fruit that belief did bear them.

How the removal of the Pitcairners was effected, the arrangements that had been entered into for their location at Otaheite, and the state of things there, will appear from the report submitted to Rear-Admiral Sir E. Owen, by Captain Sandilands, after the desired service was performed; and though it makes no allusion to the apprehension that influenced them, when consenting to abandon their old home, *that* is shown by the official document I shall quote next after that of the Commander of the *Comet*, who wrote thus:—

"*H.M. Sloop, 'Comet,' Port Jackson, May 26th, 1831.*

"*I have the honour to report to your Excellency, the proceedings of H.M. Sloop under my command, since the 5th of last Nov., when I communicated to you my intention of putting to sea, upon the arrival of the Colonial barque 'Lucy Anne,' from Norfolk Island. That vessel reached this port on the 4th Dec., 1830, and was immediately got ready for sea, with all the arrangements deemed necessary by Governor Darling, and myself, for proceeding to Pitcairn Island, and for the removal of its inhabitants, or such of them as were desirous of removing. I put to sea, with the 'Lucy Anne' in company, on the 27th Dec., arrived off Pitcairn Island on the 28th Feb., '31, and being guided on shore by natives who came off in their canoes, I landed on the same day, and made known to the inhabitants the object of the expedition.*

"*On the second day, I assembled all the heads of the families, and having most fully explained to them that they were perfectly at liberty either to remove to Otaheite, or remain where they were*" [though a barque then lay waiting to receive and take them away!]—"*I directed Mr. Henry (who was employed by the Government of New South Wales to accompany the expedition), to give them every information in his power, which—from his being thoroughly acquainted with the manners and laws of Otaheite, as well as having been present at the meeting held by the late King Pomáre, and the Chiefs, when the promise of land, protection, and assistance, was made to Captain Laws, of H.M.S. 'Satellite,' as set forth in his letter to the Secretary of the Admiralty—he was well calculated to afford. One half of the inhabitants gave me their names; having resolved to remove to Otaheite; and, on the following day, the remainder came to the same resolution. They all immediately commenced making preparations for embarking, by carrying down to the landing place yams, potatoes, and household goods, which were continued to be embarked in the ships until the 7th of March; on the morning of which the entire of the inhabitants were on board the 'Lucy Anne'—being 87 in number.*

"*I arrived at Otaheite, and anchored at Papiete Harbour, on the 23rd March, and found the island under the government of Queen Pomáre, daughter of the late King Pomáre, but, I regret to say, upon the very eve of a civil war; which, however, I have great pleasure in making known to your Excellency, terminated by the opposing parties coming to actual hostilities!*". [Captain Sandilands appears to have hailed from "the Green Isle."] "*And prior to my leaving, the Governors of Provinces, and the Chiefs opposed to the Queen and her party, having amicably arranged their difficulties, had returned from Papiete to their own districts, with their numerous armed followers. Although the island was in the most disturbed state on my arrival, I was greatly relieved from anxiety for the situation in which I was placed with the inhabitants of Pitcairn Island, by receiving from the Queen, and her Chiefs, on the one side, and the hostile party on the other, assurances that the promises made by her father, and them, would be most strictly executed. I therefore, at the request of the Queen, landed the people of Pitcairn, at her residence, about three miles from the anchorage, where houses were provided for them, and they remained until the contending parties returned to their homes; when the Queen gave up for their use a large dwelling belonging to herself in Papiete.* (a)

"*Pending these arrangements, a beautiful tract of very rich land, belonging to the Government of the island, was well examined by the Missionaries, myself, Captain Walpole, and Lieutenant Peake, and determined to be a very eligible territory for the future residence of the Pitcairners. Having made known to the Queen this determination, she assembled the Chiefs of the district in my presence, and formally communicated to them that she had assigned this land to the new comers—giving orders, at the same time, that her Tahitans should immediately commence the construction of houses when the others had chosen a site suited to their wishes; and the materials for erecting these houses were in considerable forwardness before my leaving. A feeling of great regard was universally manifested to this people by the Otaheitans, who diligently endeavored to find out those who were their relatives—a search in which they were often successful; and a person, who had come a considerable distance, discovered a sister in one of the few remaining Otaheitan women who had gone to Pitcairn with Christian, and his party* [42 years previously], *and were now returned.*

Captain Sandilands then reverts to his recent visit to Pitcairn, and states, " On my arrival there I found the islanders extremely distressed for water; and what they had was procured with difficulty " [in later years such scarcity or difficulty was but rarely experienced]; "and although the fertility of Pitcairn has reared a comparatively numerous population, this very circumstance, from their increasing numbers, renders " (he thought) " the necessity for emigration the more obvious." [In after times, the island supported considerably more than twice as many people as he took from it, in 1831; and if its resources had been properly developed, even that number might have been very largely exceeded. In

---

(a) Fresh meat and vegetables, for a period of six months, had also been secured to them by the British Government.

1833, Captain Freemantle, R.N., was "satisfied it is capable of supporting 1,000 persons;" and in 1839, Lieutenant Lowry, R.N., expressed a like opinion.] But, relying on the circumstances mentioned in his report, the gallant Sandilands "concluded there was every reason to hope that the change from Pitcairn to Otaheite would be attended with advantage to the people of the former."

He was a bad prophet. The licentiousness of the Otaheitans disgusted the moral Pitcairners from the first; sickness broke out amongst them—of which 12 of the party died, within a few weeks from their arrival. Thursday October Christian was amongst the victims; and four others sank under disease which they caught at Otaheite, and bore with them to Pitcairn, on their return thither. For, all those who were still spared speedily determined upon that step; and, ere long "the beautiful tract of very rich land" which had been allotted to them on the former island, with all the seductions it could afford, were abandoned and rejected; and the simple folks were on their mountain home once again. Upon the 24th April, '31, John Buffett, and family, two of the Youngs, three of the Christians, and one of the Quintalls, sailed from Otaheite for that spot, in a small schooner; and though, owing to contrary winds, they were landed at Lord How's Island (where another of the Christians died), and the schooner returned to Otaheite with her owners, a French brig (*Bordeaux Packet*), carried the survivors home, two months later. On 2nd Sep., '31, the remainder of the Pitcairn people arrived there, from Otaheite, in an American brig, *Charles Dagget*, chartered for that purpose by the British Consul, and other friends, at the latter place. And thus—with the four deaths that ensued at the former—terminated that sad and mad incident, entailed upon the poor islanders by the folly of a paternal Government. (*a*)

It was at day-break their old quarters came in sight of the larger party of the returning islanders; and as their vessel stood in towards the land, the sun rose from behind it in full splendour; gilding its peaks with quivering flashes of golden light; darting

---

(*a*) "It is a remarkable fact," observes Captain Freemantle, in May, 1833, "that many of the copper bolts of the *Bounty*, which had been brought to Otaheite from Pitcairn by the islanders, were taken by the Master of the *Charles Dagget*, as part payment for their freight, to the amount of 200 dollars"—a King's ship helping to pay the passage of *their* children who rose against him, and it !

a-down its steep sides, and tinging the foaming breakers that girt its base. Every eye was strained to catch the first glimpse of the dwellings they had recently left, and were now re-seeking, that nestled amid the palm, the myrtle, and the orange trees, which bent to the wind, or glistened at the touch of morn; and every heart was glad that Pitcairn was theirs again.

But the full consequences of their late absence had yet to be endured; and they were still worse than the immediate discomforts, and 17 deaths, attending it. Those results, the dread that had induced their consent to the English project, and the feelings of the returned wanderers, are fairly stated in a communication addressed to the Admiralty, by Captain Freemantle, R.N., about 20 months after they had regained the loved abode; and which ran thus, under date, 30th May, 1833 : —

"*After visiting, in the 'Challenger,' several of the islands, I proceeded to Pitcairn*" [*arriving there in Jan., '33*]. "*The ship was immediately visited by most of the islanders, who came off in their canoes, to invite the officers on shore. They were all well dressed, and in every respect had the appearance of Englishmen. But I was sorry to find they had not been improved by their visit to Tahiti; on the contrary, I had reason to think they were much altered; and that, on their return, some of them had indulged in intemperance, by distilling a spirit from the ti-root, which grows in great quantities on the island. I interrogated the most intelligent of the men respecting their removal from and return to it; and they are unanimously agreed they had never been happy or contented from their quitting until their regaining it. They added, that nothing would have induced them to leave it, except the fear of displeasing the British Government, which (it was thought) they might have done, had they not profited by the means offered to remove them; and that, being now re-established, they would ever remain at Pitcairn. They had nothing to complain of in their treatment at Tahiti; but disliked the character of its people, and were alarmed at the sickness which prevailed among them, and had carried off 17 of them in all—includiny five who had died of it since their return* [*or at Lord How's Island*].

"*The number of people on Pitcairn at present is 79; and there appears to be abundance of vegetables of every description. They seem to be under no alarm for want of water; as they said, when their numbers increased they could dig more reservoirs and wells; and as regards food, I am satisfied the island is capable of supporting 1,000 persons. The soil is particularly good; and as most part of it is uncultivated, there is little dread of scarcity. On their return from Tahiti, they found their island overrun with wild hogs, and their plantations destroyed; and they had only just succeeded in hunting down the depredators; but even so, the 'Challenger' was supplied with a large quantity of vegetables. Nothing could exceed the kindness of the people in offering every thing they had, which they thought would be acceptable. It is impossible for any person to visit this island without being pleased with a race generally so amiable; springing from the stock of the mutineers, and brought up in so extraordinary a manner; and though I think they have lost much of that simplicity of character which has been attributed to them by former visitors, they are still well disposed, well behaved, kind, and hospitable; and, if well guided, could be led to anything. . . . The present generation of children is the finest I ever saw; out of the whole number, 79, there are 53 under 20 years of age; and they appear to have been well instructed—nearly on a par with children of the same age in England. But a Clergyman would be most desirable, and acceptable to them, if means could be adopted to secure one. Government has sent them gifts from time to time; but they still require articles of clothing, and household utensils. The 'Challenger' took for them, from Sydney, some few things, but so scanty an allowance, that very little benefit could be felt from it. I remained off the island two days; the ship being under weigh, as there is no good anchorage, and the landing is particularly hazardous; it being very rarely that a ship's boat ought to land, or attempt it; though the natives are very clever with their canoes, and will land in almost any weather. Having given all the assistance and advice in my power, and arranged their little disputes to the best of my abilities, I left this tiny Colony; being much pre-possessed in its favour by everything I had seen."*

Another and very remarkable episode, in course of occurrence before and after the date of that letter, is alluded to in a passage of it not as yet quoted, and exhibits other early fruits, or evil effects, of the Pitcairners' residence in Otaheite, brief though it was. In the beginning of 1831, and before the return to Pitcairn of the majority of its islanders, they had agreed to receive Mr. Nobbs as "their sole teacher and Minister;" and the British Consul, and Missionaries stationed at Otaheite, approved of the arrangement, in Aug., '31, hoping he would prove a blessing to them all. But, in the Dec. of '32, or 15 months after the surviving islanders were re-settled at Pitcairn, Mr. Nobbs was removed from his office of teacher and schoolmaster; and the following singular document made its appearance:—"To all whom it may concern. We, the undersigned heads of families at Pitcairn, do hereby certify that Mr. George H. Nobbs has conducted himself to our satisfaction, ever since he has been on this island; also, we have no fault to find with his manner of keeping school for the space of four years; and the reason why Mr. Nobbs is dismissed from teaching, and school keeping, is in consequence of a disagreement between him and Mr. Joshua Hill, who has lately come to reside amongst us."— Signed by three of the Quintalls', one of the Youngs', one of the Adams', two of the Christians', and one of the McCoys'—though as marksmen only; while each of them could write!

Captain Freemantle's report to the Admiralty, of 30th May, 1833, which I have already cited, has this additional passage in reference to the above, and other matters connected with it, which shows that in one respect, and for a time, at least, a marked change for the worse had befallen the inhabitants of Pitcairn.—"I found on the island a Mr. Joshua Hill, a gentleman nearly 70 years of age, who appears to have come from England, by way of Otaheite, expressly to establish himself amongst these people as a kind of pastor or monitor. He had not been on Pitcairn more than two or three months, was officiating as schoolmaster, and had quite succeeded in supplanting the Englishman who had acted previously in that situation. He informed me that, on his arrival, he had found the island in the greatest state of irregularity; and that he had taken Mr. Nobbs' duties upon himself, in consequence of the other's incapacity to perform them (as Mr. Hill alleged); and wishing to render as much service as possible to the islanders. It appeared to me so extraordinary a circumstance—a person of Mr. Hill's age, and seeming respectability, coming from England for the express purpose of residing on Pitcairn—that I at first thought he must be some adventurer, more likely to do harm than good in the cause he had undertaken; but as, from the papers he showed me, he had been *in communication* with my Lords Commissioners of the Admiralty, the Colonial Office, Captain Barclay, and many respectable gentlemen—offering his services to remove the people from the island, when it was originally proposed—I was induced to think he must be interested about them! [Did Captain Freemantle also belong to the *green* island?]; and as he had succeeded in restoring them to some kind of order, by putting a stop to the intemperance which existed (having broken up their stills, and formed themselves into a Temperance society), I gave him all the assistance in my power to support him in his mission."

If the allusion, contained in the preceding extract, to the revival of distillation in the island, and its results, depended solely upon Mr. Hill's representations to Captain Freemantle, little reliance could be placed upon it. Unfortunately, however, Mr. Nobbs, himself, corroborated those representations; because, in a Petition which he forwarded in 1833 (I think) to the Admiral of the Station, he says, " A short time after our return to Pitcairn, some of the natives " (whom he names) " determined to re-commence distilling spirit—a practice they had been accustomed to in John Adams' earlier time. I remonstrated with them on the impropriety of their conduct, but to no purpose ; the answer they gave to my advice was, 'We are our own masters, we shall do as we like; no one shall control us.' Often I talked to them, and begged them to desist from distilling; but I always received abuse in return, and twice narrowly escaped a beating from one of the party" (whom he specifies): So much had their allegiance been shaken, and gratitude waned, to their best friend and teacher, since " the father " was gone, and their visit to Otaheite.

Profiting by this, Mr. Hill speedily extended his complaints so as to include Buffett and Evans, as well as Mr. Nobbs; and sought to obtain their expulsion from Pitcairn; as we find that, in May, 1833, he thus communicates with Mr. White, the British Consul at Valparaiso :—" I had the honor of addressing you a few lines by Captain Freemantle, recently sailing from this island for your port, and England—since when, I have experienced considerable trouble by the presence of two or three *foreigners*, of whom I made mention, residing here; and till they are compelled to leave there will be no peace upon Pitcairn! I have again written home to our Government on the subject, as well as to Captain Freemantle, stating that his sentence, whilst here, for them to leave the island as soon as possible" [he neither gave, nor had power to give, any such order], " will never be respected by these men. Let me beg and pray of you, sir, for the sake of the natives, that the British Commander-in-Chief, the Right Honorable Lord James Townsend, might be entreated to consider the case, and that he would be pleased to give the necessary instructions for the removal of these foreigners from this in other respects happy little island" [and which directions his Lordship had as little authority to issue, as Captain Freemantle could have had.]

Mr. Brodie has thrown considerable light upon the above cool, and fulsome epistle. He tells us, that "Mr. Nobbs' pleasant, efficient and indefatigable relations with the Pitcairn islanders, were interrupted once, and only once, in consequence of the arrival of a certain Joshua Hill, calling himself *Lord* Hill, who came from Tahiti in 1832. This man had the art to persuade the simple islanders, that he had been sent out by the Home Authorities as Governor of the island; and certainly beguiled them into the belief of same by the most extraordinary assertions it is possible to conceive. Indeed, his persuasive powers appear to have failed him but once; and that was in an attempt to seduce them from the Church of England to Wesleyanism, which was steadily resisted. George Nobbs, with the other two European residents, who had seen a little of the world, of course made light of his pretensions; and Joshua consequently declared war to the knife with the malcontents. He then contrived to enlist against them the majority of the islanders (who, I believe, were as much influenced by the fear of giving offence to the British Government, as by any predeliction in their new Governor's favor); and he forthwith commenced a system of petty persecution which eventually drove the three Europeans from the island."

All this is largely corroborated by the allegations in the before-mentioned Petition of 1833, from Mr. Nobbs, to the Admiral of the Station, in which—after referring to his original position of teacher and schoolmaster on Pitcairn, and entrusted with the charge of its spiritual affairs, after the death of John Adams; to his having accompanied the islanders to Otaheite, on their removal thither, and his appointment to be " sole teacher and Minister," in August, 1831, as already mentioned; and to the re-commencing of distillation by three of the islanders, on their return to Pitcairn, notwithstanding his entreaties to the contrary— he proceeds to state, " Afterwards, a Mr. Hill arrived, who assumed great authority; saying he was sent out by the British Government to adjust the internal affairs of the island; and that the British ships of war on the coast were under his direction! Believing these things to be true, your Petitioner gave Mr. Hill an apartment in his house, and used every means to make him comfortable, but, before one month had expired, the latter succeeded by villainous misrepresentations, atrocious falsehoods, and magnificent promises of presents, to be obtained through his influence from the Home Authorities, &c., in ejecting your Petitioner from his house. He then told the people he should act as their teacher, until a qualified one was sent out from England; .... and, shortly after Captain Freemantle's visit and departure, in the *Challenger* (Jan., 1833), Mr. Hill began to oppress your Petitioner, and the two other Englishmen. He ordered the islanders to turn us out of their houses; and our nearest relatives dared not come and visit us. So soon as a ship appeared off the island, a canoe was despatched on board, forbidding the officers and crew coming to our houses; and we were threatened with stripes if we offered to go on board. In May last, an Act was passed (by force) to deprive our children of their mothers' inheritance, merely because their fathers were "foreigners" (Englishmen). In August, Mr. Hill sent his colleagues to seize the muskets of those persons who (he said) were opposed to the Governor of the Commonwealth!; and so soon as he obtained possession of the arms, he loaded them with powder and ball, and deposited them in his bedroom, for the use of the Magistracy of the island. Every Sunday, a loaded musket is placed beneath his seat in Church, to intimidate his hearers! Since that period, your Petitioner has lived in continual alarm for the lives of himself and family. He dared not go out of his house after dark, nor up to his plantation at any time, by himself, for fear of being maltreated by the colleagues of Mr. Hill. Several of the inhabitants protested against such conduct; but he threatened to flog them; and said, too, that if they did not obey him, he would cause a military Governor to be sent out from England, with a party of soldiers, who would take their land from them, and treat them as slaves!! . . . At last, your Petitioner, by anxiety of mind, deprivation of common necessaries, and a sickness thus induced, was brought to the verge of the grave—when, providentially, he obtained a passage to Otaheite, by the *Tuscan* (a passing vessel): And now, driven from family and home, by an unauthorised person, without friends or money, and almost without clothes, . . . he prays that your Honor will cause him, and the other two unfortunate

Englishmen who are with him, to be restored to their families and possessions on Pitcairn."

The state of things revealed by the Petition of Buffett to the same Admiral—and the most material averments in which are supported by the island records—is still more astounding. He mentions that, having touched at Pitcairn, as a sailor in Dec., 1823, by desire of the islanders, and consent of his Captain, he went on shore to teach the children of the former; which he did, until the arrival of Mr. Nobbs, since which he had lived on the island as a private person; that after proceeding to, and returning from, Otaheite, he and the surviving Pitcairners all resided together in a friendly way, till Mr. Hill came, who alleged that he had been sent out by the British Government; that whatever he was in want of he could procure from England, New South Wales, or Valparaiso; and that whatever had been forwarded thence, theretofore, had been procured by his influence; that by means of such representations he had gained the favor of a few of the islanders, and had appointed three Elders, and two Privy Councillors!; that he had framed laws, and built a prison, and declared that if any of them refused to obey him, he would send to England for a Governor, and a regiment of soldiers; that he had thus persuaded the Pitcairners to sign a Petition to Government to deprive the Englishmen, and their children, of their mothers' property; and that he (Buffett), his wife, and little ones, had been ordered to leave the island—on the plea that there was not land sufficient; while, at the same time, Mr. Hill proposed to send to England for wives for the youth of the place; and because Buffett had made known the plan of transporting his wife and family, he had been subjected to a mock-trial, on which Mr. Hill was Judge, jury, and executioner; that, after that gentleman beating him over the head, breaking it in two places (likewise his finger), he was suspended by his hand in the Church! and flogged until he was not able to walk home;!! he was confined to his bed for two weeks; it was several weeks before he was able to work, or have the use of his hand; and Mr. Hill would not allow the people to visit him, or his wife—not even her own sister—but literally tried to starve them; that Charles Christian, then the oldest man on the island, was brutally treated and turned out of his house, for trying to prevent his (Buffett) being flogged;

and because the women assembled, crying shame on Mr. H.'s proceedings, he read the Riot Act on the following Sunday! and told them should they do so again, the authorities would be justified in shooting them!!; that he then sent his colleagues (as he was pleased to call them) to take possession of the Englishmen's fire-arms, which he loaded with ball, and had since kept in his possession; that he had been the means of depriving one of Buffett's children of land derived through her grandfather, Mr. Young, of the *Bounty*, and meant to deprive the others of theirs, and (as the lads grew up) to send them to sea as cabin-boys; that he (B.) was then at Otaheite (having escaped thither, with Mr. Nobbs, by the *Tuscan)*; and humbly hoped the Admiral would use his influence to get Mr. Hill removed from Pitcairn —as was likewise desired by most of the inhabitants. (*a*)

There was a Petition from Evans, very much to the same effect as Buffett's, but charging Mr. Hill with licentious conduct, and with having compelled all the "genuine islanders," from 7 years and upwards, to sign a paper declaring "they would never intermarry with a foreigner"—a term applied to the children of the Englishmen, as well as to themselves; that a law having been enacted, in July, '33, relative to high treason, Evans "requested

---

(*a*) The following extracts, from the island "Register," of the sentence passed upon Buffett, with the *Nota bene* attached to it, confirm his main allegation, and are unprecedented in British judicature:—

"*Pitcairn Island, 5th Aug., 1833.*
"*It only remains with us to declare the sentence of the law, which is* :— And the Court doth accordingly adjudge—that you receive forthwith 3 dozen lashes with a cat, upon the bare back and breech; together with a fine of 3 barrels of yams, or potatoes, to be paid within one month; or, in default, an extra barrel will be required for this reiterated contempt of Court!
"*Signed, &c., by the whole Court.*"
"*Moreover, John Buffett, the sentence of the Court is that, whether with or without your family, you are to leave this island by the first vessel that may present herself here; for if you do not, punishment and imprisonment will be the consequence.*
"*Signed by the whole Court.*"

And there is a N.B. affixed to the record, of a somewhat later date than the "sentence," which shows that poor "Buffett" had to verify his name, by receiving 24 out of the 36 lashes awarded; and that the balance of a dozen, which still remained due to him, must be settled, "if he did not, so long as he remained on it, respect the public functionaries of the island," whose authority, "with the help of the blessed Lord, the Executive has determined to maintain and enforce"!

a copy, as a guide for his future conduct;" whereupon, Mr. Hill "flew into a violent rage, and, shortly after, your Petitioner was dragged to the Church, underwent a mock-trial (no witnesses being allowed), received one dozen lashes with a cat-o'-nine tails—each tail being the size of a man's little finger—and was so much hurt about the head, eyes, and ribs, as to be confined to his bed for ten days:" And Petitioner, having (in dread of his life at the hands of Mr. Hill,) got away to Otaheite, with Mr. Nobbs, and Buffett, entreated that the Admiral would remove the usurper from Pitcairn, and restore himself to his wife and family there.

It would seem, also, that letters were addressed by the Missionaries at Otaheite to Naval officers, serving upon the Pacific Station, up to Dec., 1834, at least, complaining of the usurpation, and oppression which Mr. Hill—that self-constituted prosecutor, Judge, jury, and provost-marshal—had practised upon Mr. Nobbs, Buffett, and Evans; all of whom he had driven into exile from Pitcairn, and two of whom he had publicly flogged, and otherwise tortured, in its Church: The same letters complained of his continued tyranny over the islanders remaining on Pitcairn : And though those communications, as well as the prior Petitions, of 1833, reached the persons to whom they were directed, in due course, and found their way to the Admiralty soon afterwards, a considerable period elapsed before anything was done for the suppression of the scandalous abuses: In the meanwhile, Mr. Nobbs and Evans, unable to return with safety to Pitcairn, went to reside at the Gambier Islands as Missionaries; and Buffet remained at Tahiti: But in the early part of 1837, H.M.S. *Actæon* having touched at Pitcairn, and her Commander, Lord Edward Russell, having discovered and unmasked a false pretence of Mr. Hill, (that he was a near relative of his Lordship's father, the Duke of Bedford,) and heard of his other proceedings—the impostor's duplicity, and the subjection in which he still held the islanders, were brought under the notice of the then Admiral of the Station: And H.M.S. *Imogene* was despatched to the island, under Captain Bruce, with orders to remove his Excellency from it : He was accordingly secured and carried off to Valparaiso, much to the satisfaction of the Pitcairners, who no longer believed in him, had become heartily tired of him, and had invited Mr. Nobbs, Buffett, and Evans to return to them—which they speedily did; receiving a most affectionate welcome from the people: Nor was Mr. Hill's discomfiture the less signal when it is considered, that frequently between 1832 and 1837 (the dates of his arrival in the island and his expulsion from it), he had, both by himself and his "functionaries," addressed numerous letters to the Senior officer in the Pacific, Her Majesty's Consul in Chili, and the Missionaries at Otaheite, to himself, and those functionaries (for he was the author of several of the epistles which he represents to have proceeded from the latter to him), and that in these various communications he lauded himself in immoderate terms for the services he pretended to have rendered to the island, grossly vilified the men whom he had outraged and banished, as well as the Missionaries; and proved himself a most reckless Munchausen. Nor, after his expulsion from Pitcairn, was there any one found who could tell who or what the fellow really was, whence he had come, or whither he went from Valparaiso; though he led Captain Freemantle to believe, in 1833, that he had been in communication with my Lords Commissioners of the Admiralty, and the Colonial Office, &c., &c.! If madness and imposture, audacity and cunning, can be united in the same person, Mr. Hill seems to have embraced them in no measured degree; and he was permitted for five years to tyrannize over the properties, liberties, and almost the lives, of the Pitcairn islanders—and to do so in the name of the Imperial Government! (*a*)

I scarcely think that any Dominion which the people of Australia may establish in after years, for the protection and control of Englishmen in the Southern hemisphere, would tolerate similar outrages for an hour—though the British Parliament has now-a-days gone to the other extreme, by enacting that British-born subjects, resident in independent South Sea islands, may be seized and removed thence, when a High Commissioner is pleased to consider them troublesome!

(*a*) In a letter of 20th July, 1847, addressed by several of the islanders (including the Magistrate, and a Councillor), to the Rev. J. Murray, then Chaplain of H.M.S. *Thalia*, Mr. Hill is described as a "partially deranged impostor."

CHAPTER VIII.—Later History.

1838, Jan.—1850, Jan.: Restoration of harmony, election of "Chief Magistrate," and hoisting of the "Union Jack," at Pitcairn, in 1838—The "fossicking" Frenchman; and yearning for British nationality—Lieutenant Lowry's Elysium; land and people, in 1839—The gift-bearing *Camden*—Disease and relief—Death of Fletcher Christian's widow, in 1841—Inspection and features of "Elizabeth Island" (a proposed adjunct to Pitcairn)—A Queen to a Queen—The poor teacher—A portentous year; hurricane of the next; and rumor of war—An accident; and the island's sympathy—A desire for Ordination—Fresh benefactions, and gratitude—Hieroglyphics on sea cliff, and descents to them—Other evidences of early occupants—The testimony of Worth—Arrival of live stock—Another man-of-war! and celebration of the 60th year of the settlement.

THE banishment of Mr. Joshua Hill, and the recall of Mr. Nobbs, had a happy effect in restoring peace to the island, and in reviving the brotherly love that formerly graced it; but it was some time before the olden simplicity, and perfect harmony, again fully prevailed amongst its people: Thus we read in the "Register," under date 2nd May, 1840:—"A serious altercation took place between Edward Quintall, sen., and John Evans, sen., in which the latter received several bruises, and some scratches, in his head, back, and throat:" Nowhere else, however, would that have been considered a very "serious" matter; though, as Edward Quintall, jun., was then "Chief Magistrate," he may have felt himself somewhat embarrassed when dealing with the case of his uncle: For, about 18 months previously (29th Nov., 1838), H.M.S. *Fly* having arrived at Pitcairn (with gifts from Mr. Rowlandson, and his congregation, at Valparaiso), her Commander, Captain Russell Elliott, recommended the election of that high official; and, his suggestion having been adopted, Edward Quintall, jun., son of Matthew, and nephew of Edward Quintall, sen., "was sworn in." He was re-elected in '39 and '40; and in the former of those years, Fletcher Christian, and William Christian, were chosen as "Councillors." Pitcairn was thus becoming "municipal" in its form of Government. The "Commonwealth," and "Executive," of Mr.

Hill had wisely receded to the more reasonable position of a limited corporation; but gallantry was a leading feature in it; as *ladies* were admitted to the suffrage in the choice of their rulers; and in 1844 the female electors were more numerous than the males— 28 as against 24.

The necessity for the election of a Chief Magistrate, the mode of election enjoined by Captain Elliott, and certain other privileges which he conferred upon the islanders, are shown in his report to Rear-Admiral Ross, dated from the *Fly*, Callao, Jan. 25th, 1839, and the "Regulations" he promulgated at Pitcairn in the previous Nov. In the former he states that, having arrived there (as above), he found its interesting community preserving their deservedly high character for exemplary morality, innocence, and integrity; but they very earnestly represented to him the immediate necessity for there being some Chief, or head to their increasing community (then amounting to 99 souls), for their internal regulation and government; but more especially to meet difficulties and dangers such as they had already experienced, and were again threatened with, by lawless strangers in whale ships—as, when half the ruffian crew of a whaler were on shore for a fortnight, during which they offered constant insults to the inhabitants, and threatened to violate any women whose protectors they could overcome by force; thus occasioning the necessary concentration of the men's strength for the personal protection of the females, and so involving great damage to the crops, which demanded their incessant attention; taunting them, too, that they had no laws, no country, no position entitling them to respect from those American whalers; who denied that the islanders were under the protection of Great Britain, as they had neither "colors," nor written authority (though Captain Elliott found them flying a merchant Union Jack, procured from an English ship): Apprehending that his duty required some decided steps in this unlooked-for emergency, that gentleman considered he should best afford protection to the Pitcairners, by conferring the stamp of authority on the election of an Elder or Magistrate, to be periodically chosen from among themselves, and answerable for his proceedings to Her Majesty's Government: He accordingly drew up certain "Regulations," to be observed in the election, and prescribing the duties of, such an officer; "swore him in" (when first elected); and supplied a proper "Union Jack"—trusting the islanders would be thus insured from any renewed insults by foreigners; And they accordingly selected for the post of distinction "Edward Christian, a most able and superior Senior of their number:" I annex a copy of the Regulations above referred to. (a)

The hoisting of the "Union Jack," under the authority of the Captain of a Queen's ship, and the undisturbed occupation of Pitcairn Island (both previously and subsequently), by subjects of Her Majesty, were amply sufficient to constitute it a dependency of the British Crown: And the prudence of the step thus taken by Captain Elliott to secure to the Pitcairners a recognised position, was shown some years afterwards, when (in 1849) a Frenchman, of military air, and partly military costume, who had reached the island with some other voyagers, by the brig *Fanny*, seemed desirous of placing it under the protection of the "tricolor." Having, with the politeness characteristic of his countrymen, engaged in conversation with Mr. Nobbs, he inquired "whether the people of Pitcairn had heard of Prince Louis Napoleon, and the French Republic? and would they enlist under it?" Then, suiting

---

(a) By Russell Elliott, Esq., Commander of H.B.M. Sloop *Fly*, and Senior officer at Pitcairn:—

"Regulations for the appointment of a Magistrate at Pitcairn, on the 1st day of Jan., every year. An Elder or Magistrate is to be elected by the free votes of every native born on the island, male or female, who shall have attained the age of 18 years, or of persons who have resided five years upon the island—who are to assemble for such purpose in the school-house, the first day of every year; where the business shall be presided over by the Magistrate of the preceding year, whose period of office does not expire until the swearing in of his successor. The greatest number of votes shall determine the election or re-election of the Magistrate; whose duty it shall be to hold the chief authority on the island, and to settle all differences with the advice of his Council; which is to consist of two other natives, one to be named by the votes of the assembly, the other by the Magistrate himself; but his decision is final [on any such differences]. The Magistrate shall also keep a Journal, or Register, of all complaints made to him, and of his decisions thereon; and if any grave offence, or serious crime, be committed, he is to secure the custody of the offender, until he has an opportunity of delivering him over to justice. He will submit his account of what has occurred to the Captain of any British ship of war arriving; and hold himself responsible for the faithful and just fulfilment of the duties of his office. It will be incumbent on his countrymen, and the residents on the island, to respect his situation, and obey his authority, under pain of serious consequences, until he is superseded by the authority of Her Majesty, the Queen of Great Britain. And no one shall be eligible for the position of Magistrate, but a native-born inhabitant of the island." The Regulations supply a form of oath to be taken by him; enjoin the duties they previously prescribed; and are dated on board the *Fly*, off Pitcairn Island, the 30th Nov., 1838: R. Elliott, Commander.

the action to the word, he produced a paper, on which desired republicans could enrol themselves. Mr. Nobbs answered him by pointing to the English flag, which waved over their heads; and assuring him that the islanders knew all about Louis Napoleon, and the French Republic, but were loyal subjects of Queen Victoria. The Frenchman bowed, returned the paper to his pocket, and remarked that "he did not know that Pitcairn was a British Colony."

But its people long desired an express recognition of their *status* as British colonists; and, in a Memorial addressed by them to Her Majesty, in July, 1853, while they acknowledge "with pride and gratitude the visits of her ships of war to their island, they humbly trusted they might be allowed not only to consider themselves Her Majesty's subjects, but that it should be deemed a British Colony, in the fullest sense of the word:" They add, " several years since, the Captain of your Majesty's ship *Fly* took formal possession of our little island, and placed us under your protection: And if your Majesty's Government would grant us a document, declaring us an integral part of your dominions, we should be freed from all fears (perhaps groundless) on that head; such a gracious mark of Royal favor would also be cherished by us in the discharge of the various duties incumbent on British subjects." At same time, they "humbly trusted Her Majesty would be pleased to permit the visits of her ships of war to be continued to them, if her Government should think fit to remove them to some other place." It was intimated to them soon afterwards, through a Secretary of State, that the issuing of such a "document," as they thus applied for, "might imply doubts that did not really exist:" and so (I believe) that matter remains to this hour. But the place to which they *were* removed, three years later, has had no cause to complain of in-attention from ships of war.

Reverting now to the other proceedings of Captain Elliott, in 1838, it would appear that the office of Chief Magistrate, which he then inaugurated at Pitcairn, though indicative of the Sovereignty which it represented, and serving many other useful purposes, was not a very coveted one; and it sometimes happened that the person for whom the honor of holding it was designed by his fellow subjects, would rather be fined than accept its somewhat invidious trust. The fine generally consisted in " providing a hog for the public good;" it was slaughtered and distributed amongst the disappointed electors: But when the office was accepted, its duties were invariably discharged "without fear, favor, or affection."

On 9th November, 1839, H.M.S. *Sparrowhawk*, Capt. J. Shepherd, visited the island, having on board General Friere, ex-President of Chili, "who was pleased to examine the school children, and express his approbation of their proficiency." On this occasion, Captain Shepherd distributed presents amongst the scholars, and islanders generally; and determined several cases submitted to him for decision. And Mr. James Lowry, a Lieutenant in his vessel, has supplied this pleasing picture of Pitcairn, and its people, at that date (1839):—

"At the time of our visit they had increased in number to 102 (51 males, and 51 females)—a great part of them children, and as fine a race as ever I saw. Some of the girls, and young women, were very pretty, and would be considered beauties in Old England; all were very good looking. There was but one person ever born on Pitcairn with any bodily defect, and that was only in his eye. The island is a beautiful little spot; and I doubt if there be any other in the world, of the same size, to equal it in scenery or fertility. It is not quite one square mile in extent, and is supposed capable of maintaining 1000 inhabitants. When first taken possession of, it was divided into seven [nine] equal parts, the number of English at that time on the island. It has since been subdivided [into 22 parts], as the families have increased; still, there is abundance, and will be for some generations to come, as but a small portion of the land is cultivated. A great part of the produce the inhabitants supply to whalers, in barter for clothes, or any necessary articles they want—money there being of no value.

"They have plenty of fowls, pigs, and goats, as well as fruit and vegetables; and their yams are the finest I ever saw. We got a plentiful supply from them, in exchange for things we took them. It is good for them that there is no anchorage [except to the westward of the north-west end of the island], as they stand less chance of being corrupted by communication with the crews of whale ships—the only ones almost that touch there, except the yearly man-of-war. At present, I doubt, if among the same number of people you could find, anywhere else, so few exceptions to good moral behaviour. The islanders all came down to receive us on landing, and conducted us to their homes; each anxious to carry us away; and they had provided their best form of entertainment. There were six or seven of us in the first party that landed; so we were distributed pretty well. Before every meal, they offer up thanks—and they put us to the blush when they first dined on board (as some did daily), by asking us, after a slight pause, if we never said grace? and, on our replying, 'but seldom,' they sought permission to do so before they would begin dinner. There is not such another happy little community.

"On their first rising, they assemble, and sing the morning hymn; and, before resting, they again meet, and sing the evening hymn. A few trifling disagreements they had, which the Captain settled to their satisfaction. They have also made a brief code of laws; and one of their punishments is flogging, with a cat-o'-nine tails, for theft; but only once have they had occasion to apply it. There are but three persons staying on the island who were not born there; they are Englishmen; and no more will now be admitted. These three have resided a long time, and have families. One of them acts as schoolmaster and Parson; and, in return, the rest of the males cultivate his land. We all visited their school, and were much pleased with their progress, the seniors could write, read, and understand arithmetic; and every one can now read—which they could not do formerly for want of books; as they had during the earlier years but one Bible amongst them. I was not on shore on Sunday, but from the accounts of those who were, the sight then presented must have been very gratifying. All attend Divine Service; no manner of work is done; not even meals cooked; that being seen to on Saturdays. They did not forget in their prayers our little Queen, and all people in England. The service was of the Church of England. Generally, the girls marry at 14 or 15, and the men under 20. One of the girls at the school, who was only 15, had been married for upwards of 12 months, and had a child. There has been only one old maid on the island; she is now nearly 50; is as cross and crabbed [the Lieutenant has forgotten here the gallantry of his cloth] as any old maid need be; and she rails against the early marriages most heartily.

"Their manner of living is so simple, that they have but few diseases, and death rarely visits them except from old age. There are 13 families who live in comfortable homes, constructed of wood. One end is partitioned off for the bedroom of the father and mother of the flock; there are bed places along one side of the wall, facing the door of the other apartment. They are not very clean in their houses; but that could be easily remedied if they had any Lady to put them in the way of better habits. And there are neither fleas, bugs, lice, nor any poisonous reptile, whatever, on the island. The Admiral, and his wife, sent them a present of carpenter's tools, needles, thread, and some cottons for gowns; and there were some books sent from England. . . . The women and girls wear a loose sort of dressing gown, not confined at the waist, and coming up close to the neck. Neither sex wear shoes; although the females have pretty little feet of their own; and the present generation have good hair; that of the first families was curly; but it has gradually became the same as Europeans. When they have no visitors, they partake of meat but twice a week; there is abundance of vegetables at all times; and they only drink water and cocoa-nut milk. They have numerous goats; but never milk them; letting them run wild to breed. Some years ago, they managed to distil a spirit; but when, after a short time, its injurious effects were experienced, they passed a law that no more should be made.

"They have no springs; but have plenty of water from the rain, as there are now several reservoirs." Mr. Lowry then refers to their temporary migration to Otaheite, in 1831, and speedy return from it; and continues—The experience there gained " has done them this good, that they will not again be anxious " [induced] " to leave their own sweet isle; and they seem quite aware that they are far better off, and happier, than the generality of mankind. (*a*) . . . Little is now left of the *Bounty*; as every person who touches at Pitcairn tries to get a part of her. I got a small piece of her wood, which I have made into a box, and a bit of her keel. . . . On our leaving, all the islanders followed us to the beach to see us off; with many kind wishes for our health,

---

(*a*) Accordingly, when an offer was made in 1849, by Consul-General Miller, and other persons at Otaheite, to provide land and other necessaries, for any families who might wish to emigrate there, it was not even entertained. The Pitcairners had had enough of Otaheite in 1831.

and a happy return to our friends in England. Such was our parting from what I consider the most interesting spot in the universe."

The presence in it of an ex-President, such as the *Sparrowhawk* had brought as a passenger, seems, however, to have induced a slight appreciation of worldly distinction; for in the following month, the "Register" was honored with the entry of "Joseph Napoleon Quintall," and " L. Victoria Rose Quintall," amongst the names of the newly born.

On the 9th Nov., 1840, there came to the island the Missionary packet, *Camden*, having on board the Rev. Mr. Heath, of the London Missionary Society, who was the bearer of valuable presents from the Governor of New South Wales, from the Bishop, and from Dr. Ross. During this visit, the island school was examined "collectively, and individually," and both teacher and pupils were commended.

Heretofore, Pitcairn was singularly free from diseases; but in 1841 it was visited by so general, and so severe an attack of influenza, attended by a distressing cough, that there were not a sufficient number of able persons left to dig the yams, then in harvest, "and nearly every house was like an hospital;" but the visitation was relieved by the services of Dr. Guin, Surgeon of H.M.S. *Curacoa* (Captain Jenkins Jones), which came from Callao on the 18th Aug. of that year. The same vessel bore presentations from the Admiral, and Mr. Miller, of Valparaiso. Captain Jenkins was also generous to the islanders. So that, when the *Curacoa* left, she carried with her their prayers that " God might preserve the worthy Captain, officers, and crew, from every untoward circumstance."

In the same year died " Isabella," a native of Otaheite, widow of Fletcher Christian, the mutineer; her age was not known; but she frequently said she remembered Captain Cook arriving at that island (his first landing there was in Aug., 1773). And though her sphere was humble, her life was an eventful one. Sprung from that sensuous land, she had formed an attachment, in 1789, to the young Englishman " of bright, pleasing countenance, and tall commanding figure," who had designed and led the Mutiny of the *Bounty*; for him she had left country and kin; remained faithful to him until his death; and though afterwards, in 1831, she (with the other Pitcairners) had been persuaded to revisit Otaheite, it was soon forsaken by them all for the little isle where her children were born, and he had fallen (if the current story be correct). And now many a lithesome fisherman, and winsome girl, of Norfolk and Pitcairn Islands, claim descent from "Dark Isabelle."

By 1841, communication between Pitcairn and the outer world had largely increased from the days of Martin Folger, and Captains Staines and Pipon; so much so, that in that year, 19 ships touched at Pitcairn; in 1842, 31 ships did the like; 29 in 1843: and in 1846, there were 49, of which 46 were American; though in 1849, the American vessels had dwindled down to 7 (owing to the decline of whalers visiting the South Seas). There were, however, 8 from the Australian Colonies, bound for California. But this extended intercourse with strangers, though offering a market for the island supplies of fruit, vegetables, hogs, and poultry, may have brought the new maladies that assailed it in 1842-5-6— during which, fevers of various descriptions broke out amongst the people; and in 1849, there was so much sickness, that the public school had to be closed, and Divine service could be performed but once on each Sabbath.

In 1843, the idea of extending their possessions seems to have entered the minds of the Pitcairners; for, on 4th March of that year, John Evans, and 10 of the others, sailed in the barque *America*, "in order" (as the "Register" tells) "to explore Elizabeth Island; but they returned some days later, bringing a very unfavourable, general, report of it." That island was first visited by the crew of the *Essex*, an American whaler, two of whom landed on it after the loss of their ship, and were subsequently taken off by an English whaler, which heard of their fate at Valparaiso. The place was next touched at by the ship *Hercules*, of Calcutta—after whose Captain it is now sometimes called "Henderson Island." It lies about 120 miles from Pitcairn (lat. 24° 0' 2" S., and long. 124° 45' W.); is considerably larger than the other, and covered with timber of a small size, similar to that with which the houses were originally built upon Pitcairn (but which was nearly all used up by 1850). The 11 explorers of 1843 found the landing at Elizabeth Island anything but easy; and the soil not nearly so rich as that of their own; being of a much more sandy nature. Of water there appeared at first to be none; but after a long search they discovered a spring below high tide mark. Some cocoa-nuts, which had been purposely carried there, were planted upon the best ground they could find. The party were only a few hours on this island, and were therefore unable to give any detailed description of it on their return to Pitcairn; but it is about five miles in length, one in breadth, some 80 feet above sea level, strewn with dead coral; and difficult to penetrate, owing to the shrubs that covered it. Evans and his comrades had gone to inspect it, with a view of ascertaining whether it would be suitable as a run for the live stock of Pitcairn, and thus permit the latter to be reserved exclusively for cultivation. (*a*) Water may be had on the north-west part of the island, dripping from the roof of a cave, but which cannot be reached without the aid of ropes. (" Register ").

It was in the same year (1843), that Queen Pomáre, who had done her best to reconcile the Pitcairners to Otaheite, during their sojourn there in 1831, by the grant of land, and other considerate treatment, to which reference has been previously made, began to feel that the Protectorate which France had forced upon that island was becoming intolerable, and gave expression to her trials in the following touching letter, or cry for help, which she addressed to the Queen of England, and of Pitcairn, with whom she had been in prior correspondence:—

" *Tahite, Jan.*, 1843.

"*My dear Friend, and Sister, Queen Victoria, of Great Britain—Health, and peace to you: And saved may you be by Jehovah, the foundation of our power as Queens of our respective countries. . . . This is my speech to you, my sister friend. Commiserate me in my affliction —in my helplessness. . . . The existing Protectorate Government of France in my dominions I do not acknowledge. I knew nothing of what my Chiefs and the French Consul had done before I wrote to you, by Captain Jones; I being absent at Raiate.*" . . . After bemoaning the dependent condition into which she had been thrown by French intervention, and the machinations of her Chiefs, the hapless Lady proceeds: *And now, my friend, think of me; have compassion on me, and assist*

(*a*) Mr. Brodie's " Pitcairn Island and the Islanders in 1850." During a visit paid to this island by 88 of the Pitcairners, in Nov., 1851, they discovered eight human skeletons lying in caves; probably the remains of shipwrecked mariners, who, unable to procure food or water, had lain down to die. Mr. Murray's Pitcairn, &c. A few months previously, another skeleton had been discovered by 12 of the Pitcairners.

me; let thine aid be powerful, let it be timely, and saving, that I may be reinstated in my Government. . . . I fly to you for shelter—to be covered under your great shadow—as my fathers were by your fathers, who are now dead, and whose Kingdoms have descended to us, the weaker vessels. I renew the agreement; let it be lasting, and for ever; extending not only to ourselves, but to our children's children. . . . My only hope of being restored is in you. Be quick to help me, for I am nearly dead. I am like a captive pursued by a warrior, and nearly taken; his spear is close to me. My friend, send quickly a large ship of war to assist me. A French ship of war is daily expected here. Speedily send a ship of yours to assist me, and I shall be saved. . . . Continually send here your ships of war. Let not a month pass away without one, until all my present difficulties are over. . . . Health and peace to you! May you be blessed, my sister friend, Queen of Great Britain," &c. (a)

But her Majesty of Otaheite either forgot, or knew not, that her "sister dear" was Queen of a limited Monarchy; and, as Lord Aberdeen was then Secretary of State for Foreign Affairs, nothing was done, or sought to be done, for the former. On the contrary, France was permitted to tighten her grip on the fairest and most fertile island in the Southern Seas (which Captain Wallis had named "King George's Isle," and taken possession of for the Crown of England, in 1767, and which Captain Cook had visited so often, and loved so well), and to convert it into a listless, withered, and helpless region—that is now "*united* to France under the law of 1880:" And Toubouai (where Christian and his party first settled, after the Mutiny in the *Bounty*,) is at present claimed by the same country, as a dependency of Otaheite. (b)

When will there be an end of such apathy—of such truckling to France, that now threatens to absorb, and blight the New

---

(a) In Sep., 1842, Admiral Du Petit Thomas extorted from Queen Pomáre a convention, under which the right of sovereignty over Tahiti was assumed; and, though the French Government, out of deference to England, ignored the claim to dominion thus extorted, and professed themselves satisfied with the more moderate assumption of a Protectorate merely, the result has been the same; the "toils" were equally ensnaring, and have been equally fatal to the independence of the Tahitians.

(b) In his "Greater Britain," Sir C. W. Dilke observes, "Now that the French are rapidly occupying most of the Polynesian groups, Pitcairn becomes of importance as a solitary British post on the very border of the French dominions"—though he adds, in that spirit of tradesmanism which distinguishes English Radicals, "and it has for us the stronger claim to notice which is raised by the fact, that it has figured, for the last few years, on the wrong side of our British *budget!*"

Hebrides, as well as many another Pacific isle, to which both her claim and necessities are far less than ours? Not until the Australian Colonies shall insist, in unmistakable terms, upon the Crown of England discharging that duty to the British people, and especially to her Southern sons, which is the price of their allegiance, by annexing on their behalf every such isle that is still unappropriated, is of British heritage by discovery or early service, and essential to the protection of their commerce, and the maintenance of that moral atmosphere in which alone they can exist: And if England ignore that duty, then Australia should, by herself and for herself, take her own course, by appropriating the New Hebrides at least, and holding them against all comers. She is both strong enough, and rich enough, to do so. Tanna, one of the most important of the Group, has petitioned for annexation to Great Britain; most of the other isles also desire it; and it would be well for the interests of all, and of humanity and religion, if the lawless kidnapping, bloodshed, and heathenism, that now prevail throughout them, were displaced, and uprooted, by a settled form of Government, and their dusky races be ruled by the foremost men we can lend to the cause of civilization, peace, and Christ. (*a*)

(*a*) The New Hebrides—which France seeks to overrun with her vilest criminals—are the most convenient to the eastern seaboard of Australia, of all the Pacific isles that are still "un-annexed" by European powers; are well watered and fertile; and England has a much stronger right to their possession than has her Gallic sister.

They may be described as lying about 1,200 miles east of that portion of that seaboard which would be included within parallel lines drawn at Cape Bedford and Cardwell, on the Queensland coast—a favored zone of sugar growing land; and they consist (irrespective of various smaller ones) of five islands, of considerable size—which are named Espiritu Santo, Mallicolo, Sandwich, Terramongo, and Tanna. The group was discovered by De Quir and De Torres, when on that voyage of discovery in the service of Philip III. of Spain, in 1606, which resulted in the finding and passage of De Torres through that Strait which now bears his name—and during the exploration of which he must have sighted parts of the northern shores of Australia (though he was preceded in their discovery by the Dutch, by a few months). But from that time to the present, neither the Spaniard nor the Dutch have ever laid claim in any way to those islands: And M. De Bougainville, a gallant Frenchman, and distinguished sailor, was their next European visitor. He reached them in 1768, passed between some, landed upon one of them, and observed two or three which had not been noticed by De Quir, or De Torres. That, however, was the entire of his service. He did nothing else. And so matters rested until Aug., 1773, when Captain Cook, during his second famous voyage, visited this collection of islands, ascertained that it embraced several which neither the Spanish nor French navigators had revealed,

LATER HISTORY. 149

The years 1843 and 1845 were marked by the arrival at Pitcairn of H.M.S.S. *Talbot* and *Basilisk*, under Captains Sir T. Thompson, Bart., and Henry Hunt; each of whom disposed of such Judicial cases as were presented to him; and the latter vessel bore gifts from the British Government, Admiral Thomas, the Rev. Mr. Armstrong, and other friends at Valparaiso. Captain Hunt also appointed a " Commercial Agent " (says the " Register "): And boundaries having become confused, their survey and adjustment were attended to in the latter year. In the interval, the clerical wardrobe of Mr. Nobbs had been reduced to a sad strait: In writing to a Clergyman at Valparaiso, in Aug., 1844, he says:—" My stock of clothing which I brought from England in 1828, is, as you may suppose, very nearly exhausted, and I have no friends there to whom I can with propriety apply for more Until the last three years, it was my custom to wear a black coat on the Sabbath; but since that period I have been obliged to substitute a nankeen jacket, of my own making. My only remaining coat, which is quite threadbare, is reserved for marriages and

---

sailed round and determined the extent of each of the larger ones, and discovered the splendid harbors which he named "Port Sandwich," and "Port Resolution: He also surveyed the north bay of St. Philip and St. James, in which the Spaniards had rested, in 1606, but which the Frenchman had not seen in 1768; and, conceiving that the services he had rendered to navigation and geography by those investigations, entitled him to do so, he ignored the name of the "Great Cyclades," which De Bougainville had previously given to the group, and styled them the "New Hebrides"—a title they have ever since borne amongst all European nations—including France,

Again, Australia, which may be fairly considered as a Continent, is the nearest mainland to the New Hebrides; is occupied and owned by nearly 3,000,000 of English speaking people; and has a very large trade along its eastern and northern shores, Colony with Colony, and with Batavia, China, and India: Whereas New Caledonia, on which France must rest any pretence she may advance to the New Hebrides, is a comparatively small island (contrasted with that Continent); is no more than a most unsuccessful penal settlement, inhabited by a mere handful of prisoners and guards, with their dependents, and has no such trade.

But a still more conclusive argument in favor, either, of England's, or Australia's, acquisition of supremacy over the New Hebrides, is that drawn from the *necessity of the case*: Australian commerce would be at the mercy of French privateers, issuing from the secure harbors which De Quir and Cook discovered, striking at every helpless sail, and either destroying or bearing her away to the same retreats. And Australian cities would be inundated by the reflux of the vilest ruffians whom France produces, if the group were allowed to pass under her dominion: No effort —no struggle—that can be made should therefore be omitted to secure us against those calamities; and they are no friends to our community "who cry 'peace! peace!' where there is no peace.

burials; so that it is customary to say, when a wedding is going to take place, 'Teacher! you will have to put on your black coat next Sunday;' which is equivalent to informing me that a couple are going to be married." If ever there was an instance of honorable poverty, that was one; and it may be that the "nankeen jacket" may yet vie with many a vestment of lawn, or of purple and fine linen.

The year 1845 was a portentous one; for it is recorded, "Worms infest the potatoes; weeds over-run the island; and there is a comet in sight"—which, it was thought, had some connection with a calamity occurring on the night of 16th April—when there was a hurricane, accompanied by almost incessant thunder and lightning; the whole 'concave of the heavens being in a continued blaze;' and the roar of the elements deafening; a small portion of the island gave way, and fell into the sea, carrying with it about 200 cocoa-nut trees, and a piece of yam ground; destroying several fishing boats; washing the *Bounty's* guns (now raised from ocean's bed) to the edge of the reef, and levelling many plantain patches; thus causing a dearth of food for five weeks: But these calamities did not shake the faith of the sufferers; since (as the "Register" declares), "'God tempers the wind to the shorn lamb'; and we humbly trust that the late munitions of Providence—drought, sickness, and storm—which have been now inflicted upon us, may be sanctified to us, and be the means of bringing us, one and all, into close communion with our God; may we remember the rod, and He who appointed it." In the same year, a rumor of war reached the island; and its people besought the Almighty "to watch over the fatherland; and prayed that, whether engaged in hostilities, or enjoying peace, it might never succumb to insult, nor advocate oppression."

By 12th June, 1846, a new Church-and school-house, upon which the people had been engaged for some time, was completed; and is described as "a very decent building, that reflects much credit upon those employed in its construction." Still, secular things ran their course, and the usual accidents of life were not absent from the little community. The "Register" records a serious mishap which befel a son of Mr Nobbs; and the account shows the tender solicitude of the islanders towards each other:—

"1847, Feb. 20th.—This afternoon, as Reuben Nobbs was out in the mountains, shooting goats, his foot slipped, and he let fall his musket, which exploded, and wounded him severely. The ball entered a little below the hip-joint, and passing downwards, came through on the inside of the thigh, about half way between the groin and the knee. Providentially, some persons were in sight, who immediately ran to his assistance, and tore up their shirts to stay the blood, which was pouring forth profusely. A messenger was sent to the village with the melancholy news; and in a few minutes all the inhabitants, capable of going, were on their way to afford relief; headed by his loving mother, who was almost frantic with grief. In about an hour, they returned, bearing Reuben in a canoe: After some difficulty the blood was stanched; and the lad suffered but little pain. . . . Many remained by his father's house all night, to be ready at a moment's warning to do anything that might be required; towards midnight he fell asleep—and so ends this melancholy day.

"Feb. 21st.—About daylight, the wounded boy awoke; very much refreshed; he does not complain much, and has but little fever. Three watches have been formed, to attend his wants, both day and night. 22nd.—Reuben is free from pain; but there is a considerable accession of fever; it does not appear that either the thigh or hip bone is injured, as he can move his leg without much difficulty or pain. From the great length of the internal wound, it is hard to ascertain whether any of the wadding remains where the ball must have passed through. Feb. 26th.—This morning a ship was reported; everybody was rejoiced; hoping to get assistance and some necessaries for their wounded friend. On her nearing the island, the vessel proved to be H.M.S. *Spy*, Captain Woodbridge. 'Thank God!' was the grateful exclamation of many, on learning this, and that therefore there was a Surgeon on board. At 1 p.m. Capt. Woodbridge and Dr. Bowder landed; the latter immediately visited young Nobbs; and, after probing the wound, and ascertaining the extent of the injury, gave it as his opinion, there was not much danger; and that, with proper attention, the patient would, in all probability, recover; although his escape from immediate death was very narrow."

But his constitution had sustained a shock which it never recovered; and in Dec., 1849, he went to Valparaiso, hoping to earn his living in some mercantile pursuit there, rather than be in any way a burden upon the island, where his diminished strength no longer enabled him to be of much service. (*a*) On Reuben's now quitting Pitcairn, his father insisted upon his taking all the money he, himself, possessed (about eight dollars); and the families joined in fitting him out to the best of their power; furnishing him with a supply of clothes, and making up a purse of more than forty dollars; several contributing every cent. they had. Churlish fathers! and churlish rich! who will deny to their fellow men, as well as to their own flesh and blood, every farthing they can withhold, what a lesson might ye derive from the poor Pastor, and poor islanders, of Pitcairn?

The *Spy* brought them a present from the Rev. J. Moody, Chaplain to H.M.S. *Thalia*, then on the Pacific Station; and in their letter of grateful acknowledgment, dated 20th July, 1847, after mentioning that the whole of their community were members of the Church of England, admitted thereto in infancy, by the rite of baptism, and that the Chaplain's procuring of some Prayer Books, Psalms, and Watts' Hymns for public use in the

---

(*a*) At Valparaiso, Reuben Nobbs acquired the esteem and confidence of the merchants by whom he was employed; but, after a few years' residence in that city, where his health continued to be frail, he returned to Pitcairn, in compliance with the wishes of his mother, in April, '53, in H.M.S. *Portland*. The desire, however to earn his own bread, impelled him to re-visit the former place, which he did in H.M.S. *Dido*, some months later. But his strength still sinking, it was found necessary he should again seek the mild atmosphere of his native isle; and he reached it, via Otaheite, in Dec., '54. The touching sequel is told by his father, in a letter to the Rev. Mr. Murray, of 29th Jan., '55:—"*My poor boy sank rapidly after his return. I saw from the first there was no probability of his recovering; but this stroke of domestic affliction was divested of much of its severity, on finding that he was perfectly aware of his situation, and not only resigned to it, but actually desirous to depart, and enter into the joys of his Lord. Sometimes, his mother flattered by the specious appearance of his insidious disease, would hint at the possibility of his being yet spared to us. But, with a gentle shake of the head, he would reply, 'No, dear mother, I feel I am rapidly approaching the grave; humanly speaking, my recovery is impossible; and that my dear father knows as well as I do; and if it be not improper to entertain such a wish, I would rather not return to health again: 'My earnest desire and prayer is to depart, and be with Christ, which is far better.' Such was the tenor of his discourse during the short time he was spared to us: He died strong in the faith, giving glory to God. An hour before his death, he was seized with a violent spasm, which we thought would have carried him off, but he rallied again. Seeing his mother weeping, he said, 'Do not weep, mother; one more such stroke, and I shall be in the arms of my Saviour.' Shortly after, he had another attack; and nothing remained but his attenuated form.*"

island, together with a few school books, and a medicine chest, would be conferring a most essential service—they approach a subject which had been long one of deep moment amongst them :

"One thing more, before concluding, we earnestly present to your consideration, and as it comes in a special manner within the province of your holy office, we would indulge the hope that our application will be attended with success. Our teacher, who has been with us for 19 years in that capacity, and whose services to us are invaluable, has never received the license of the proper authority in that Church of which we are a component part This circumstance is a source of much anxiety, both to him and us; and as our number now amounts to 138, and is rapidly increasing, we do most urgently, but respectfully, solicit your application to the proper quarter for a pastoral letter, inducting or sanctioning him in the holy office he has so long unceasingly, untiringly, and worthily filled on this island. That he is deserving such a mark of Ecclesiastical approbation and favor is justly and cheerfully acknowledged by the whole community; and of the great benefit which will accrue to us therefrom, no one can be more competent to judge than yourself."

A similar entreaty was urged in a communication forwarded by the islanders, in the same month of July, 1847, to Captain Charles Hope, who commanded the *Thalia*; and "for this purpose" (they wrote), "our humble request to you is, that you will (if it can be done with propriety) make our case known to the Bishop of London, or some other competent Dignitary, who would send a pastoral letter to our teacher, confirming him in the sacred office he has so long held among us": But it was not until five years later, that practical, or more immediate, steps were taken to obtain the Ordination of Mr. Nobbs

On the 9th March, 1848, H.M.S. *Calypso* reached Pitcairn; and her Captain (H. J. Worth) landed with a party of his officers. The greeting on both sides was most cordial; men, women and children were almost beside themselves; for two whale-boats, and several large cases of useful articles, were landed- contributions to the island from the Admiral and officers on the Station, and foreigners resident in Valparaiso—among whom, the Rev. Messrs. Armstrong and Turnbull, ("our untiring benefactors," say the islanders), were prominent; and the "Register's" notice of these benefactions concludes with the aspiration—" May God have them in His holy keeping; and may they long hold a place in our grateful recollections." (*a*)

Three days after the arrival of the *Calypso*, Dr. Donnet, her Surgeon, hearing there were hieroglyphics, supposed to have been inscribed by original inhabitants of Pitcairn, on the face of a cliff on the east side of the island, determined to inspect them. He was informed that the path was not only difficult, but dangerous; yet he would not be turned from his purpose. Accordingly, he started with one of the islanders, and succeeded in his undertaking; being the first European who ever went down the face of that cliff (which is very precipitous), without the assistance of a rope. On the same day, Lieutenant M'Leod, and Mr. Midshipman Lock, of the same ship, descended the "ridge of the rope." We are not informed what either they, or Dr. Donnet, saw on the cliffs, as the result of their hazardous enterprise. But Mr. Brodie, who inspected the hieroglyphics, during his visit to the place, two years later, has been more communicative: He thus writes:—

"*March 27th*, 1850.

"*This afternoon, Mr. Carleton, John Adams, and myself, went to the east side of the island, to try and get to a place where there were some unknown characters, believed to have been cut into the solid rock by the original inhabitants. It was called the "Rope"—a rope having been used in former days with which to descend the precipice. Upon our arrival at the edge of the perpendicular cliff, we did not like the look of it; it was a very dizzy height; of nearly 600 feet perpendicular; and broken necks would have been the inevitable consequence of missing a single step. Adams strongly dissuaded us, on account of the slippery state of the ground, from attempting it; we therefore returned home with disappointed curiosity.*" . . .

"*March 28th.*

"*Hearing there was another road to the hieroglyphics, rather more circuitous than the one we attempted yesterday in vain, and not quite so dangerous, Carleton, Adams, and myself, made another attempt to reach them. Upon arriving at the edge of the precipice, it was an awful looking place to go down; but, if anything, rather more easy to the eye than the*

(*a*) This was after the young women of the island had "presented a Petition' to Captain Worth, praying "that he would remain another day."

other road. The first 100 yards we slid down in a sitting position, on our haunches, having but little regard for the seat of our trousers. We then came to a spot, in my opinion, far worse than what we looked at yesterday; it was a ledge of rock about ten feet long, and of only a few inches in breadth. I must say it made me feel rather nervous; but our guide having told us it was the worst place we had to cross, I hurried over it as quickly as I could, but with as much caution as possible. Though Adams tried to persuade us there was no danger, I could not agree with him; still, to him it was as nothing, and he skipped across it like a goat. It is extraordinary with what agility these islanders go up and down the precipices, and jump from rock to rock. After crossing this bad spot, the remainder of our journey down to the sea was still very steep; but with a few rests, to recover breath, we at last reached the seashore in safety, with no other mishap than a few scratches, and broken trousers. We then proceeded along the coast, for about one-third of a mile. The walking here was very bad, being over large and loose rocks; fortunately, it was low water, or I should have had to swim round a headland that formed one side of the bay. We now arrived at the destination which had cost us so much trouble and anxiety to reach. The hieroglyphics were carved at from two to ten feet from the ground, many of them appearing to be nearly obliterated. The rock in which they were cut was exceedingly hard, and much resembled the French burr stones."

They consisted of rude outline figures of three men; of the sun, and a little sun; of the moon in two phases; of four stars, and a bird; of a straight line placed in a slanting position, and supporting semblances to our letters e, i, j, and l; to a moon having a star within it, and to our numeral 5; with something which I can only describe as tolerably like the handle of a whip, whose lash is doubled back, and tied in the centre.

"After remaining about an hour, we returned home, not by the way we came, but by the road we attempted yesterday, which made a difference of nearly a mile in shortening the distance. Adams took the lead, with a rope and a hoe in his hand, making holes in the ground, and soft rock, wherever they could be made to our advantage, in scaling this far from delightful ascent. When nearly up to the top of the first ridge, I squeezed myself between two rocks to rest, and requested Adams to pass the rope down to fasten round my waist, as immediately above me the rocks were perpendicular. He then hauled or assisted me up the difficult pass. Carleton would not use the rope, preferring his own hands and feet to the assistance of others. Upon arriving here, which was the place we looked down upon yesterday, I was most thankful. How curiosity could have tempted me to undertake so dangerous an excursion I know not;! but I strongly recommend Europeans never to attempt the same from any such motive: And the figures can be visited in a canoe or boat, though only in very fine weather on account of the great surf running on that side."

In connection with these figures, Mr. Brodie adds, there is no doubt but that Pitcairn must have been inhabited many years prior to the arrival of the *Bounty;* though the original race had then disappeared. "Ancient burial places are still to be seen; so are large, flat, hewn stones, in different parts of the island, which served for pavement in front of their houses—such as are still in use among tribes in the South Seas. These stones, when first observed by the crew of the *Bounty*, had very large trees growing up amongst, and frequently displacing, them. Stone images were likewise found, supposed to have been objects of worship." [Overlooking Bounty Bay is a lofty peak, within 100 yards of which these images were discovered. They were four in number; each about six feet high, placed on a platform, and not unlike those in Easter Island. One of these has been preserved; and is the rude representation of the human figure to the hips; hewn out of a piece of red lava—as were all the others.] " Stone spear heads, and small axes, are very common; and round stone balls, each of about 2 lbs. weight, are occasionally met with, when working up new ground. A large stone bowl has also been unearthed. All of these are made from a bluish-black stone, very fine grained, and smooth; and the spots where such images and stoneware were fabricated, may still be recognised by the large accumulation of chips in various parts of the island. Human bones have been repeatedly dug up; although not during the last eight years; and in one instance a perfect skeleton was discovered, in the last stage of decay, with a large pearl shell, of a sort not belonging to the island, placed under the skull. This is a custom with the natives of the Gambier Islands, Bow Island, High Island, Toubouai, and nearly all the Pumutu or Low Islands. The cocoa-nut tree, bananas, plantains, and bread fruit trees, as well as the yams and sweet potatoes, found here by the mutineers, are an additional sign of the previous occupation of the island—more especially as those bread-fruit trees were confined to one single spot; and it is very unlikely they were indigenous so far to the southward, as they will not grow upon every part of the island, but merely upon a few of the warmest situations on the lower ridges. The aborigines who occupied Pitcairn in former times were, most probably, drifted there upon a raft; it having been a custom, many years ago, especially at the Gambier Islands (which lie to the W.N.W., and about 300 miles from Pitcairn), to put those who were vanquished in war upon a raft, when the wind was off the land ; sending them to drift to whatever place they could fetch. Two instances of this practice, and one of which came under his immediate cognizance, while he himself was at the Gambier Group, were mentioned to me by Mr. Nobbs."

Captain Worth bore the following testimony to the happy state of Pitcairn, and amiable character of its people, when visited by the *Calypso* :—

"We arrived here on the 9th March, 1848, from Callao ; but the weather being very bad, stormy, and squally, and as there is no landing except in a small nook called Bounty Bay, and very frequently not even there, I did not communicate with the shore till next day ; when, having landed safely all the presents I brought for the inhabitants from Valparaiso, I went ashore myself with half the officers and youngsters; the ship standing off and on. I made the officers divide the day between them—one half on shore, the other half on board ; so that they all might be enabled to visit these interesting people. I never was so gratified by any visit to any other place ; and I would rather have gone there than to any part of the world. They are the most contented, moral, and happy community that can be conceived.

"Their delight at our arrival was beyond everything. The comfort, peace, strict morality, industry, and excessive cleanliness and neatness, that were apparent about everything around them, were really such as I was not prepared to witness. Their learning, and attainments in general education, and information, were astonishing. All dressed in English style ; the men, a fine race ; the women and children very pretty ; and their manner of a superior order, ever smiling and joyous. But one mind, and one wish, seemed to animate them. Crime appears to be unknown ; and if there be true happiness on earth, surely it is theirs. (*a*)

(*a*) The following letter, written in 1855, by Mrs. Nobbs (grand-daughter of Fletcher Christian), to Mrs. Heywood and Lady Belcher widow and daughter of his old comrade, Peter Heywood), affords good proof not only of the simple, unaffected piety, but of the intellectual culture, of the descendants of the mutineers

"The island is romantic and beautiful; the soil of the richest description; yielding almost every tropical fruit and vegetable; in short, it is a little Paradise. I examined their laws; added a few to them; assembled them all in the Church, and addressed them, saying how delighted I was to find them in the happy state they were; advising them to follow in the steps of virtue and rectitude they had hitherto pursued; and that they need never want the sympathies of their countrymen in England, who were greatly interested in them. It was strangely affecting to see these primitive and excellent islanders, both old and young, 140 in the whole, looking up to me, and almost devouring every word I uttered, with eager attention, and scarcely a dry eye amongst them. Although 'unused to the melting mood,' I found a moisture collecting in my own, which I could scarcely restrain—they were so grateful, so truly thankful, for all the kindness that had from time to time been shown them, and for the interest in their welfare evinced by us, and their countrymen at large. I had all the men, and most of the women on board; but there was such a sea on, that the poor girls were dreadfully sick. I fired some guns, and let off rockets, on the night of our departure. And they returned the compliment by firing an old honeycombed gun belonging to the *Bounty*. I set them completely up before leaving,

---

though reared and educated on a mere rock of the ocean, and far from the beaten track of civilisation:—

"*My dear Ladies,*—My husband has left room in his letter for me to say a few words; and I address you without any hesitation; for you seem to me as personal acquaintances. The circumstances which brought my grandfather to this island have made the name of your husband, and father, as familiar to us as 'household words.' And now that I have heard my husband speak of the kind reception you accorded him, when in England, and have myself become the recipient of your benevolence, I cannot let this opportunity pass without testifying my gratitude for so much kindness to me, and mine.

"It has pleased God in His inscrutable wisdom to call from time to eternity my beloved, my first-born. But though the tears of natural affection will flow, and I do not restrain them, still, I sorrow not as those which have no hope. For my dear child displayed so much of humility, faith, and trust, that I think I may conclude, on scriptural grounds, he is now with those who are washed in the blood of the Lamb. 'Not lost, but gone before.' Several others from amongst us have been called from time into eternity, very recently; but I perceive my husband has given you the particulars of this. Yet the circumstance speaks to every member of this community, 'Therefore, be ye also ready.' My daughters bid me offer their respects, and thanks. Wishing you, dear sisters in Christ, every needful blessing, believe me, yours most gratefully,—SARAH CHRISTIAN NOBBS."

by giving them 100 lbs. of powder, ensign and Union Jack, casks of salt beef and pork, implements of agriculture of all kinds, clothes, books, &c.; and sailed on the evening of the 11th for Tahiti." (*a*)

During the following year (11th Aug., 1849), H.M.S. *Daphne* (Captain Fanshaw), reached Pitcairn from Valparaiso, *via* Callao, bringing a bull, cow, and some rabbits, which produced a great sensation; also several boxes of very acceptable articles from the islanders' old friend, the Rev. Mr. Armstrong, and a large case of books from the Christian Knowledge Society. "Surely" (adds the "Register") "no community of people were ever so kindly cared for as we are." And the account given in the same record, of the arrival, about a month previously, of H.M.S. *Pandora* (Captain James Wood), from Oahu and Otaheite (bringing back John Buffett, who had gone to the Sandwich Islands, on some commercial enterprise, in the preceding year), shows with what delight the appearance of a man-of-war off their coast was still hailed by the Pitcairners:—"July 10th. This morning, at daylight, our 'city' was scared from its propriety by the booming of a cannon. Those who had already risen ran to the edge of the precipice; and those who had not turned out, lost no time in doing so. A brigantine was discovered in the offing, with a flag of some kind flying; but from the want of light we could not distinguish her heraldic bearings. After peering through the somewhat hazy atmosphere for nearly half-an-hour, and stretching our necks and eyelids in a most extraordinary manner, the increased light enabled us to discern that the vessel wore the St. George's ensign; and now the shout of 'a man-of-war'! sounded from house to house. Two whaleboats were speedily manned, and soon got on board. As the weather was lowering, we were fearful on shore that a ship's boat

---

(*a*) When writing to the Rev. Mr. Armstrong, after the arrival of the *Calypso*, George Adams, the then Chief Magistrate of Pitcairn, thus expresses himself:— "The presents are divided equally amongst us all, from the oldest woman to the youngest child. Kind friend! this is the first opportunity I have had to write to you. I will thank you very much if you will take 'the fund of money' which you will find in this paper, and buy me a few fish-hooks, of the size you will see in the paper; and also, for my family's use, six copies of Watts' Hymn-books, and one family Bible. Friend! I bid you farewell. Perhaps it may not be our chance to meet in this world; but I hope we may in a better, where saints and angels meet; and if it be our luck to meet there, then we shall part no more."

would not land; but, after an hour's anxious suspense, we were gratified by seeing one lowered, and pull for the shore, accompanied by our boats. On nearing the surf, a party from the ship's boat shifted into ours, and passed through the breakers quite dry. The brigantine proved to be H.M.S. *Pandora*." And in the note to this Chapter will be found a full account of her mission, the island, and its inhabitants, at that time, from the pen of Captain Wood.

About three score years had now passed since the mutineers had landed on Pitcairn; and on the 23rd of Jan., 1850, that period, exactly, had elapsed since the *Bounty* was burned and sunk. This day was therefore observed (states the "Register"), "as the anniversary of the settlement, 60 years previously. One survivor of that event (an Otaheitan woman) witnessed the present celebration. At daylight, the *Bounty's* gun was discharged, awakening, the sleeping echoes, and every drowsy inhabitant. At 10 a.m., Divine service was performed. After the sermon, the various letters received from the British Government, and principal friends, were read from the pulpit, and commented upon. At noon, a number of musketeers assembled under the flag-staff, and fired a volley in honour of the day. After dinner, males and females assembled in front of the Church (where the British flag was flying), and gave three cheers for the Queen, three for the Government at home, three for the Magistrate, three for absent friends, and three for the community in general, amid the firing of muskets, and ringing of the bell. At sunset, the gun of the *Bounty* was again fired, and the day closed in harmony and peace towards God and man. It is voted that an annual celebration be observed." (*a*)

(*a*) Under date, July, 1849, Captain Wood writes from on board the *Pandora* :

"*H.M.S.* '*Pandora*,' *July*, 1849.

"*I ran on till very close to the island (which appeared in the moonlight like a high rock, with its summit in the clouds), and then hove to. At daybreak I bore up, and at seven a.m. was near enough to see the houses, and perceive there was a heavy swell breaking on the rocks. We fired a gun, which soon drew attention ; at first a red ensign, and then a white flag, was displayed from a staff in front of the school-house.*

"*The village is on the northern face of the island, and appeared buried in trees, but the cleared fields showed out well.*

"*At first, some doubts were expressed by Mr. Buffett of the possibility of boats getting through the surf, but the white flag, which is a signal that landing is practicable, eased my mind on that score, and, soon after eight, two whale boats were seen coming off. They were quite laden with men, a fine, hardy, athletic set of* fellows as ever I saw, and but little tinged with their mother's blood; indeed those of the third generation are nearly as white as Europeans. They soon dispersed themselves all over the ship, as eager to see their countrymen as ever; indeed they seemed quite beside themselves. Buffett's meeting with his son, a fine and rather handsome young man, was most affecting, as was his greeting from them all. 'It is never old Buffett come back,'/ was passed from one to the other, with every appearance of affection for him. Arthur Quintall, son of the mutineer, a fine, strong-made man, upwards of fifty, with an honest, open countenance, was the senior of the party; but a strapping stout fellow, John Adams, was pilot for the time; this berth they take in rotation, each family according to their seniority, and that family has the privilege of entertaining the Captain of a war ship when on shore. When asked down to breakfast, in the midst of their laughter and glee, and before they touched anything, they joined their hands, and in a devout and unaffected way prayed for a blessing on their food. This is their invariable custom, and, like much we saw there, read a lesson to us all which we shall not easily forget.

"Arrangements having been made for landing Buffett's traps (not very easily accomplished, owing to the high surf, and the difficulty of getting a boat's crew together to take them), I at last saw most of them off, and, accompanied by Buffett and some of my officers, pulled in towards the landing place, which is in a small cove called 'Bounty Bay.' The wind was fresh, and the swell high, so that it seemed to me when I got to the spot, that I was more likely to go on shore out of my boat, than in it, but as both the whale boats had just passed in, I determined to try it, and in two trips we were all safely deposited on the beach. The way they effect a landing is this—one whose experience can be trusted, mounts a rock that commands a view of the sea, and he watches for the proper moment, when at a signal from him, the boat, which has been lying as close to the breakers as possible, makes a rush, and by taking one of the less heavy breakers, goes flying in before it, frequently without a stroke of the oars being necessary, except to steer her, till they get within the rocks, when all danger is over; but as the turn is very narrow and sharp, it requires skill and experience to get a boat in safely, for a trifling deviation on either side would dash it to pieces on the rocks.

"The beach and the heights above were lined with inhabitants (mostly females), with Mr. Nobbs, pastor and teacher, at their head. I cannot describe the scene which took place so as to do it justice. After shaking hands with Mr. Nobbs, a pretty-looking girl came up to me, and almost shaking my hand off, said, 'Thank you, Sir, for bringing my father home,' her countenance beaming with joy. The entire sisterhood now crowded round me, and as I could not shake all their hands at once, I thought it better to kiss them, and they appeared to like this as well; their warm and simple hearts were strangers to concealment, and they gave themselves up with the most complete and childish joy to again seeing a man-of-war off their island. I soon found my cap ornamented with a garland of flowers, and amidst laughter and jokes we began to ascend the cliffs. This is no easy task, even to a strong man, and to me would have been quite impracticable, had not Mr. Nobbs called to one of the young ladies to come and help me,—two or three volunteered, but my prop and support was Jemima Young, a stout, good-natured girl, who seized my arm, and almost carried me up without the aid of my feet, and this without any apparent effort on her part. All my officers were similarly treated, and decorated with garlands, not only round their hats, but their necks; in this array, and almost as excited as themselves, we were marched to the top of the hill or cliff, and there met with the remainder

M

of the community, consisting principally of the elder females, and those with young children in their arms.

"Here another scene of introduction was gone through, and amongst others I was introduced to the only remaining female of the original Tahitians. She is very old, and has lost an eye, but still continues to walk about. From this we went to the school-room, the path leading at first through a grove of cocoa-nut trees, and then across some nicely cultivated potato fields. Here I sat for some time, and gave the letters I had brought, as well as explained the object of my visit, but I do not think much attention was paid to either myself, or Mr. Nobbs, who read one of the letters addressed to the islanders—they were all too much excited to be serious.

"The school-room or house is a long room, furnished with cross benches, fitted with forms, inkstands, &c.; at the upper end a square compartment is formed by the benches, with a table and seat for the master; and against the end is the pulpit or reading desk, for the school-room is the Church on Sundays. Their form of worship is the Church of England ritual; and now, whilst on the subject, I cannot but add my testimony to those who have gone before me, as to the excellent moral and religious character of these people. Evil and crime seem unknown amongst them; their very simplicity and open-hearted kindness towards us showed such a consciousness of innocence, or rather ignorance of evil, that familiarities such as pass between brothers and sisters were soon established, and all the freshness and warmth of their hearts had free scope, without a thought of prudery to check it.

"The young people are generally good-looking, some of them very pretty; all of them have good eyes and teeth, and the most engaging expression of countenance I ever saw; their figures are good, inclining to embonpoint, but their carriage excellent, and a most charming modesty characterizes all their actions. Their dress is as varied as their methods of wearing it, but the most useful is a kind of long white jacket or short skirt, with a dark-coloured wrapper; which is fastened round the waist, and hangs down to the ankles. They wear no shoes nor stockings, and from their working so hard in the fields, and the mountainous nature of the country, their feet are large and broad, and their legs very stout. Their heads are uncovered; but the hair, which is very long (a dark brown or black), is kept clean, neat, and very glossy, by the aid of cocoa-nut oil, which they contrive to scent very agreeably with the orange blossom. It is turned up behind in an ingenious manner, which needs no comb or other aid to keep it in its place. This, they say, is necessary when at work in the fields, or going through the woods; combs also would be sadly in their way when conveying a load of yams, and they pride themselves on the weight they are able to bear from the landing place to the top of the cliff—a girl of 16 or 17 will carry over one hundredweight. They had once two donkeys to do this work, but they did not answer, and now the only conveyance they possess is a kind of wheelbarrow.

"After I left the school-room, I paid visits, with Mr. Nobbs, to all the families in their houses. They are all lodged alike; the houses are built of wood, and show progressive improvement, in the mechanical part of them, which would not disgrace an European tradesman. They consist of one long room, divided by two or more partitions, and are raised upon huge sleepers, placed upon large stones to clear them some two or two and a-half feet from the ground. They all lie nearly east and west, with the door fronting the north, and the same front contains windows, forming nearly the whole side of the house, and closed by sliding shutters; their roofs have a moderately high pitch, and are formed of the pandanus leaf, which, being bent over a long light stick, forms a kind of board. Several of these laid nearly close form an excellent thatch, lasting from five to seven years. The side opposite the windows is occupied by bed places, which are similar to the sleeping berths in the old packets. These have again a smaller window, or scuttle, as a sailor would call it, which admits air when they are shut out from the common room or hall, by drawing the curtains. Their bedclothes are, without exception, formed of the tappa cloth, both white and tanned. This they manufacture themselves from the bark of the paper mulberry tree, which till lately has formed the staple article of their clothes. Most of the houses are now ornamented with prints and looking-glasses. One had an American clock, which however would not go, nor did its owner seem to care whether it went or not; ' the sun,' he said, ' was the best timepiece.'

"They rise before the sun, eat when they are hungry, sleep when they are tired, and, in fact, are barred by no rules as to the disposal of their time, except on Sundays, when they attend Church twice, at stated times; and on that day alone Mr. Nobbs winds up his watch, and sets it, so as to ensure punctuality; but he prefers the sun as a guide, and for this purpose has a meridian at ten a.m. and two p.m. marked on the floor of his house.

"I went to visit the grave of old John Adams. He is buried close to his house, with a daughter and grand-daughter lying by his side. A stone, with his name and the date of his death, is placed at the head. From thence I visited the 'Bounty's' forge, which is still in being, with the exception of the bellows, which have long since gone to pieces; the anvil had lost its nose. This, with a large copper fish-kettle, are the only considerable remains of the 'Bounty' that I saw; but I got pieces of her copper, wood, &c., of which they all possessed a portion.

"I dined with the pilot, John Adams, and his family; a boiled fowl, some pig and yams, and sweet potatoes, with roasted bread-fruit, and a cake made of yams and plantains beaten up, and baked in leaves, formed our repast. Knives and forks were, as well as spoons and tumblers, not wanting at the table, which was covered with a clean cloth; and dishes and plates seemed by no means scarce. This was a great improvement since Captain Beechy's visit, when but three of the latter conveniences were to be found. The women do not eat with the men when strangers are present—so my kindhostess and cook, and her pretty daughter, had only the cold remains of our dinner. The mode of cooking is well worth notice, and answers admirably. A hole in the ground forms an oven, the bottom of which is covered with fresh plantain leaves; heated stones are then spread over, and, strewn with leaves; on these are laid the articles which are to be cooked, wrapped in leaves, but potatoes and yams go without any covering. Some more hot stones are then placed among the meat, &c.; the whole being overlaid with another large layer of leaves; and when the top has been duly covered with green leaves in bunches, a mass of dirty-looking rubbish is piled upon it so as to keep in all heat. This, they confessed, was a very dirty plan, but it answered the purpose admirably, and from the quantity of clean leaves all over, no dust can get to the food. Twenty minutes to half-an-hour suffices to cook a fowl, or small piece of meat; and it is only necessary in opening the oven to be careful not to let the dust pass the outer covering of green leaves, and all is clean and wholesome as if cooked in our way.

"In the evening, we had a general meeting to consider the offers of removal we made them, this being the only time they could all attend; field labour, cooking, and other necessary work, keeping them employed during the day. They all expressed themselves pleased and thankful for the interest our Government evinced in their welfare, but it was evident that none of them had as yet made up their minds to the dreaded evil *of a removal.* They wished for time to consider the matter. However, they promised to give some kind of answer next day, but even that they found impossible, so they undertook to send a reply by the next vessel, which called at the island. I myself think there is no necessity for any of them leaving the island at present. They allow that there is much land uncultivated, and a more equal distribution of it would make what they have go much farther.

"The plan they adopt, and which could not now be disturbed without some injustice, is this. The original settlers, the mutineers, marked out and divided the land into nine equal parts; these parts were again equally subdivided among their children; and again the children of the third generation have also a portion of their sub-divisions. This, though apparently fair enough at first, has led to evils they did not anticipate; for instance, one of the original settlers had a family of eleven, his ninth was, therefore, divided into eleven parts. Again, one of his daughters married, and has a family of eleven, so that each of her children will have but the eleventh of her eleventh portion; whereas, another of the first lot, who had only one son and daughter (the latter of whom survives, unmarried) left, by the same rule, the whole of his ninth to her, so that she now has as much land as twenty-two of the first-named family. This system cannot last long, unless the landlords emigrate, which they seem very unwilling to do, though this want of sufficient ground is a bar to many of them marrying.

"The children generally run alone at a twelvemonth, and are not swaddled or tormented as they are in England, in consequence of which they are strong, independent-looking imps; not an ill-formed or deformed child was to be seen; the only cripple being Mr. Nobbs' eldest son, who had become so from a gunshot wound in his hip. They go into the water when very young; and this habit, of which they are very fond, as well as the scanty allowance of garments, tans their skin, and render them some shades darker than their original colour. The women are said to be as expert as the men in making their way through the surf; some of them are able to swim entirely round the island.

"I walked up the hill some little way, next morning, to a pool they call Brown's water. This supplies them with drinking water, which is brought to the village by the women and girls. The path was rather steep, and slippery from the over-night's rain. The pool is situated in a small natural hollow, and is fed from a spring. It never increases or decreases.

"The trees we saw on the road were the pandanus, banyan, cocoa, breadfruit (a very large tree), a fern, the mountain plantain, some species of acacia, orange and lime trees, &c. Besides these, they have the Vhe tree, but it is now very scarce, as are also the two most valuable trees on the island, of which they build their houses—the Tafano, or flower wood, and the Aruni, or Mero. The former is a yellow wood, very hard and durable, when not exposed to wet—of this most of the joiners' work is done. The latter wood is in still more general use; it is very dark, like rosewood, very durable, standing exposure to the sun, wind, and rain, for many years without showing any symptoms of decay. The first settlers' houses were made entirely of it, and are as sound now as the day they were erected, though without paint or covering of any kind: indeed, Mr. Nobbs' house and the school are the only two that have been painted or whitewashed even in part.

"The soil is very rich and prolific. I was shown a field that for ten years had yielded two crops per annum, without suffering any deterioration, and yet no manure was supplied. The soil appears a mixture of mould and volcanic matter; it has a considerable portion of iron in it, as its red colour abundantly testifies. The rocks are composed of basalt or green stone, and I should say there was lava on the island, as they told me of a stone which rings like metal when struck.

"There is but one kind of bird, a sort of sparrow. I tried to get a specimen of it, but there was not time to catch one. Sea birds come there to breed, but there are so many looking out for them that they seldom show themselves. I took them some sheep, which I hope will thrive. Lizards are plentiful. They are plagued by a caterpillar, which destroys their peas, and the ordinary bean, so as to render it almost useless to cultivate them; but a bean was introduced some little time back which has spread wonderfully, and now grows wild all over the place, supplying them with a wholesome, agreeable, addition to their food seven months in the year. Flies are very troublesome, and they have had mosquitoes since their return from Tahiti, of which they much complain. Cockroaches are also plentiful and destructive.

"After having had as many young ladies to see the ship as the boats could conveniently carry, and made them all very sea-sick, received my letters, and supplied my men with a good stock of yams, I took leave of these kind and simple-hearted people, with many regrets and good wishes. Amongst the younger portion, many had contrived to establish flirtations, which, though short enough, brought long faces and wet eyes at parting; and many were the locks of hair, &c., which changed owners, and the promises of writing by the first opportunity. In this I believe them sincere, as I received whole heaps of letters from them, entrusted to the care of the officers of almost every man-of-war that had been at Pitcairn for some time back. They, in fact, look upon us as their fellow-countrymen; and a few hours' acquaintance with them, establishes a friendship which, though not likely to be renewed personally in this world, I feel convinced will last with their lives—for the questions they asked about those who had visited them, and the interest they took in all that concerned them, clearly showed that, however brief their stay, they had not been forgotten.

"As it was dark when I made sail, I gave them at their request a gun, burnt two blue lights, and sent up a rocket, as a farewell signal; and I must say, in common with all on board, I felt more regret in parting with the Pitcairn Islanders, than I had in parting with any one since leaving England."

It was in the following Sept. (1849), that George Adams refused ("with surprise at the proposal") a bag full of dollars, which an overjoyed father offered to him, on his having rescued, at the risk of his own life, a drowning child who had fallen into the sea from an Australian vessel touching at Pitcairn. The islander felt and said, he "had done nothing more than his duty."

CHAPTER IX.— Mr. Brodie ; and Matters Domestic.

1850, March—April : Mr. Brodie's dilemma; with his account of Pitcairn, and its people, physically and socially ; its agriculture, fish, and animals ; fruits and plants; dwelling houses, dress, and aspect of islanders—Relics of the *Bounty*—House-keeping; and house-warming—The picnic; music lessons; and "laws."

IT was in March, 1850, that Mr. Brodie, from whose little Book I have already quoted, happened to be left upon Pitcairn ; the vessel (the *Noble*, bound for San Francisco,) from which he landed, having been blown off the island during the night, and deserted him. Four other gentlemen (including Baron De Therry, and Mr. Carleton) were in the same predicament as himself ; and their worldly possessions consisted of the clothes they stood in ; whilst the chances of being able to pursue their journey, within any reasonable time, were quite uncertain. Thrown thus upon the hospitality of the islanders, avowedly destitute of the means of making any return, they were not only received with the most cordial welcome, but treated with a delicacy, and constancy of attention (the offspring of natural politeness), which could not have been exceeded in the most polished European society ; and which enabled Mr. Brodie, in spite of his interrupted voyage, to reckon the few weeks spent on the island amongst the happiest of his life. (A passing vessel took him, and his fellow visitors off, after eighteen days' sojourn.)

The following is a condensed account of the visit which he thus paid to Pitcairn : — 23rd March, 1850.— The Captain of the *Noble*, thinking it advisable to procure some water, bore up for the island. . . . March 24th, Sunday.—At daylight off the settlement, which is on the north side. At 8 a.m., we saw a red flag hoisted near the precipice in front ; and, soon afterwards, we perceived a boat coming from the shore under sail, which proved to be a whale-boat, with nine islanders in her. After the usual ceremonies of question-putting to each other, we prepared to go on shore. The Captain asked them to get some water off immediately; but they objected to do so, as the day was Sunday; telling him, however, if it were a matter of necessity, they would bring him a little—which they did. . . . At 10 a.m., the ship's boat went on shore; bearing Mr. Brodie and others, with an islander, to pilot them through the surf to the landing place—which they safely reached, and where they were met by a few islanders; the remainder being at Church: After conversing with the former for a short time, they made a start for the settlement; ascending a very steep hill (at an angle of 45 degrees), which was very slippery after rain that had fallen heavily in the morning, and was the first the island had enjoyed for two months. Climbing about 200 feet, and then getting over a stile (so placed as to prevent the cattle from approaching the settlement), they came to the Market place, a small open space surrounded by cocoa-nut trees; and, a few hundred yards farther, gained the village, to which the inhabitants had not then given a name. It is very prettily located; with a lovely view of the sea between the trees.

In passing the Church, they found that the service had only just commenced, ... and were soon engaged in prayer among the Pitcairners. Upon thus joining them, hardly one so much as turned to see what they were like. After the service they congratulated a bashful young couple who had been married during it, and shook hands with every one; introduced themselves to Mr. Nobbs, the Minister, and proceeded to his house, where they ate some fruit; then walked about. . . . On nearing the island, vessels should make the north-east end, St. Paul's Point—off which are a few large rocks, all above water; the largest of these is a square, basaltic islet; and in shore are several high pointed pinnacles, which the pious islanders have named after the most zealous of the Apostles; they stand about 50 feet above water, with room for a boat to pass between them and the mainland. About a quarter of a mile to the westward is a small boat harbor, the only landing place which a stranger would be at all likely to find; the surf appearing to break heavily all around the northern end of the island; (and the *Bounty's* crew had to pull twice right round the latter, before they hit upon this harbor). There is very good anchorage, when there is easting in the wind, for vessels of any size, about a quarter of a mile to the southward of Pitcairn's north-west end; off which lie a few large rocks above water, similar to those by the north-east end; and the depth of water is from 8 to 25 fathoms, at from a quarter to three-quarters of a mile off shore. There are neither shoals nor sunken rocks off the island, over a quarter of a mile from land; and during seven months out of the twelve (Sep. to March, inclusive), the winds are from south-east to east.

In the bight of the first little bay, after rounding the northeast end of the island, and about a quarter of a mile to the westward of same, clumps of cocoa-nut trees, and boat houses, might be observed (adds Mr. Brodie). The landing place is below these; it consists of a shingly beach of sufficient breadth to allow of two boats abreast to come in at one time; care must be taken to observe the rollers, which are very irregular; and the channel in winds between rocks, close to the shore, and to one another. When a stranger enters, a native generally takes his station upon a rock, and waves his hat, to indicate a favorable opportunity for pushing ahead; but ships' boats seldom come in till some of the natives board them. Having set foot on shore, the visitor ascends a steep hill, almost a cliff, for about 300 yards, to a table-land, planted with cocoa-nut trees, which is called the 'Market-place;' about a quarter of a mile beyond which, at the north end of the island, lies the settlement, flanked by a grove of cocoa-nut trees, rumeras, and plantains; making the approach very picturesque. On the arrival of any vessel, there was a general holiday, as everyone was employed in collecting trade, and refreshments for her. The islanders seldom went off to a whaler in a boat —using a canoe, generally; but when an English ship appeared in sight, a boat made for her, so soon as she came within reasonable distance of the settlement: And great was the rejoicing when a man-of-war arrived; the women went on board freely; which they did not venture to do with a merchantman; while the men asked the Captain's advice, should it be needed, with regard to their own internal government; and were guided by it.

"The island is evidently of volcanic origin. The highest point (Look-out ridge) is about 1008 feet above the sea. Scoriæ are scattered here and there, but not to an extent to interfere with cultivation. The soil generally is of a deep red color, apparently decomposed lava, and very productive. But the system of agriculture was as primitive, as were the manners of the people. Unversed in the mysteries of sub-soil ploughing, and ignorant of the virtues of guano, all their field labor was performed with the hoe—by the unsparing use of which they contrived to raise abundant crops of food. Mr. Brodie observed many patches of the tobacco plant; but the art of curing the leaf was not well understood. There was a common wooden sugar mill, but of an inferior description. The largest quantity of sugar ever made at one time was 6 cwt. The inhabitants preferred making molasses to sugar; it went so much further in their food; more especially among the children. The cane did not grow very large, and was but little cultivated, on account of the great number of rats, which did much damage amongst it. The following is a list of the provisions that could be annually spared from the island, and their prices:—

200 to 300 barrels sweet potatoes, at per barrel	8s.
100 to 150 „ Irish ditto „ „	12s.
100 to 120 „ Yams „ „	8s.
1,500 to 2,000 cocoa-nuts, at per hundred	8s.
300 to 400 bunches of plantains; 3 bunches for	4s.
50 dozen fowls, at per dozen	12s.
40,000 to 50,000 oranges, at per hundred	4s.
10,000 „ at per barrel	8s.
100 gallons limèjuice, at per gallon	2s.

Water melons, pumpkins, and beans, in almost any quantity (*a*.)

Fish were not very numerous; but whenever the weather was fine, the chance of catching them was seldom lost; the largest were a sort of cod; some of which were very fine eating; there was also the red schnapper, caught near the shore, in shallow water; but the former was sought for in 100 to 200 fathoms, about one and a-half or two miles from shore. The fishers made their own lines, which they much prefer to English twisted lines; their's being heavier, formed of sail twine, and not so liable to twist in deep water as the other. Crawfish were numerous at certain seasons; and were procured by diving under water, alongside the rocks. There were not many eatable shell fish. The islanders had three whale-boats; two presented by the English Government;

(*a*) Yams came in Sep.; potatoes nearly all the year round; oranges in March; cocoa-nuts, plantains, and bananas, all the year; pumpkins in March; and watermelons in November.

the other was purchased from a whaling vessel. Their canoes were about 20 in number; held generally two persons each; and were so light that a man could carry one of them; with constant painting a canoe would last five years; but the tree from which they were made was getting very scarce.

There were but five head of cattle on the island in 1850—the bull (which "soon came to grief" by tumbling over a precipice), and the cow, brought from Valparaiso by Captain Fanshaw, in 1849, and their calf; with a heifer and young bull, gifts from gentlemen in New Zealand. (*) Many goats ran wild; and about a score of rabbits were skipping round the houses: Cats were numerous, wild in the bush, and their increase encouraged, that they might kill the rats; though they probably destroyed more fowls than rats. There were many dogs, useless animals, and very currish in appearance. The island rat, which is small, and the lizard, were the only quadrupeds indigenous to the place. Merely one sort of land bird was then known to breed there—a small species of fly-catcher (white and brown); and three species of sea birds—a white "skiff," a brown "skiff," and the man-of-war bird, or hawk: all of which the islanders ate. But few insects were to be seen; though at certain times, the caterpillar made its appearance, in large swarms, and was very destructive. Of land shells, there were only three kinds, and those very minute; while of sea shells, Mr. Brodie collected about 40 varieties on portions of two sides of the islands. (*a*)

Their domestic animals were in reality a loss to them; the quantity of food they supplied being small as compared with the produce of cultivated land which they consumed. A few of the goats were allowed to run loose upon some parts of the island; the number which each family was allowed to keep at one time being

---

(*) In Aug., 1852, Admiral Moresby brought the islanders a young bull, a cow, and a ram; and he sent to them by the *Dido*, in Sep., '53, a cow, a calf, and three heifers.

(*a*) The island "Register" states (under date, Sep. 6th, 1849), "A large seal was obtained on the west side of the island. Fletcher Christian first discovered it among the rocks, and was much alarmed at the sight of it. He feared to go near it, lest it should be a ghost (of which he has a great dread), or some beast of prey;! but he quickly ascended the hill which overlooks the town, and gave the alarm. Some persons went to his assistance, and shot the animal, just as it was making its retreat into the sea."

proportioned to that of its members; but it must never exceed nine. Those which ran loose were generally "nannies;" the males being kept at home, and fed three or four times a day, until two years old, when they were killed, or sold to shipping ; the females were always brought home a few days before kidding ; after which, they were again turned out until the kids were from three to four months old ; when they were brought home afresh, and the latter were marked ; then the female kids and their mothers were turned out once more, and the males detained at home. . . . . Pigs were fed much in the same manner as the goats, which made them very expensive to rear; and what few they had they did not care to sell, as "they were ashamed to ask a remunerating price for what the animals had actually cost in labour and potatoes." Each family generally killed a large hog, at the yam digging, as they then worked very hard ; but, except at this season, they ate animal food very sparsely. Mr. Nobbs mentioned, that by the time a large hog (300lb. weight) was fit to kill, it had usually eaten about 30 barrels of potatoes, which at 8s. a barrel, would be £12. . . . Their fowls were small, but bred in large numbers, and (for the most part) at some distance from the settlement, on account of the destruction they would otherwise cause amongst the gardens, and to the banana and plantain trees, into which they flew, and where they ate the fruit so soon as ripe : And it was feared that rabbits would prove a great pest some day, there being only one species of hawk, and no other enemy, to keep them under, when they got into the bush.

The culinary vegetables were numerous—potatoes (Irish and sweet), yams, pumpkins, and a sort of bean, which the islanders dried, and could keep for many months. Cabbages and onions were then scarce ; herbs, they had none: Their fruits were pines, four species of plantain, and banana, oranges, limes, melons, paw-paw apples—a fruit somewhat resembling a small English apple ; and cocoa-nuts. Pitcairn was not rich in indigenous flora ; but many valuable trees and plants had been imported from Tahiti.

The dwelling houses were from 40 to 50 feet long, about 13 feet high, and 15 feet wide. There was no glass upon the island, except one small window, which came out of the *Bounty*, and was in Mr. Nobbs' house. The windows, more like portholes of a ship, went all round the houses, and closed with sliding shutters in bad weather. One end of each house, about 10 feet long, was partitioned off as the sleeping apartment for the head of the family, and his wife. Sometimes, the other end was separated off in like manner, and occupied by one of the married sons or daughters, and their children. The entire side of the house, opposite the doorway, was fitted up with sleeping berths, raised about three feet from the ground, for the rest of the inmates; each bed place having its own "window." . . . No house had any fireplace in it; the thermometer ranging from 55° to 85°. Their cooking-houses were always detached from their dwellings. The fashion of other South Sea islanders, in forming ovens with hot stones in the ground, was generally followed; the ovens were built of large flat stones, which were banked up with earth a foot wide; and that earth was encased by another outside square of similar stones; so that the heat was most effectually kept in. The islanders were cleanly in their cooking, and took much trouble over it. Their food was chiefly fruit and vegetables; fish, when they could procure it; and occasionally the flesh of goats, which they shot "in the mountains." They were very ingenious cabinet-makers; constructing neat workboxes, "and dressing-cases," of a reddish, streaked wood, like that they built their houses of, very handsome, and rather lighter than rosewood in color; many of these "wares" were inlaid with a yellowish wood, which added to their beauty; and they readily sold from 20s. to 30s. each, to parties visiting Pitcairn. The islanders also formed very handsome walking canes of the same wood, as well as of the cocoa-nut and palm trees. The women manufactured hats and baskets from the leaves of the *pandanus*—which were also used in thatching the houses; and there was sale for as many of those various articles as could well be made; every person landing on it being desirous of carrying away some memorial from this interesting island. The population was then 156 souls; 79 females as against 77 men; 20 married couples; 15 males unmarried between the ages of 16 and 25; and 11 females between the same ages; with (amongst others) the Tahitan widow of Mr. Edward Young, as well as of Thursday October Christian. . . . .

The women generally wore a petticoat from the hip downwards, and over that a loose gown; often with a handkerchief thrown over the shoulders. A wreath of flowers round the head denoted that a woman was unmarried. The hair was worn in bands, with what (to Mr. Brodie's eye), " was an incomprehensible knob." The men always wore short trousers, the legs of which were cut off about six inches above the knee. A shirt, and a cap or hat, completed the costume; but on Sundays both men and women were very particular about their dress; and they expected their guests to be equally so; since they sent to Mr. Brodie, and his companions, white shirts for the first Sunday of their visit (they generally donned colored ones), and requested they would wear them at Church. Until they were two years of age, " children usually ran about in a state of nature." The men were mostly well formed and muscular; standing rather above the ordinary height; the women were neither tall nor short; but inclined to be rather stout, with a fine skin; some of them very fair; while others were as dark as Spaniards. Both men and women had splendid teeth, especially the latter. The children came very early to the use of their limbs. " I have seen " (writes Mr. Brodie) " one of these little imps walking about at the age of ten months, and was assured that he had been able to do so two months previously. Quarrels and swearing were unknown amongst these islanders, who were as one large family bred up together; they were, in point of fact, all more or less related to each other (owing to frequent intermarriages); and looked upon each other more as brothers and sisters than anything else. Indeed, the children appeared to be more nursed by their relations than by their mothers (so universal was the affection for them); and thus it was difficult to distinguish the married from the unmarried adults. Whenever any officer, passenger, or boat's crew, visiting the island, remained on shore over night, each person was lodged in a different house; that more information might be so obtained, than could be if all remained together in the same dwelling; for then " only one would be able to speak at a time, and contributions from the others to the common stock of knowledge would be lost."

Mr. Brodie then refers to matters of a more personal character to himself, and the people of Pitcairn, or relating to its past history. Thus, he was shown two guns (nineteen-pounders), a large copper boiler, pigs of iron kentledge, part of an armourer's bellows, an anvil, two sledge hammers, and a quantity of loose copper, which came out of the *Bounty*, 60 years previously, or was raised from the sea in 1845, close by where she had been sunk in 1790. (*a*) He took some lessons in tappa making, under Mrs. Nobbs', and her married daughter's tuition; but, the process being a very noisy one, he did not long remain a scholar; tappa cloth was used by the islanders in place of sheets; and, before they received presents in clothing from the British Government, they used it for the purpose of dress. Nearly all the men were smokers; but there was not more than half a pound of tobacco upon the whole island, at the time of Mr. Brodie's visit. There being an unoccupied house, Mr. Carleton proposed that all those whom the *Noble* had deserted should go into it, and keep house for themselves, so as to relieve their individual hosts (amongst whom they had been distributed until then) from the burden of their maintenance; though they would still be dependent upon the community for an occasional basket of yams, &c., &c.: They all agreed (except Baron De Therry) to this proposal; as such an arrangement would enable them to have their own house, without disturbing anyone, as well as allow their hosts, and hostesses, to take possession of their own sleeping apartments, which they had given up to the strangers from the time they came on shore: But the islanders would not listen to the project of the others keeping house for themselves; neither did they at all like the idea of their sleeping in the new place by themselves; and when one of the wayfarers offered to work in Adams' garden, after the departure of the *Noble*, the reply of the latter was, "I have now three times more pleasure in having you in my house than before; for while the vessel was here, it might perhaps be supposed I looked for some return; but since she is gone, it is quite clear none can be made:" Indeed, the islanders appeared "to rack their ingenuity in trying to put their visitors at ease, and to make them believe the advantage was upon the side of the Pitcairners—and this with a delicacy, and natural good breeding, which it was refreshing to witness." At last, however, it was determined that the meals of the former should be taken as usual at the separate houses; and towards evening (that there might be no intermediate wants), oranges, pine apples, bananas, plantains, &c., &c., came raining in upon them at their sleeping mansion; together

---

(*a*) Portion of one of her boat's anchors has found its way to the Sydney Museum, and is now carefully preserved there.

with two large bags of new clothes (voted at a meeting of the people), from which their guests were to appropriate whatever happened to fit them: Mr. Brodie took a shirt, a pair of trousers, and a waistcoat; "shoes and stockings being luxuries, he did not meddle with them":—Mr. Carleton, having commenced teaching all the adults upon the island to sing (of which more anon), gave an extra lesson on the evening of "possession-taking," which ended in a house-warming: Edward Quintall, one of the "Councillors" brought his fiddle; he had picked up some hornpipe and reel tunes by ear, on board ships, and played them with spirit, "and true artistic twang—not omitting the stamp and wriggle, or the grind upon the fourth string:" Some of the islanders danced very well, not waltzes, but reels. The women never dance now. Three of the hosts danced a Scotch reel, which threw the spectators into ecstacies. The women shrieked with laughing. The entertainment ended with blind-man's buff; and many other innocent games, in which all shared.

One day, Mr. Brodie joined a large party of the islanders (men and women) in an expedition, in their whale-boats, and canoes, to the west side of the island, that they might bring in a store of cocoa-nuts; which are very abundant there, and thrive better than elsewhere upon it, on account of the greater warmth. In cultivating the cocoa-nut tree, nuts which are perfectly dry and ripe are chosen, and put into a piece of ground by themselves; and so soon as they begin to shoot, they are taken up, and planted where they are meant to remain—a plan that is adopted in consequence of many of the nuts failing to germinate. The cocoa-nut tree generally takes eight years before it bears; and a good tree in full bearing will produce from 100 to 300 nuts annually: But not even while feasting upon this delicious fruit, on a slope of their own fair isle, were the natural simplicity, and candor, of the holiday makers to be lulled by harmless compliment; for when Mr. Brodie alluded to the beauty of the girls of the party, one of them observed she "did not think he was an Englishman;" and when he asked what had led her to that conclusion,? she answered, that he "flattered too much to be British born." That impression did not, however, prevent either them, or their male relatives, from endeavouring to provide the wanderers with some barrels of lime juice (then worth 60 dollars a barrel at San Francisco), when the

Colonist, bound thither from Auckland, touched at Pitcairn, and gave them a passage there; the fear being that "they might otherwise be unprovided for, in case they should arrive at San Francisco before the *Noble* did." It will be long, too (resumes Mr. Brodie), "before I forget the pretty faces of some of the women, their cheeks covered with tears, when they were made aware of our intention to leave them—which, they said, was very unkind upon our part: I told them it was our duty to others to go; but that we should ever bear them in mind: And, that the departing guests should not want for provisions during the voyage, a large whale-boat was filled with "pigs, goats, ducks, fowls, pines, oranges, lemons, bananas, plantains, and cocoa-nuts, along with two large sacks of sweet potatoes, and yams;" and sent off to the *Colonist*.

This notice of Mr. Brodie's visit to Pitcairn, in 1850, will (with his summary of it) be appropriately closed by an account of the only acknowledgment which any of his party could make for all the kindness shown them; and which token, though slight in itself, and such as might have been lightly thought of by some at the time, was productive of great pleasure, and lasting usefulness (perhaps of still higher results), both to their hosts, and their descendants up to the present hour. "As might be supposed" (he writes), "our anxiety from the first was to make some little return for the warm hospitality with which we were treated; a wish, however, which it was not so easy to gratify; seeing that our sole possessions, when we found ourselves left on shore, consisted of the clothes we wore, and a tuning fork, which happened to be in the Baron's pocket. But when we had been about a week amongst them, it luckily occurred to Mr. Carleton, who had observed their imperfect attempt at psalmody in Church, that a little musical instruction might prove of interest to them: The islanders caught at the proposal with eagerness; and on the very day of it, the needful apparatus—a ruled board, conductor's baton, &c., were prepared; and the first lesson was given to the whole population, in the new house. . . . . They proved remarkably intelligent; not one among the number being deficient in ear; while many had exceedingly fine voices. Their progress surpassed the most sanguine expectation of the teacher; on the fourth day from the commencement, his pupils sang through a catch, in four parts, with great steadiness; and for persons who had been hitherto unaware even of the existence of *harmony* in singing, the performance was very remarkable. Both scholars and preceptor appeared to take equal delight in the task; and after a fortnight's instruction, they sang in the open air trios and quartettes (for the most part performed in chorus), during the greater part of the night." They had among them some books of instruction in this delightful art, (sent them from England previously,) and were now sufficiently advanced to be able to pursue the study without assistance. They did pursue it, too, with such effect, that, for many a long year, the charm of song —catch, glee, and psalmody—oft filled the homes of Pitcairn, and floated through the morning or evening air, by valley, hill side, and landing place, or lent to God's praise its highest excellence.

And Mr. Brodie thus justly summarises all that he saw, felt, and heard, at Pitcairn: "Such a society, so free, not only from vice, but even from the petty bickerings and jealousies—those mild infirmities which we are accustomed to believe are ingrained in human nature—cannot, probably, be paralleled elsewhere. It is the realization of Arcadia, or of the golden age, which we have usually supposed had existence only in poetic imagination— all loving as one family; a commonwealth of brothers and sisters (as, indeed, they almost are by ties of relationship); the earth yielding them her fruits in abundance, and requiring only so much labor as suffices to save its occupants from the listlessness of inactivity; where there is neither wealth, nor want; a primitive simplicity of life and manner, absolute equality in rank and station, and perfect content: While their practical morality, and strong sense of religion, promise a lasting continuance of the blessings they enjoy; with a warm loyalty to their Queen, and fond attachment to Fatherland."

Mr. Brodie was at pains to collect the "laws," written and unwritten, that prevailed amongst this favored people in 1850, and to the earlier of which Lieutenant Lowry alludes in his report of 1839. They relate mainly to "government," preservation of property for the general good; and public education. With scarcely an exception, they are distinguishable from most codes I have met with, by their appropriateness, thoroughness, and brevity;

and in some respects (as in that of compulsory schooling), they were long in advance of legislation both in England, and in the Australian Colonies—though the penalties for "cat killing" are somewhat severe; the number of body-guards on women, visiting ships, apparently excessive; and the prohibition against "cutting their names on trees" hard on youthful lovers. (*a*)

(*a*) LAWS AND REGULATIONS OF PITCAIRN ISLAND.

No. 1.—THE ⸍MAGISTRATE.

Is to convene the public on occasions of complaints being made to him; and, on hearing both sides of the question, commit it to a jury. He is to see all fines levied, and all public works executed; and every one must treat him with respect. He is not to assume any power or authority on his own responsibility, or without the consent of the majority of the people. A public Journal shall be kept by the Magistrate, and shall from time to time be read; so that no one shall plead ignorance of the law for any crime he may commit. This Journal shall be submitted to the inspection of those Captains of British men-of-war which touch at the island.

Nos. 2 AND 4.—LAWS FOR DOGS, FOWLS, AND PIGS.

If any one's dog be found chasing a goat, the owner of that dog shall pay a fine of one dollar-and-a-half; one dollar to the owner of the goat, and the other half to the informer. If a dog kill or otherwise injure a goat, the owner of the dog so offending must pay the damage; but should suspicion rest on no particular dog, the owners of dogs generally must pay the damage. The present law is of no effect when the goat was upon cultivated ground. Persons who have fowls or hogs in the bush may take dogs to hunt them; but should the dogs commit damage during the hunt, the person taking them to it must pay the damage. . . . . If a fowl be seen trespassing in a garden, the proprietor of the garden is allowed to shoot and keep it, while the owner of the fowl is obliged to return the charge of powder and shot expended in killing the bird [This is the law; but the practice is to send back the dead fowl, and drop the claim for ammunition] . . . . If a pig be seen trespassing, no one is allowed to give information, except to the owner of the land, that he may not be baulked in whatever course he may think to adopt. . . . . If a pig do any damage, the person who sustains the damage may take the pig so trespassing—no matter whether he or any other person see the pig committing the damage. And if any person see a pig committing damage, and neglect to inform the person sustaining the damage, the former must pay that damage.

No. 3.—LAWS FOR CATS.

If any person under the age of 10 years shall kill a cat, he or she shall receive corporal punishment. If any one between the age of 10 and 15 kill a cat, he or she shall pay a fine of 25 dollars; half the fine to be given to the informer, the other half to the public. Any master of a family convicted of killing a cat shall be fined 50 dollars; half the fine to be disposed of as above. And every person, from the age of 15 upwards, who is so convicted, shall pay a fine similar to that of a master of a family.

No. 5.—LAWS REGARDING THE SCHOOL.

There must be a school kept, to which all parents shall be obliged to send their children; who must previously be able to repeat the alphabet, Lord's Prayer, and Belief; and be of the age from six to sixteen years. The school hours shall be from 7 o'clock in the morning until noon, on all days except Saturdays and Sundays, casualties and sickness excepted. One shilling, or an equivalent, as marked below, shall be paid for each child per month, by the parents, whether the child attends school or not.

Equivalent for money:—

	s.	d.
One barrel of yams, valued at	8	0
One barrel of sweet potatoes, valued at	8	0
One barrel of Irish potatoes ,,	12	0
Three good bunches of plantains ,,	4	0
One day's labor ,,	2	0

The Chief Magistrate is to see the labor well performed : and goods which may be given for money shall be delivered either at the market place, or at the house of the schoolmaster (Saturday was a sort of holiday, in which to collect provisions, &c., for Sunday).

No. 6.—LAWS FOR WOOD.

If any person want any wood [for house building], and is cultivating any land, he is to go on that land and get it. If any person cut more wood than is sufficient to build his house, the wood that remains after his house is finished is to be given to the next person who may want to build a house. This extends only to the *mero* and *brou* timber. Any person who may want any trees to break off the wind from his plantations, or houses, is to make it known ; and no one is allowed to cut them down, even if they be upon his own land [without consent of the Magistrate]. . . . . If any person go to cut logs, to enclose a piece of ground, or for any other purpose, he is not to cut any fit for building a dwelling house. The Magistrate is to appoint four men to inspect the logs after they are brought home ; and should any be found serviceable for building dwelling houses, they are to be taken from that person and given to the next person who builds a house. The third year from the time a person commences cutting wood for his house, he is to build it ; and the second year he is to pick a store of thatch for covering it. If the wood be left longer than the time specified, it is to be taken from the loiterer, and given to the next person who builds a house. Any person wanting logs must not cut green ones, so long as dry ones can be found. . . . . No one is allowed to cut down any trees for logs on which there are young ones growing, that might become valuable for building in future. Any person having a large enclosure which needs repair, and cutting down any tree on which there is any good log, is not allowed to take the log ; he must leave it for the benefit of those who have no enclosure ; and inform them where it is to be found ; but if they do not remove it within two weeks, anyone may do so, and keep it for such service as he pleases.

No. 7.—LAWS RESPECTING LANDMARKS.

On the 1st day of Jan., after the Magistrate is elected, or other earliest opportunity, he shall assemble all those deemed necessary ; and with them he is to visit all landmarks that are upon the island, and replace those that are lost.

No. 8.—LAWS FOR TRADING WITH SHIPS.

No person shall be allowed to get spirits of any sort from any vessel, or sell it to strangers, or anyone upon the island. Anyone found guilty of so doing, shall be punished by fine, or such other punishment as a jury shall determine on. No intoxicating liquor of any kind shall be allowed to be taken on shore, unless it be for medical purposes. Any person found guilty of transgressing this law shall be severely punished by a jury. No females are allowed to go on board of a foreign vessel, of any size or description, without permission of the Magistrate; and if he do not go on board himself, he is to appoint four men to look after the females.

No. 9.—LAWS FOR THE PUBLIC ANVIL, &c.

Any person taking the public anvil, and public sledge hammer from the blacksmith's shop, is to take it back after he has done with it; and in case the anvil, or sledge hammer should get lost by his neglecting to take it back, he is to get another in its stead, and pay a fine of four shillings.

No. 10.—PUBLIC WORKS.

The Magistrate for the time being is obliged to superintend the execution of all public works—among which are ranked the building of houses; fresh thatching them (which is necessary every seven years); reparations and alterations of the Church, roads, and water tanks. And in the execution of these public works, one member of each family (except Mr. Nobbs') is obliged to assist.

No. 11.—MISCELLANEOUS.

At any meeting which may take place, there shall be no bringing up things that are past to criminate others, with a view to prevent justice in the case before the Magistrate. Anyone doing so shall be punished by such fine as a jury may think proper to award. The Magistrate is to appoint churchwardens, four in number, beginning on the 1st of every month. Any person detected in shooting, or in any way killing white birds (unless it be for the sick), shall, for each bird that is killed, pay a dollar. . . . Carving upon trees is forbidden. . . . When a man marries he takes his share of his father's land, which is equally divided among his children; and the wife takes her proportion from her own father's land, and joins it to her husband's land; so that the young couple come immediately into their landed property.

CHAPTER X.—By Land and Sea.

1851, July—close of 1853 : Daily occupations at Pitcairn—Reception of visitors—The Admiral, and his Lady petitioners—A flag-ship ! in the offing ; and consequent doings, arrangements, observations, and amusements—Anniversary Ode—Ordination of Mr. Nobbs—Second and third visits of the *Portland ;* with "hard times," sickness, and endearments ; strolls by sunrise ; and ship's band ; evening adventure ; blind-man's buff ; and the parting—The Chaplain ; *Virago ;* and Consul ; peace, and welcome ; song, and woe ; the funeral ; goat hunting ; and Nicolas' epitome.

IF it be asked how the Pitcairners passed their time, and what they could have to do in a spot whose utmost limits is only about four miles and a half in circumference, or of less extent than Hyde Park and Kensington Gardens conjoined ? the question may be answered by an account of their ordinary daily occupations.

They generally rose so soon as it was light ; each family had early prayer, preceded by Scripture reading ; two chapters of the Bible being usually selected for the purpose ; and, after some slight refreshment, or without any (for they had only two regular meals every 24 hours), the business of their day began. The young people were sent to school, in accordance with a law of the island ; and, after the "graver hours that bring restraint and sweeten liberty," they had their needful food, and amusements. They were fond of kite-flying, and of games at ball ; though the narrow limits of the island had a corresponding influence on the nature and number of the out-door diversions, both of young and old.

. The men were occupied in cultivating their land ; looking after their gardens, building or improving their houses (which were neat, clean, and commodious); rearing stock; fencing in their plantations ; manufacturing hats from the leaf of the palm ; making fancy boxes and canes, which they kept in store for barter with whalers, or other vessels that might call at Pitcairn for refreshment.

At about 12 o'clock, they had a plain but not stinted meal, consisting of fruit, yams, and sweet potatoes, made into a kind of bread—with fish, meat, or poultry, once or twice a week. Fishing for a kind of cod, grey mullet, and red schnapper, though no very hopeful pursuit in the deep water round the island, occasionally formed part of the day's employment; and sometimes the islanders went forth at night amongst the rocks close to the shore, or rowed out in a canoe; and, flashing a light from its bows, attracted the fish, which they then struck with a five-pronged spear, and so took. The evening meal was partaken about seven o'clock, and mostly consisted of like materials to the breakfast, or dinner. After this repast, it was usual to attend the singing-school, to call on Mr. Nobbs, or meet to have a chat. (*a*)

The women had their daily task to perform; preparing the ground for cultivation, taking up yams, and doing other work requiring diligence and strength; and as there were no servants, the sisters or daughters of each family made and mended the clothes, and attended to all the requisite household affairs. The women also manufactured *tappa*, or native cloth, from the bark of the "anti," or paper-mulberry, which was rolled up, soaked in water, beaten out with wooden mallets, and spread forth to dry—a very laborious work; but the cloth was exceedingly durable. Mr. Murray had in his possession, in 1860, a piece of beautifully wrought white tappa, given him by Mrs. Heywood (Captain Heywood's wife), and bearing a label which stated it was made by the widow of Fletcher Christian, the mutineer. It was entrusted by Mrs. Christian to Captain Jones, when he visited the island in H.M.S. *Curacoa*, in 1841, as already mentioned; and she particularly desired him to give it to "*Peter's wife*."

Cooking was performed by the females; their cooking places were apart from the dwellings; and (from prudential motives), there were no fire-places in any of their wooden houses. Baked,

---

(*a*) As the difference in longitude between England and Pitcairn is about 130 degrees, or nearly nine hours in time, seven in the morning at the latter corresponded with four in the afternoon of the former.

not roasted, meats were the substantial luxuries of the table at Pitcairn. Captain Beechy says in a portion (not yet quoted) of his description of the manners and customs of the islanders, as observed by him, during the stay of the *Blossom*, in 1825, that an oven was formed in the ground, sufficiently large to receive a good sized pig, and was lined throughout with stones, nearly equal in size. These, having been made as hot as possible, were strewn with some broad leaves, generally of the ti-plant, and on them was placed the meat. If it were a pig, its inside was lined with heated stones, as well as the oven. Such vegetables as were to accompany the meal were then placed round the meat that was to be dressed. The whole was covered with leaves of the ti-plant, and buried beneath a heap of earth, straw, or rushes and boughs, which became matted into one mass. In about an hour and a quarter, the meat was sufficiently cooked. The Pitcairners were sparing in their use of lights; they had no candles; but employed oil, "and torches made with nuts" of the Doodoe-tree (*Aleurites triloba*); they have no glass for windows (except one piece); and the shutters, which served the purpose of admitting light and air, were closed in bad weather. There were no springs on the island, except the one mentioned by Captain Wood; and the water used by the inhabitants came mostly from reservoirs or tanks, neatly excavated, which collected the rain: Of these, there were five or six, holding from three to four thousand gallons of water each, and sufficient not only for the consumption of the islanders, but for supplies to whalers, and other vessels.

Formerly, all their books were considered as public property, but in 1849 a regulation was made for the distribution of them among the different families, and the placing of them on shelves so as to be easily accessible to anyone. It was believed they would be more read and valued in that way; the islanders, "being in the habit of walking into each others houses with the same freedom as into their own; and, taking up a book, will sit down and read it aloud, or not, as they feel disposed."

When the shades of evening drew on, these simple, pure-hearted people, one and all, again remembered their Maker, by reading His Word, and singing His praise. Then, without any thought of locks, bolts, or bars—for they neither had nor required any such defence — they committed themselves to His keeping, who had protected and blessed them throughout the day. (*a*)

As additional circumstances bearing on, and in proof of the kindly, primitive, state of society that prevailed in Pitcairn at the period above described (as well as previously and subsequently), and of the confidence with which its people were regarded by all visitors to them, we learn on the authority last referred to, that when the Captain, officers, or company, of any vessel touching at their island, came on shore, they were at once greeted and attended by a number of the natives, descending for the purpose from the village to the landing place. All then went up the hill--usually to the school-house, where the strangers obtained a sight of the island "Register," examined the shipping list, and entered the name of their own vessel, whence came, and whither bound. After some preliminary conversation, as to the health of the Queen, and the Pitcairners, respectively, or such like, the representatives of the several families, or one at least for each house, assembled; and after a further hearty welcome, and the interchange of friendly expressions, these inquired what was wanted by the vessel in the way of vegetables, and other refreshments—the price of which was always the same in time of scarcity, as of plenty. On a list being handed in of the articles required, such as yams, sweet potatoes, &c., the islanders asked of the Captain, or principal officer, what *he*, or the ship, had to dispose of—which was mostly found to be coarse cotton clothes, soap, oil, &c., with perhaps, small quantities of lead or iron. Then, the representatives retired and consulted among themselves what each family's proportion of the ship's wants amounted to; and, this being settled, each of them repaired to his own plantation to procure his part. When the things needed were collected, no Captain, or other officer, ever thought it necessary (such was the reliance on the honesty and integrity of the islanders), to be present, either himself, or by proxy, at the weighing or measuring of the articles; but one of the islanders remained at the Market place to take an account of those sent on board; and his "tally" was always acceded to by the ship's authorities.

(*a*) Mr. Murray's Pitcairn, pp. 157-164.

Thus "ran their world away," trustful in God, and contented with the lot which had befallen them. And heretofore, the Commanders of vessels of war visiting Pitcairn had been of the rank of Captains only; but Rear-Admiral Fairfax Moresby, C.B., being in charge of the Pacific station, received in July, 1851, the following warm and hearty invitation, signed by thirteen of the female inhabitants of the island, in the name of all their sex, to favor it with his presence:—

"*Pitcairn, July 28th,* 1851.

"*Honorable Sir,—From the kind interest you have evinced for our little community, in the letter you have sent to our excellent and worthy Pastor, Mr. Nobbs, we are emboldened to send you the following request, which is, that you will visit us before you leave this Station; or if it be impossible for you to do so, certainly we, as loyal subjects of our gracious Queen, ought to be visited annually, if not more frequently, by one of her ships of war.*

"*We have never had the pleasure of welcoming an English Admiral to our little island: and we therefore earnestly solicit a visit from you. How inexpressibly happy shall we be, if you think fit to grant us this our warmest wish. We trust that our very secluded and isolated position, and the very few visits we have of late had from British ships of war, will be sufficient apology for our addressing the above request to you. With fervent prayers for your present and future happiness, and for that of our Queen and Nation, we remain, honored Sir, your sincere and affectionate well-wishers,"*—[signed by three of the Adams', three of the Youngs', one of the McCoys', one of the Christians', four of the Quintalls', one of the Evans, and one of the Nobbs'], "*in the names and on behalf of all the rest of the female sex on the island.*"

What sailor could decline such an invitation? Admiral Moresby could not; on the contrary, it was cordially accepted; and early in Aug., 1852, his flagship, the *Portland,* graced the island waters. This is Mr. Nobbs' pleasant narrative of what followed on her appearance:—"On the 7th Aug., '52 (at noon), a vessel was reported, which at sunset was strongly suspected to be a ship of war. The hours of the night passed tediously away; and before sunrise next morning, several of our people were seated on the precipice in front of the town, anxiously awaiting the report of a gun from the ship, which would give positive confirmation to the over-night's anticipation. Nor were they kept long in suspense; the booming of a cannon soon electrified the town; and the whole community was thrown into a state of intense excitement; especially as it was soon observed that she bore an Admiral's flag.

"Our boat repaired on board; and, after a short time, another from the ship was seen approaching the shore. The teacher and some others went to the landing place, and had the honor of welcoming to Pitcairn, Rear-Admiral Moresby, Commander-in-Chief of the Pacific Station, and the first officer of that rank who ever visited their island: He received our greetings of welcome very urbanely; attended Divine service, and was evidently surprised at the excellency of the singing; particularly, as friend Carleton had so very limited a time for instructing our people. In the afternoon, the Rev. Mr. Holman, Chaplain to the *Portland*, read prayers, and preached most appropriately to the occasion, from 1st Cor., 15th ch., last verse—' Therefore, my beloved brethren, be ye steadfast, immovable, always abounding in the work of the Lord; forasmuch as ye know that your labor is not in vain in the Lord.'

"In the course of conversation, the Admiral learned from the inhabitants that they had a great desire for the ordination of their Pastor (that he might be qualified to administer the sacrament of the Lord's supper); and, with great kindness, he proposed to send Mr. Nobbs to England for that purpose, and to leave the Rev. Mr. Holman to officiate in the others stead, during his absence from the island. The inhabitants did not accede to this most generous offer as readily as they ought to have done; and the reason they gave was, that in case of sickness they would have no one to prescribe for them. The Admiral told them they might do as they liked; but that they would be much wanting to themselves, and their children, if they let so favorable an opportunity pass without improving it. He explained to them, clearly and forcibly, the necessity of an ordained Clergyman being established among them, and the disabilities their children labored under until such an event took place. They listened with breathless attention to his paternal advice, and readily admitted that the subjects of it were most vitally connected with their welfare. But still they evinced a backwardness in agreeing to part with their teacher. The Admiral, on perceiving this, kindly told them he would give them till eleven o'clock that night, to come to a decision, and that he would not retire to rest until then.

"During their debate, one of them came to inquire of the Admiral, whether Mr. Holman would teach the public school, as well as be Chaplain to them. Sir Fairfax replied, 'Certainly:' On this the man went away; and at eleven o'clock, as no answer had arrived, the former went to bed. About twelve o'clock, word was brought that the community had agreed to let their teacher go; which was only reported next morning to the Admiral; who remarked that they had done well in consenting to Mr. Nobbs' departure; and that he would take upon himself the responsibility of the expenses to be necessarily incurred by the other; although he had no doubt there were friends of the Pitcairn islanders in England who would cheerfully unite with him; and, further, that the islanders would never lack friends, so long as they continued to deserve them.

"As the point was now decided, Mr. Nobbs was requested to hold himself in readiness to embark; the Admiral generously undertaking to supply him with articles in which his scanty wardrobe was deficient. On observing, too, the necessity there was for the presence of an educated female on the island, to improve the domestic habits of the women and children—and hearing Mr. Nobbs remark that he would send one of his daughters to Valparaiso, to gain the acquirements needed for the work, but that he could not command funds for doing so—Sir Fairfax said, 'Take your child with you as far as Valparaiso; I will put her to school there while you are gone to England; and when you come back, you can take her to the island with you' [and this was done].

"The ship remained off the island for three days; and now comes the leave-taking on the 11th Aug. The venerable Commander-in-Chief of Her Majesty's Forces in the Pacific, standing on the rocky beach at Bounty Bay (the very spot where the mutineers had landed 62 years before), himself the oldest person there by 15 years, surrounded by stalwart men and matronly women, youths, maidens, and little children, every one in tears, and deeply affected, formed a truly impressive scene. The boat was some time in readiness before the Admiral could avail himself of an opportunity to embark. Some held him by the hand; the elder women hanging on his neck; and the younger ones endeavouring to obtain a promise that he would re-visit them. As a number of the islanders went on board the *Portland* with the

Admiral, a similar scene occurred there; and as the latest boat pushed off from the ship, some of the hardy tars, standing in the the gangway, brushed away many a tear. The frigate now stood in for the last time, and, hoisting the Royal standard, fired a salute of 21 guns; while the seamen manned the rigging, and gave three hearty cheers, and one cheer more. The islanders responded; the band struck up 'God save the Queen,' and the stately *Portland* started on her cruise." (*a*)

This is what the fine old sailor (whose memory is still cherished on Pitcairn as that of one of its best friends), wrote to the Admiralty on the following day [12th Aug., '52): "Of all the eventful periods which have chequered my life, none have surpassed in interest, and (I trust and hope), in future good, our visit to Pitcairn; and surely the hand of God is in all this: for, by chances the most unexpected, and by fortunate winds out of the usual course of the trades, we were carried in 11 days from Borobora. It is impossible to describe the charm that the society of the islanders throws around them, under the providence of God. The hour and the occasion served; and I have brought away their Pastor and teacher, for the purpose of sending him to England to be ordained; while one of his daughters will be placed at the English Clergyman's, at Valparaiso, until her father's return. The islanders depend principally for their necessary supplies on the whaling ships, which are mostly American; and, greatly to their credit, these whalers [with scarcely an exception], behave in a most exemplary manner, and very differently from what I had expected. One rough seaman of the *Portland*, whom I spoke to in praise of such conduct, said, 'Sir, I think if one of our fellows was to misbehave himself here, we should not leave him alive': They are guileless and unsophisticated beyond description."

And the Admiral's son and Secretary, Mr. Fortescue Moresby, when referring to the arrival of the *Portland*, and the three days spent at Pitcairn by her people, thus describes what he saw and felt:—"At 6.30 a.m. on the morning of the 6th August ('52), as we were dancing along about eight knots an hour, before a fresh

---

(*a*) The crew of the *Portland* requested and had permission to present the Pitcairners with three casks of rice, 12 bags of bread, and one cask of sugar, the value of these articles being charged against their wages.

breeze, we discovered a thin blue shadow, whose outline appeared to be too well defined to be a cloud; and at 9 it was certain we saw Pitcairn Island. Having read so much about the Mutiny of the *Bounty*, and the subsequent romantic history of the mutineers, which has resulted in the formation of a Colony, celebrated for the virtue, simplicity, and religion of its citizens; I experienced a feeling, on approaching the island, such as filled my heart when visiting some spot held sacred as the scene of Biblical relation, or historical interest. Having a fair wind, we hoped about noon to be on shore; but, while we were yet 20 miles from the island, it came directly foul, and fell light; so that we hardly held our own, owing to the heavy swell; and all day we remained endeavouring to work up. . . . . During the night, we got a slant of wind; and at 6 o'clock, Sunday morning, the 8th, we were close to the shore. A whale-boat, full of islanders, soon came off; but, before drawing alongside, they asked permission to board; then jumped up the side seven or eight fine, tall, robust fellows; and assured us of a hearty welcome when we went on shore.

"I was in my cabin with Philip McCoy, one of our visitors, when the sentry came to tell me it was prayer time, in the Admiral's cabin; and I said to Philip, 'I shall be up again directly, if you will wait!' He paused a moment, and then said, 'May I come, sir?' 'Oh, yes!' I answered; and, on going down we met his companions, whom he told of the sentry's message, and, coming in, they all knelt down to prayers. We then got a hurried breakfast; and the Admiral and myself immediately landed in the cutter, the water being pretty smooth. Mr. Nobbs received us at the landing ground; and we at once ascended the cliffs by a steep, winding path to a plantation of cocoa trees, called the Market place, as all trade is carried on there. Here some of the islanders met us and gave us a hearty welcome; and it is here all the inhabitants assemble to welcome the officers of a man-of-war landing upon a week day: But as this was a Sunday, and the hour early, the majority of them had not as yet arrived. We continued our way, by a pretty path winding through the trees, to the town; meeting occasional detachments coming towards us. These all followed in our wake; and by the time we reached Mr. Nobbs' cottage, which is situate on the opposite end of the town, we had pretty well all the islanders about us.

"Never were so many happy, smiling faces, all eager to look at the first Admiral that ever came to their happy home; but not one tried to push his way, or make any attempt to get before another. If we said a kind word to any of them, they looked so happy and pleased; and we did not neglect to gratify them. There is not one in whose face good humor, virtue, amiability and kindness, do not beam, and (consequently), not one whose face is not pleasing.

"It was now the prayer time and away we all went to Church. Mr. Nobbs officiated, and read the prayers impressively and earnestly; the most solemn attention was paid by all present. The islanders sang two hymns in most magnificent style; I have never heard any Church singing that could equal theirs, except at Cathedrals; and the credit is largely due to Mr. Carleton, who was left behind by accident from a whaler, in 1850. . . . . . .

"Boys and girls can swim through the largest surf, and play about amid the broken water, by the rocks, that we looked upon with terror. One of their greatest amusements is to have a 'slide,' as they term it; that is, to take a piece of wood, about three feet long, shaped like a canoe, but having a small keel—called a surf-board—hold this before them, dive under the first heavy sea, and come up on the other side. They then swim out a little way, until they meet a rapid, heavy sea coming rolling in—the higher the better—when they rest their breasts upon the surf-board, and are carried along upon the very apex of the roller at a prodigious rate right upon the rocks. One thinks nothing can save them from being dashed to pieces; but in a moment they are upon their legs, and prepared for another 'slide.' The method of fishing adopted by the women is equally dangerous. They walk upon the rocks until they see a 'squid;' then watching the retreating wave they run in, and try to pick up the 'squid' before the advancing surf can wash them off; but frequently they are taken with it, and have to exercise their skill to gain a footing, and land, for they have no surf-boards to help them in this pursuit.

"Christmas Day is a grand feast day among these islanders, and they keep it in good style. But the Queen's birthday is *the* day of days (for all secular purposes at least), and it is observed accordingly. 'How is the Queen?' is a question everybody asks of a stranger." And their own special song (which was written by Mr. Nobbs, and is sung in general assemblage on Her Majesty's birthday) is at least a hearty one:—

> " The Queen ! the Queen ! our gracious Queen !
> Come raise on high your voices,
> And let it by your smiles be seen
> That every heart rejoices :
> Her natal day we'll celebrate
> With ardour and devotion ;
> And Britain's festal emulate
> In the Pacific Ocean.
>
> " Now let old England's flag be spread,
> That flag long famed in story ;
> And, as it waves above our head,
> We'll think upon its glory :
> Then fire the gun ! the *Bounty's* gun,!
> And set the bells a-ringing ;
> Till,—with hearts and voices one,
> We'll all unite in singing :
>
> " The Queen ! the Queen ! God bless the Queen !
> And all her Royal kindred ;
> Prolonged and happy be her reign,
> By faction never hindered :
> May high and low, the rich and poor,
> The happy, or distressed,
> O'er her wide realm, from shore to shore,
> Arise, and call her blessed.'

Mr. Nobbs and his daughter left Pitcairn in the *Portland*, amidst the tears and blessings of his little flock, and arrived at Valparaiso on the 30th Aug., '52 ; then he crossed the Isthmus of Panama, and landed at Portsmouth, 16th Oct. ; Admiral Moresby having supplied him with the means of obtaining a passage from Valparaiso to London, and contributed £100 towards his expenses whilst absent from the island. Dr. Blomfield (then Bishop of London), made no difficulty about his ordination ; on the contrary, in consideration of his long and faithful services at Pitcairn, and the high character given of him by the Admiral, he readily acceded to Mr. Nobbs' request to be admitted to holy orders. On the 24th Oct., in the parish church of St. Mary Islington, and under a special commission from Dr. Blomfield, he was admitted to Deacon's orders ; and on the 30th Nov. he was ordained Priest, in Fulham church, by his Lordship; his description in the letters of orders being " Chaplain of Pitcairn Island." He received marked attention from many distinguished persons during his stay in England; was admitted to an audience with the Queen, at Osborne, by her desire, and presented with Her Majesty's portrait, as well as with portraits of Prince Albert, and the Royal children, as gifts to her faithful subjects, the islanders (whose fathers the Admiralty would have strung to the yard arm, had they been taken sixty-three years previously). (*a*) On 17th Dec., '52 (after he had been placed by the Society for the Propagation of the Gospel on its list of Missionaries, with a munificent salary of £50 per annum,! and assisting in raising a fund amongst generous persons in England for the purchase of a whale-boat, labourers' and carpenters' tools, a proper bell for the Church, medicine, a few clocks, clothing of various sorts, simple articles of furniture and cooking—and of which contributions, £500 balance was left for investment in the stocks, for the future benefit of the Pitcairners—this excellent man sailed from Portsmouth, reached St. Thomas' early in 1853, proceeded to Navy Bay, re-crossed the Isthmus of Panama, and on 12th Feb. arrived at Valparaiso. (*b*)

The following extract from a letter to a friend, by Fortescue Moresby, of 25th June, '53, details what followed: " On 15th April, the *Portland*, having Mr. Nobbs and his children, Reuben and Jane, on board, left Valparaiso, in order to return them to their island home." [Reuben was going there on account of his continued illness; but Jane, that she might impart to its people the knowledge and habits she had gained during her absence from it.] " The Admiral was much pleased with the

---

(*a*) In a sermon preached by Mr. Nobbs during his stay in England, after picturing the early history of the Pitcairn settlement, he was able to add : " Its population now amounts to 170 persons, who are living without any dissensions, and with but one form of Church government—that of the Church of England. The Holy Bible and the Church Prayer Book are their rules of guidance; their motto—one Faith, one Lord, one Baptism ! And when I took a sorrowful leave of them, about three months since, they were strong in faith, giving glory to God."

(*b*) In a letter of June, '55, Mr. Nobbs gratefully alludes to the fact, that so large a balance had been received for the future wants of the islanders; and adds, " I do not think there will be a necessity for drawing any portion of it for the next two years, if we should remain at Pitcairn so long ; but if there should be a removal to Norfolk Island, that may alter the case."

progress made by her, whilst at Valparaiso; she had learned to sew neatly, and acquired many other useful domestic accomplishments, without losing, in the least degree, her pristine simplicity and modesty. On Saturday, 14th May, we sighted Pitcairn, about 60 miles distant; and on Sunday, at sunrise, it was looming large from the deck. Before going to morning Service, we fired three guns, to let the islanders know we had as many passengers on board. After Service, we were close enough to see people on the shore, and we observed them come out of Church, and launch their whale-boat. This was a most anxious time for Mr. Nobbs. In half-an-hour, the boat came alongside, followed by a canoe, in which were old John Adams' son, and grandson. The crew manifested the same honest, generous, feeling of delight at Mr: Nobbs' return, as the islanders had of sorrow at his departure; and of course they were delighted to see *us*, also, once more. The Admiral, with Mr. Nobbs, Reuben, Jane, and myself, immediately landed in the cutter, and got rather wet in the surf. Every soul was on the beach to receive us; and to attempt describing their joy at again having amongst them their old and beloved Pastor, would be a task my pen is totally unequal to. But we observed, that all the men looked ill, and poor; which (they told us) was the effect of a long drought, that had disappointed them in their harvest. This had not caused quite a famine, but so nearly so, that for months they had been reduced to pumpkins, berries, cocoa-nuts, and beans, for existence. Nor were they the same gay people we had previously known: one and all looked thin, and careworn.

"We proceeded in a body to the village; and then they told us, how close they were pressed, and how they had been pushed for food. The officers and crew of H.M.S. *Virago*, which visited the island in Jan. 1853, had presented them with all their savings of provisions; and except for that timely supply, the distress in the island would have been much more sharply felt. They made the best of their position, at same time; saying they generally fared so well that the least privation seemed to them a great hardship; but their thin figures, and low spirits, spoke of their sufferings. We staid from Monday until Thursday morning, and passed our time in much the same manner as before; in taking walks over the island; sketching, talking, and singing. Truly, a more innocent and delightful race could not exist.

"On Thursday we left, and shaped our course for the Gambier Islands; we sighted them the same evening; but the weather was so bad, we dared not attempt to pass through the narrow entrance in the reef. For some days this state of things continued—grew worse, indeed; and, as the wind was fair for Pitcairn, at the same time, we bore up, and soon made the island again; but as squalls were still general, and heavy, no boat came off as we stood in; so we thought they could not communicate. We stood off and on, for a few hours; thinking the weather would moderate, and then bore round; intending to fire a gun or two, and away! Just then, I caught the flash of an oar, and said to the Flag-lieutenant, 'There's a boat, Sir!' He thought what I had seen was a glint upon a rock; but, as I observed it rise on each wave, I replied, 'it is a living rock, then.' At last he was convinced; so we hove to; and five of the islanders came on board in their whale-boat. They had a sad tale to tell; all were sick on shore; having been attacked with influenza the day after we had sailed. We gave the poor fellows a good supper, and they related their woes. It was thought the malady had been communicated from some cases on board the *Portland*, during her recent stay at the island; and it was decided that, early next morning, the Captain, Dr. Palmer, and myself, should land and see what could be done. Meanwhile, a quantity of tea, sugar, biscuit, &c., was got ready for the sufferers. On Sunday morning, we landed, and found most of the poor things in bed. Some, not so bad as the others, got up to receive us. The Doctor visited and did all he could to relieve, them; three or four of the cases were very serious ones, and he would willingly have remained some days to attend upon them; but as he had given the necessary directions, and done all he immediately could, the Admiral decided to leave, as his stock of water was failing.

"You can hardly think how sad it was, seeing four-fifths of our friends so ill. We visited each house, and spoke a word of comfort, here and there, to those most desponding. Tea was their great want; and they were very thankful for the little stock I took them: Some at once made a kettle-full, and said they felt better on partaking of it. Mr. Nobbs, Reuben, and

Jane, were almost the only ones entirely free from sickness; showing that the strong food they had been living on was their medicine; for the poor islanders, famine-struck and weak, had no strength to resist the disease. At 4 p.m. on Sunday, we were compelled to depart once more; and our distress was great, because we left them nearly all ill. Now we are fairly off, I suppose. Never more, most probably, shall I see Pitcairn; but though I never behold it again, I can never forget it. To me it will ever be the gem of all the places I have ever visited, or shall visit, in the varied roamings of a sailor's life."

Indeed, one can scarcely conjure to the mind, a spot more inviting to any man, untrammelled by worldly ties and cares, than Pitcairn usually was—in mountain, sea, and sky, forest, cliff, and shore; presenting, too, a great variety of soil and aspect, well wooded, and generally healthy; the cocoa-nut, plantain, banana, bread fruit, banyan, and orange trees, numerous and flourishing; the sweet and ordinary potato, yams, watermelons, sugar-cane, tobacco, ti-plant, and maize, still more abundant; and goats, hogs, and poultry equally so; the thermometer ranging from 59° to 89°; and a state of society prevailing which, for virtue and goodness, has never yet been excelled, if ever equalled, throughout the world.

The sickness above alluded to soon passed away; and I think the exquisite picture that is next presented, from the same pen (Fortescue Moresby's), in Aug., 1854, has reference to the *Portland's* visit to Pitcairn, and to the occurrences there, between the 15th and 19th May, '53, that are already referred to:—" The most implicit confidence is placed in English officers; no restraint is thought necessary; and girls walk about with them by day or night, alone, or together. I was generally accompanied by one or two, with their arms round me; almost as often by three or four. Captain Chads, and one or two more, who remained on shore as long as I did, were similarly attended. All the time, the stream of fun and laughter was uninterrupted; but their demeanor is so virtuous, modest, and natural, while they show so much affection, that I could not help feeling quite a love towards them all; and I am convinced the most heartless villain, and the greatest reprobate, must loathe himself, and detest his sins, in contemplating the high moral standard to which these simple islanders have attained. The delight and pleasure our company seemed to give them could hardly be believed; they could not restrain such expressions as the following; all the time clinging round us, and looking up into our faces:—' Ah, I do love the English so'!—' How good, how kind, you are, to come and see us;'! and the pleasure that filled their pure hearts was evident from their faces. This familiarity only exists with English officers, who have, by their right and steady conduct, tried to deserve so high a mark of esteem. Successful they have been; for but one person rises above us in their estimation, and that is her Majesty, who is more loved here than in any other part of her wide dominions.

"*Monday.*—At day-break, accompanied by a troop of young girls, we walked to the highest ridge on the island, and obtained a splendid view of the settlement, and whole island. We also got a good idea of the risk the men run while hunting the goats. It is wonderful how they can cling on; for, to our weak heads, it appeared a feat to stand on the edge, and look down. I said to one, 'You cannot go down there;'! he immediately clung to the side, and in a moment was six or eight feet down—proof that he could accomplish the remaining 300. We had great fun coming back; running with the girls down the steep hills, &c.; but we were quite amused to see with what care those appointed to look after the Admiral performed their task; helping him up any difficult places; and they were not weak young ladies. At last we got down, and had a splendid breakfast of yams, done in two or three different ways, bananas, oranges, cocoa-nuts, fowls, and pork. After breakfast, all the girls that could be spared, we took on board, to see the ship; and though they were sick before they got alongside, and continued so, they still maintained their cheerfulness, and ran about, and looked at everything. We made them dance a country dance; but the band was their greatest treat; for it was the first they ever heard, and occupied a great share of their attention. They also sang us several of their beautiful songs—with 'God Save the Queen,'—and they sang the latter better than I can pretend to describe. We got on shore about 4 p.m., and supped. I had supper with Jemima Young, and afterwards went to the singing-school. They entertained us pleasantly until 10 p.m. We then proposed 'blind-man's buff;' and it was fun, I can tell you, to hear their laughing and screams. This lasted until midnight, when we retired.

"*Tuesday.*—Up at day-break, and until breakfast walked about the village. All those who could not go on board yesterday, went to-day; and the band came on shore to amuse the others. The intense excitement it caused, and the curiosity with which they followed it, were very amusing. After it had played for some time, the girls sang us some of their exquisite glees, catches, songs, &c.; then the band played again. This lasted until 4 o'clock, when it was time for the sailors to go on board, much to the regret of the whole community. I went down to the sea side, to meet the girls who were coming on shore; they had been very sick indeed; and one poor thing, half dead, I took home. She was so weak that twice she had to rest, coming up the hill; and she lay down and put her head in my lap. It was quite dark when we reached her house, and she was so grateful; but I could not stay to supper (which was a disappointment to her), because I was engaged to sup with Rebecca Christian, who had also asked the Admiral, Captain Chads, and Mr. Nobbs. . . . After supper, we all repaired to the singing-school; and were, for the last time, enchanted with their admirable singing. It is really wonderful after only six or seven weeks' tuition. About 10, we repaired to John Adams' house, and had a splendid game of 'blind-man's buff.' The way the active creatures elude you, running and dodging in every direction, was most amusing. It was 1 o'clock before we got to bed; and I was to sleep at Jemima Young's house.

"I was awakened in the morning, by Jemima, Martha Young, and Dinah Quintall, standing round me; I had so completely got hid in the feather bed they gave me to sleep in, that I was almost lost. We took a walk to a cave up the mountains, and came down to breakfast. This was our last day, and it was rather *triste*. When 2 p.m. came, and we all (the whole village) assembled at the landing place, the scene was most affecting. Never in my life have I seen anything to equal it; all the kind, affectionate people crying; the girls clinging round us; and begging us to come back soon again. I tried for a few moments to bear up, but it was a sad failure; I broke down, and am not ashamed to say I cried as much as they did (as I kissed them all round).

One big, stout fellow came and said, 'God bless you, sir,' and gave me a kiss. I thought his heart would break. I could not have believed that a few days would have made me feel such an affection for any single person, much more for a great number, as I did for them; but so it is; their honest, pure character produces an impression that can never be effaced. Nearly all the men came on board with us; and we stood close to the island, hoisted the Royal Standard, and fired a Royal Salute. We then gave three hearty cheers, and the band played 'God Save the Queen,' 'Rule Britannia,' &c. We were so close in, that we could see them all collected under the trees, and we heard their cheers in answer to ours. The parting with the men was worse almost than with the girls; to see big stout fellows crying, and hardly able to look up, was too much. All the officers were deeply affected; and I saw some of the men nearest me, old hardy seamen, and big marines, not only wipe away a tear, but regularly crying. (a)

It should have been mentioned (in the order of time), that, in the December of the preceding year (1852), the Rev. W. H. Holman, (Chaplain of the *Portland*), who was left at Pitcairn during the absence of Mr. Nobbs in England, on his ordination visit, wrote thus to Admiral Moresby:—" From my experience, the Pitcairn islanders are fully deserving of the high social and religious character which they bear: I have seen no instance, whatever, of disagreement or ill temper; but, on the contrary, everything is done in peace and goodwill. They vie with each other in their attempts to make me comfortable, and have so loaded me with presents (which I dare not refuse without wounding their feelings), that I have a large stake in the property of the island."
. . . Each family " provided his food in turn."

And when, toward the close of Jan., '53, H.M.S. *Virago* visited Pitcairn, bearing (amongst other things) some roses, myrtles, and fig-trees, which the thought and kindliness of Lord Palmerston had procured for its inhabitants, the extract next presented, from the diary of Mr. B. T. Nicholas, British Consul

---

(a) About three years from date of the above, it was Mr. Moresby's fate to again meet his friends, the Pitcairners; and though they were then located upon Norfolk Island, "never" (he says) "did any man receive a warmer welcome than I did—much to the wonder of the officers who were with me."

at Raiatea, then a passenger, and who spent on the island the week that vessel lay off it, furnishes an agreeable and animated sketch of life there—showing that seamen were not the only persons who estimated its attractions very highly:—" At daylight, on Monday, 24th Jan., Pitcairn Island was in sight from the masthead of the *Virago*, apparently about forty-five miles off; and as it peeped from the horizon, it recalled the top of St. Paul's Cathedral. We reached the anchorage in Bounty Bay, at half-past two, under steam; and, being the first steamer that had ever visited the island, we made up our minds to astonish the natives, with the unusual display of a ship going through the water at the rate of some six knots an hour, in a dead calm. But they knew the monster at once to be a steamer; and though much delighted, were not equally surprised at her performances. A boat came off with Mr. Holman, who had been left to fill the place of Mr. Nobbs, whilst the latter was in England for ordination purposes. The people supposed we had brought Mr. Nobbs back; and his wife and a daughter were in the boat to welcome him, that came off to the vessel. They, of course, were disappointed; but glad as the islanders would undoubtedly have been to receive Mr. Nobbs, they would, I believe, have been little less sorry to lose Mr. Holman. We landed (the *Virago* saluting me with seven guns), without much trouble, in Captain Prevost's whale-boat, steered by one of the Quintalls, and experienced a hearty and truly English welcome; the natives shaking us warmly by the hand, and telling us how glad they were to see us—professions which their after kindness fully confirmed.

"From the landing place, we scaled a kind of zig-zag goat path, for about 200 yards, which brought us to the 'Marketplace;' but instead of buildings, benches, butchers' shops, and all that constitutes an English market-place, one must fancy a floor of shrubs, and a roof of cocoa-nut trees; a small space of a few yards being cleared; and to this the different families bring their stock for sale, when any merchant vessel calls at the island for provisions. Here were assembled all those who were either too old, or too young, to reach the landing place, and who renewed the expressions of good will made to us by their relatives below. We then walked towards their village, or rather the succession of detached houses, each on its own little terrace, embowered in orange and cocoa-nut trees; and, as it was nearly tea-time, we were billeted, generally two in a house. My friend Hassan, the Turkish lieutenant, and myself, were quartered on John Adams, with whom Mr. Holman lives. Soon afterwards, it being a beautiful moonlight night, we all met in front of the house where the organ is kept. The islanders then sang several hymns, and touching melodies, one of which, from its simple pathos, and from the exquisite manner in which it was rendered, to the tune of 'Long, long ago,' I shall never forget. (*a*) Their voices are both powerful and sweet; and the thrill of rare and unexpected pleasure I experienced, on hearing them sing that song, was never surpassed in me, not even when listening to Jenny Lind. This may seem going too far; and so may other of the statements I make in speaking of the Pitcairn islanders. I came prepared to do them justice, it is true; but no more; for I could not help believing there must be some exaggeration in the florid

---

(*a*) THE SAILOR-BOY'S EARLY GRAVE.

Shed not a tear o'er your friend's early bier,
When I am gone, when I am gone;
Nor, if the slow-tolling bell you should hear,
When I am gone, when I am gone.

Weep not for me when you stand round my grave:
Think Who has died, His beloved to save:
Think of the crown all the ransom'd shall have,
When I am gone, when I am gone.

Plant ye a tree, which may wave over me,
When I am gone, when I am gone :
Sing ye a song, if my grave you should see,
When I am gone, when I am gone.

Come at the close of a bright summer's day—
Come when the sun sheds his last ling'ring ray;
Come, and rejoice that I thus pass'd away,
When I am gone, when I am gone.

Plant ye a tree that may bloom o'er my bed,
When I am gone, when I am gone;
Breathe out a sigh for the bless'd, early, dead,
When I am gone, when I am gone.

Praise ye the Lord, that I'm free from all care,
Love ye the Lord, that my bliss ye may share
Look ye on high, and believe I am there,
When I am gone, when I am gone.

accounts given by voyagers who had touched at their island. I came, therefore, with a mind disposed to test and to criticise; and I leave them with the feeling that few, if any, of their qualities would not stand the severest test; and that their conduct, generally (that is, on all main points), may triumphantly challenge the sternest criticism. This is my deliberate opinion, after having been domesticated amongst them for a week, and with every opportunity given me for arriving at a just conclusion; going in and out of their houses at any hour I chose; and asking any questions I thought proper; seeing them, too, in their joy, and afterwards in their affliction.

"Captain Prevost having offered to take all the inhabitants round the island, in the *Virago*, under steam, on the following day (*Tuesday*), the offer was joyfully accepted; and about ten o'clock on that morning, our own boats, and their whale-boats, brought successive cargoes of men, women, and children on board, until only six persons were left on the island. We then got under weigh, and slowly steamed from point to point; and, in about an hour, again anchored in Bounty Bay,—where, after partaking of cake and wine, the people were safely landed. The engine room afforded constant interest to those who were not sea-sick; but, unfortunately, most of the women and children were very much so. We went ashore in the afternoon; and in the evening the islanders again sang the songs we were never tired of hearing; and we amused them by dancing among ourselves, and playing at leap-frog, blind-man's buff, &c., at which they laughed heartily.

"The next day (*Wednesday*), having planted the rose-trees, myrtles, fig trees, &c., we felt it was time to hasten on our way, and accordingly wished our friends good bye—except the few who accompanied us on board, intending to return in their whale-boat. At half-past one, the capstan was manned, and we were about to get under weigh, when our attention was arrested by the firing of the *Bounty's* gun, in farewell salute. Scarcely had the sound died away, when it was succeeded by what we at first took to be cheers; but which, alas! proved to be shrieks from women and children along the cliffs. A boat was instantly manned, and sent on shore, with the two Surgeons. With the aid of a glass, we could see the women carrying two forms along the cliffs towards the houses—by which we feared that some fatal accident had occurred; and a canoe soon came from the shore with the melancholy tidings, that, in loading the gun, the Chief Magistrate, Matthew McCoy, and two others—Driver Christian and William Evans—were seriously, if not fatally injured.

"When the Surgeons reached the village, they found that poor McCoy, who had suffered the most severely, had had his arm amputated above the elbow, as it had been perfectly shattered. The arm was going on well; but there was very little hope of his life, owing to the shock his system had received. He had pleaded very hard that his arm should not be taken off; as without it (he said), he would be of little use to his family; but on being told *that* was his only chance of life, he submitted to the amputation with unflinching nerve. It was a necessary expedient, though useless infliction, as the result proved. He remained hovering between life and death until about 2 o'clock the next morning, when he died. The two other sufferers were severely wounded and burnt, but not dangerously [and they recovered]. This dreadful accident has overwhelmed the little community with grief; there is nothing but weeping; they are truly one family, bound together in heart, as they are by the ties of relationship.

"*Thursday.*—At sunset, the officers and petty-officers of the *Virago*, myself, and the islanders, assembled outside the house where the body of McCoy lay. His widow had begged to be allowed to take a last look of what was her husband; and touching indeed was the scene when she, and her eight children, came to look on the dead. . . . . All in the *Virago* gave her, and the little ones, their best sympathy, and made a subscription for them, amounting to nearly £30. . . . . Few scenes have made a stronger impression upon my mind than McCoy's funeral. It was deeply impressive from the earnestness of those engaged in it, and from the absence of that form, and those trappings, with which civilization too often 'mocks its dead.' The grave was dug in a little garden, consecrated by the ashes of his father and brother, beside whose remains his own were about to be laid. The burial service was impressively read by the Rev. Mr. Holman, after which a hymn was sung—or attempted to be sung—for the accents of the distressed islanders were stifled by sobs; and amidst these the body was lowered into the grave. An exquisite sunset fell around; the tall, plume-like, cocoa-nut palms waved gently above our heads. Borne upwards from the sea, mournfully, but not discordantly, came the sound of the breakers, as they burst against the shore; while from orange, lime, and a thousand fragrant herbs, a delicious fragrance filled the air. Quietly, and thoughtfully, the sailors and I retired from the spot, and gradually found our way to the ship, to avoid giving the afflicted people any trouble we could help.

"*Friday.*—Went with Captain Prevost; and, with the full consent of the islanders, spiked the *Bounty's* gun, to prevent a recurrence of the late dreadful accident; which seems to have been caused by using a rammer made from a house rafter, that had a nail at the end; the friction thus occasioned effecting an explosion of the powder with which the gun was charged.

"*Saturday.*—Finding there was no chance of sailing to-day, it having come on to blow, and the *Virago* standing out to sea, I accompanied the rear guard of a party of goat hunters to the mountains, armed with a clumsy-looking, but I believe a true, German rifle, lent me by George Adams—whose maker, boasting a name of some seven syllables, could have little anticipated that his handiwork would awake echoes from the picturesque crags of an island in the South Pacific. I returned to the settlement dead beaten, with a very vivid recollection of the awfulness of the precipices, and of the wariness and activity of the goats.

"The Pitcairn islanders are undoubtedly a fine race; the figures of the men being, however, better than those of the women, which betray their Tahitan origin. The expression of the face in both sexes is generally good; often singularly good, and intellectual; their skin is dark—darker than I had expected; though exceptions occur, particularly in children, when it is sometimes nearly white; their eyes are large and lustrous, and their teeth beautiful.

"The week spent at Pitcairn Island was one of the most interesting in my life. A state of society is there beheld which cannot be believed in, unless seen. In many points, particularly in the culture of their minds, a high state of civilization presents itself, without vice or luxury; the community living in the most primitive simplicity. But the most remarkable feature in their character is that of earnest and universal piety. And from this fountain springs their brotherly love, so true, so touching, so unlike anything I had ever seen or dreamt of, as dominating a whole community, that it can only be likened to the feeling that exists in a deeply religious and united private family in England. So earnest is their piety, so directly does it appear to spring from Him who is the Divine source of all religion, that I almost fancied myself in a Theocracy of the primitive ages.

"If I be asked, 'Have they no faults?' I answer, 'Yes, two' —to show that they are children of Adam. The first is, that the men seemed to allow the women to work harder than themselves: The second, that there is a want of energy apparent in all they do—always except in religious matters, whaling, and swimming. In these, I have summed up everything I know to their disadvantage. How proud may England be, that it is to her this virtuous and most interesting community look as to their Fatherland!" Nor scarcely less gratifying to New South Wales should be the thought, that numerous descendants of the same community are now enrolled amongst her island citizens. (*a*)

And when (towards the end of 1853,) H.M.S. *Dido* came to Pitcairn, laden with good things, and a few head of cattle—contributions from friends abroad (especially from *the* Admiral, and his officers)—with the portraits entrusted by Her Majesty to Mr. Nobbs, but which *he* had been unable to bear with him to the island—and one of "the grand old sailor" himself—we find that Captain Morshead (Commander of that vessel) paid a like tribute to its people; though then suffering from a very adverse season.

(*a*) In July, '53, or between the departure of the *Virago* and arrival of the *Dido*, the Pitcairn islanders forwarded to the Queen the little gift which is described in the Memorial of that date, to which reference has been previously made (for another purpose), and wrote thus:—"At the suggestion of our worthy benefactor, Rear-Admiral Moresby, we have ventured to present your gracious Majesty with a small chest of drawers, of our own manufacture, from the island wood. The native name of the dark wood is *miro*. The bottoms of the drawers are made of the bread-fruit tree. Our means are very limited; and our mechanical skill also; but we will esteem it a great favor if your Majesty will accept the offering as a token of our loyalty and respect." The Queen did so, "most graciously;" the Duke of Newcastle being directed to "express her gratification at receiving that mark of loyalty and esteem from her subjects on Pitcairn Island;" and it is probable that humble offering is more highly prized by Her Majesty, than many a more costly tribute, from King, or Czar.

He thus writes to Admiral Moresby, on 15th Dec. of that year:—
"With reference to the provisions you entrusted to my discretion, I have left them on the island. Their yam harvest has been a fair average; but, owing to a long drought, great fears were entertained for the potato crop, on which they are equally dependent. One whaler only had been supplied for the year; yet there was not on the island a single yam, potato, hog, or goat, available for traffic; although, if they had them, they would exchange them for an equal amount of nutriment in biscuit, or flour. Their famine has caused them to tie up to the beams small parcels of biscuit, to await a still more imminent scarcity. Under these circumstances, I was induced to leave the supplies, with directions that they were to be retained for the contingency.

"It has long been their custom to reserve any cases at issue for the decision of a Captain of a man-of-war, as a final appeal. Only one was left for me to decide; it had previously been before the Magistrate, and submitted to a jury; and upon my confirming the opinion of their own tribunal, all the litigants shook hands.

"I trust I may be allowed to add my testimony to their already established reputation for morality and virtue: With the Scriptures daily, even hourly, in their hands, it is impossible that any can act from higher principles or purer motives; and all their impulses appear for good; while that goodness ever inclines them to judge charitably of the faults of others: But so simple and confiding is their nature, that any designing person, thrown among them, might easily destroy their peace and harmony. It has never been my lot to witness a community more entitled to admiration and respect; and from this estimation of their character, it is impossible to separate the credit that is due to Mr. Nobbs, who has been their friend and teacher for 25 years, and is now, happily, their spiritual guide and Minister."

CHAPTER XI.—Parting Days; and Removal to Norfolk Island.

1854—1868 : Suggestions for removal of Pitcairners to Norfolk Island; and the grounds—Mr. Batchelor's description of its features, products, buildings, fish, and birds—A Post Captain's view of the position—Deaths of a little boy, and grown man, at Pitcairn—Duty and devotion—*Pro* and *con* on the removal question—The special mission, discussion, and decisive vote—Unavailing requests—Freemantle to the minority—Second visit of the *Dido*—Last days and departure (in 1856) of the islanders to Norfolk Island, in the *Morayshire* ; passage thither, first appearance, and landing there—Arrangements for their reception, and settlement—The "Ocean Hell," and "Earthly Paradise"—What the Bishop's Chaplain, and Mr. Augustus Robinson, thought of the Pitcairners—Glance at their after history, on Norfolk Island—Return to Pitcairn, in '58 and '63, of certain of them; and instance of the pluck and devotion of the race.

AN event of the utmost importance to the Pitcairn islanders was now approaching. It may be remembered, that Captain Wood, of H.M.S. *Pandora*, could not, in July, 1849, obtain any expression of assent to a suggestion for their removal to some other place, which he then submitted to them. Still more marked must have been their feeling, when, in the following month, Captain Fanshawe, of H.M.S. *Daphne*, visited the place, and thus wrote:— " I could not trace in any of them the slightest desire to remove elsewhere. On the contrary, they expressed the greatest repugnance to do so, whilst a sweet potato remained to them—a repugnance much enhanced by the failure of their emigration to Otaheite, about eighteen years ago." And George Adams, son of the "original John," declared, subsequently, that he would " prefer continuing at Pitcairn to going anywhere else, so that, when his time should come, he might die on his native isle, and be buried in the grave of his father: " While Mr. Nobbs had said, in the hearing of the Rev. Mr. Murray, in Nov., 1852, that " so long as two families remained at Pitcairn he would remain also."

These opinions had been expressed in consequence of other suggestions, that removal to some larger and better provided island than their own tiny one, might (some day) become desirable on the part of its people; and occasional drought, failing crop, and increasing population, with the sufferings they had undergone towards the close of '52, and the beginning of '53, gave to the idea a show of countenance at least. Yet they could scarcely have ignored their own knowledge, or forgotten the favorable reports of Captain Freemantle, and Lieutenant Lowry, as to the productive capability of Pitcairn, and its other resources, if turned to proper account Any such removal would also have involved an uprooting of all the bonds that linked them to their own loved home, and of the happy life that adorned it. But Baron de Therry (who, it may be recollected, was one of Mr. Brodie's companions, when he visited Pitcairn in the beginning of 1850) was not troubled with any sentiment in the matter; " the tuning-fork," which was his sole possession at that time, seems to imply that he was a worshipper of *sound* only; and, being apprehensive that its inhabitants might be pinched from scarcity of food and water, during a season of drought, urged them (before he departed from the island), to consider the advisability of an early emigration. In June, '52, he also wrote to them, to like effect, from Honolulu, and recommended an application to Her Majesty's Secretary of State for the Colonies, that they might be transferred to Norfolk Island, in the event of its abandonment as a penal settlement of New South Wales. And the desirability of such an arrangement had evidently presented itself, about that time, to that Department; for in a despatch by Sir John Pakington to Governor Denison, dated Downing Street, Dec. 15, 1852, the latter was requested to transmit a report respecting the arrangements that might be requisite for the evacuation of Norfolk Island as a convict depôt, and as to its resources, buildings, and other suitableness, for the reception of the people of Pitcairn.

It would appear, too, that Admiral Moresby tendered to the latter, during the few days he spent amongst them, in May, '53, similar advice to that of the Baron; since, on the 18th of that month and year, in a letter addressed to him by the Chief Magistrate, and first and second Councillors, they say that, " having, according to your request, convened a public meeting of the inhabitants of this island, we have the satisfaction to inform you, as regards the necessity of removing to some other place, it is very evident the time is not far distant when Pitcairn Island will be altogether inadequate to the rapidly extending population; and the inhabitants do unanimously agree in soliciting the aid of the British Government in transferring them to Norfolk Island, or some other appropriate abode; and they desire that the funds, which you and other benefactors raised in England for the benefit of this community, be reserved, and appropriated in assisting them in such a step, whenever it shall become necessary."(*a*)

That "solicitation" was forwarded by the Admiral to the Home authorities, from Callao, in June, '53; and at an assemblage of the islanders, in the Nov. of the same year, they were informed of the circumstance by Captain Morshead, of H.M.S. *Dido*. The Rev. Mr. Murray also states, that "an official communication respecting the necessity of a removal from Pitcairn was made by Mr. B. T. Nicholas, Her Majesty's Consul at Raiatea, in a communication to the Earl of Malmesbury, in April, '53, or three months after the former's visit, in the *Virago*: The same Rev. gentleman adds: "In that year it was determined, by the British Government, to accede to the request of the people, and to transfer to Norfolk Island such of them as should desire to go thither. The benevolent plan thus decided upon was notified to the Pitcairn Fund Committee, by letters from H. Merivale, Esq., Under Secretary for the Colonies, dated Dec. 14, 1853, and April 6, 1854: And it is stated, that "instructions were given to the Lieutenant-Governor of the former island not to allow the land upon it to be occupied by any other class of settlers." But any such instructions would have been given to the Governor of New South Wales, rather than to his deputy at Norfolk; and the letters referred to must have indicated a probable intention, rather than a fixed decision, as it will be found that, so late as Aug., '55, the question whether the islanders would remove from Pitcairn to Norfolk was still an open one, and left by the British Government to their own decision.

It may be mentioned, meanwhile, that the latter island was discovered by Captain Cook, in Oct., 1773, taken possession of by England, from, and as a dependency of, New South Wales, in Feb., 1788, and is situate in lat. 29° 0′ 50″ S., and long. 167° 57′ E.; is elevated above the sea 1,039 feet; and visible at a distance of

---

(*a*) At one time, some of them thought of Juan Fernandez as a suitable place of residence; but as that island belonged to Chili, and not to England, the project did not receive much favour.

36 miles from a ship's deck. The following interesting account has been given of it by the Rev. F. S. Batchelor, who resided upon it between three and four years :—" The island is about 20 miles in circumference, with an average breadth of five or six. It is beautifully diversified with hills and dales, or (as the latter are generally designated) ' gullies,' and these lowlands are exuberantly fertile. On the same plot of earth are growing pine-apples, figs, guavas, lemons, pomegranates, Cape gooseberries, bananas, plantains, grapes, peaches, strawberries, apples, quinces, potatoes, cabbages, peas, and beans. Cinnamon and other spices abound ; while tobacco, arrowroot, red pepper, and sweet potatoes, can be cultivated to any extent. Maize, barley, wheat, and rye grow on the higher and more level land. In my time, Mr. Price, the Commandant, introduced the cocoa-nut tree, and planted orange trees in all directions, which, doubtless, before this have brought forth fruit to perfection. Hundreds of acres are in high cultivation, and much more of the island can be speedily reclaimed, and made available for any purpose. Fortunately, too, there are a number of capital stone-built houses, really large and handsome edifices, which would not disgrace our large cities, and plenty of store-houses, granaries, barns, &c., with a neat Chapel, capable of accommodating 1000 persons, and another similar building, formerly used by the Roman Catholics for Divine service. Indeed, I should think it might be designated an island of palaces, compared with Pitcairn and its belongings ; and, besides tools and other implements of husbandry, now in use by the convict population, there is a good stock of cows, sheep, horses, pigs, and poultry, which would be invaluable to a new community.

" There are plenty of fish to be caught at all seasons ; such as salmon, herrings, trumpeter, kingfish, schnapper, garfish and mullet; some of which are very delicate and delicious, and all eatable ; while in the fresh water streams, which intersect the island in all directions, there are magnificent eels, weighing from one to seven pounds. There is doubtless great danger in fishing from the rocks which stud the coast, as the sea often rises, in a moment, by seven or ten feet; and the receding of the waves is absolutely terrific— so that few Europeans, washed off, have been able to make the land again. However, as the Pitcairners have been accustomed from their infancy to fish in like dangerous waters, they would feel quite at home. The whole island teems with life. Parrots and paroquets, of various kinds, swarm on your path. Pigeons (originally the common English pigeon let loose), are in innumerable flocks; and magnificent woodquests and plovers are often to be had. No venomous reptile of any kind is on the island; and it is very rarely indeed that you ever feel or see the mosquito, which seems indigenous to all warm localities."

And on 12th June, 1855, Captain H. M. Denham, of H.M.S. *Herald*, thus alluded to the expected resting place of the Pitcairners (a):—" I found Norfolk Island no longer a penal settlement. The convict establishment was withdrawn on the 7th of May; and it is at present occupied by an Assistant Commissary Storekeeper, with a few hands employed in rendering into tallow the surplus of the sheep intended for the Pitcairners, who are soon expected to occupy this island, and will not fail in gratitude to the Queen, and country, which are about to put them in possession, with fostering solicitude, of the most lovely island conceivable (with numerous facilities for industry and comfort), comprising 15 square miles of land capable of tillage; 800 acres cleared and fenced; excellent roads intersecting it ; 81 substantial buildings, including Chapel, schoolroom, hospital, barracks, dwelling houses, mills and workshops; together with household furniture, artizans' tools, and agricultural implements; the gardens stocked with seeds, and the farms with 2,000 sheep, 300 cattle, horses, pigs, and poultry. A bounteous bestowal indeed !"

But while a change in their place of residence was thus probably looming over the Pitcairners, the issues between death and life to which man is ever exposed, be his habitation where it may, were not absent from their isle; and the story of two of these "passages," as detailed by Mr. Nobbs, in his letter of 29th June, 1855, to the Rev. Mr. Murray, from which I have already quoted, is, I think, worthy of record :—" Three weeks after the departure of my son, death made another inroad among us. A little boy, 10 years of age, son of my wife's sister, Maria Quintall, pierced his foot with a barbed arrow (used for taking fish from holes in the rocks) ; this induced *tetanus,* and in 48 hours after the terrible disease had commenced, his happy spirit fled to the realms of

---

(a) Hydrographic Notice of Islands and Reefs in the South-western Pacific Ocean.

bliss. During the intervals of the violent contortions of the suffering body, the dear child would speak of his blessed Saviour, and ask to be taken by Him to those whom He took in his arms when on earth. He was aware he could not recover; still, he never expressed the least fear of death. At the time of his departure, I was praying with him; his parents and several other persons kneeling round his bed—when he gave a slight shudder, and exclaimed, in a clear and audible voice, 'Lord Jesus, receive my spirit!' and then he went to see Him as he is.

"Only one fortnight had elapsed from this event, when another sad and awful bereavement fell upon the community. Daniel McCoy and his wife went to the north-west side of the island in quest of fish. After descending to the rocks, Daniel left her, and re-ascended, with the intention of passing the head of a small inlet of the sea, and then going down to the rocks on the other side. While doing so he fell; his wife saw him fall; and though there was the inlet between them, into which a very heavy surf was running, without an instant's hesitation, beyond calling to a lad, who was fishing at some distance, to go for help, she plunged into the waters, and, landing on the opposite side of the inlet, found him stretched on the rugged lava of the shore, a corpse. But a few minutes previously, he had left her with a smile on his countenance, for Daniel was always in a cheerful mood; and what must have been her agony now, as she sat by her dead husband, with his head resting on her lap, for more than an hour, ere any one could get to her assistance! Her feelings I will not attempt to describe; but I will tell you what she did. On finding life extinct, she knelt down, and prayed that God would give her grace so to live that she might rejoin her dear Daniel in heaven; 'for I am sure' (she said, when speaking to me on the subject), 'that he was prepared for death; and the consciousness of that takes away the pain of my great loss.'"

In the same letter, Mr. Nobbs asks the advice of his correspondent, respecting the proposed removal from the island: "The next time you favor me with a letter, I want your opinion as to what I ought to do, if some families remain at Pitcairn, rather than remove to Norfolk Island, whenever an opportunity is offered them. Personally, I have no choice on the subject. I have mentioned it to my Diocesan, the Bishop of London, but I should like to have your advice also. I think it probable some families will remain, and I have no objection to stay with them; but I hold myself in readiness to go, if desired to do so. In all the vicissitudes through which I have passed—whether on the Galopagus Islands, almost perishing from thirst, or laboring in chains among malefactors of the deepest dye, on the batteries of Callao, or awaiting with some anxiety my turn to be the subject of a *fusillade*, for the amusement of Benevideis in Arauco—I have never regretted, nor desired to abandon, the course prescribed by my duty."

Yet this is his account of the position in which Christian England, and its wealthy State Church (of which he was an Ordained Priest), permitted that faithful "Chaplain of Pitcairn" to be, at that time, and to remain so long as the settlement there was maintained. After referring to the monthly celebration of the Holy Communion, to the number of Communicants (78), and to the day school (with its 55 scholars), held from 8 in the morning till 1, during five days in the week, he tells Mr. Murray, on 19th July, '55: "I attend that school every day from 10 until the dismissal. These duties, with the maintenance of Divine services (twice on the Sabbath, and once on every week day, except Saturday), assistance at Sunday school, and the care of the sick, keep me in constant employment, and, I am happy to say, beneficially so. Edward Quintall, the young man who has the school, being incapacitated by bodily infirmity for any other occupation, I have made over to him its pecuniary resources, to wit, one shilling per month for each scholar, paid in potatoes, &c.! So that I am altogether dependent on my stipend from the Society for the Propagation of the Gospel" [it was less than £1 a week]; "more especially, as I have now no beloved son in Valparaiso to contribute to my necessities. Nevertheless, I will take my stand upon the declaration of the Son of Jesse, 'Trust in the Lord, and be doing good; dwell in the land, and verily thou shalt be fed.' 'He hath given meat unto them that fear Him. He will ever be mindful of His covenant.' But a greater than either the son, or grandson of Jesse, has prescribed the line of conduct imperative on the believer: 'Therefore I say unto you, take no thought for your life, what ye shall eat, or what ye shall drink; nor yet for your body, what ye shall put on.'" And Mr. Nobbs had the love and gratitude of his people at least: as one of them wrote in Oct., '54, so it was to the end of his Ministerial life—"Ever since his ordination, our *Pastor* has borne himself in a manner honorable to his high calling, and profession. His whole aim seems to be devoted to one object—that of doing good to his flock, both in spiritual and temporal things."

But in July, '55, Mr. Nobbs must have felt that "coming events were casting their shadows before them;" since he records, "the greater part of the community are holding themselves in readiness for a removal; and several have relinquished house building. We are now on the eve of yam harvest; and though the crop is quite a poor one, we have a good stock of sweet potatoes to turn to, though few or none to spare for ships. However, humanly speaking, the pinch of the year is over; and perhaps by March next, we may, if it please God, be on our route for Norfolk Island."

But whether it was wise or unwise on the part of the British Government, either to effect, or countenance, the removal of the Pitcairners to Norfolk Island, ample time was given them to decide the question for themselves. And there were arguments that might have been and were used in favor of either position. Norfolk Island was not only very much larger than Pitcairn, but would afford many facilities to prosperous, comfortable existence, and to development of the race, which Pitcairn could not. On the other hand, a considerable portion of the latter island still remained uncultivated, though capable of cultivation: it was also (for its extent) more fertile and better wooded; a continued residence there would have preserved, for some time at least, all the early associations, and home ties, of its people; and, should the period arrive when any migration became absolutely necessary, the swarming hive could then proceed to some of the rich and yet unoccupied isles of the Society or Friendly Groups that lay much nearer, and were more similar in climate and product, to Pitcairn, than was Norfolk Island—which was still more subject to drought than the other; whatever might be its advantages in some respects.

Thus stood the facts, and attending circumstances, when in Aug., '55, Sir William Denison, by the direction of the then Secretary of State for the Colonies, despatched from Sydney, H.M.S. *Juno*, (Captain Freemantle) for the object and with the results detailed in the following statement by the latter:—" Having left Port Jackson on the 6th, I arrived off Pitcairn Island on the 18th Aug. (17th according to Pitcairn date). As we approached Bounty Bay, a whale-boat, containing the Magistrate, and several other natives, came alongside; and having assured us that landing was practicable, I accompanied them on shore, with half the officers. Mention of the cordial reception which is invariably accorded to officers of men-of-war by the ingenuous, warm hearted, and loyal inhabitants of the island, need not be repeated here. The visit of one of these ships is always a season of gaiety and innocent excitement—labor and studies are suspended; and all occupy themselves in the service and entertainment of their welcome visitors.

" Having been heartily greeted by the whole population, we proceeded to the Church-and-school-house—the spot usually chosen for assembling the community upon public matters. Here the object of our mission [to obtain a final decision on the question of their removal to Norfolk Island, which (it was proposed) should be granted to them,] was explained at length. The Rev. Mr. Nobbs also read out a brief description of that island, which had been drawn up and furnished by the Governor-General of New South Wales. The generous proposal of Her Majesty's Government was not unexpected; rumors of such intention had already reached Pitcairn " [rather, the matter had been the subject of prior deliberation and correspondence]; and, though the mind of the people generally was made up, they asked for a day or two for inquiry and consultation before finally deciding upon so grave a question, and one so closely affecting their future destiny.

"The following evening, a general meeting of the community was held; and a very large majority at once closed with the offer which had been made. Some there were, however, whose attachment to Pitcairn was apparently too strong to reconcile them to the thoughts of abandoning it. Among these, was George Adams, son of old John, of the *Bounty*. All felt the necessity of some change " (thought Captain Freemantle), " for another subdivision of land would reduce the portions to mere insignificant patches, scarcely worth cultivating; and all were most grateful for the solicitude and liberality manifested on their behalf, by Her Majesty's Government; yet the anticipated removal was a melancholy topic for deliberation : The addresses were abrupt, and in some instances confined to the monosyllable, 'Go.' But the discussion ended by 153, out of a population of 187, determining for Norfolk Island: As to the rest, I will not say they determined to remain on Pitcairn; but they would not then acquiesce in the voice of the majority. The lamentable migration to Tahiti, in 1831, still fresh in the recollection of the older and more influential part of the community, no doubt prompted misgivings as to the present scheme; although they seemed re-animated by the assuring prospects held out by Sir William Denison's summary, and the account of Norfolk Island given by the officers."

The issue of the meeting was conveyed in writing, signed by the Magistrate and Chaplain of Pitcairn: But the islanders expressed a hope, that they might be allowed to live on Norfolk Island in the same seclusion from the rest of the world, as they had hitherto done at Pitcairn (though that would have been scarcely possible—the former place being a dependency of what was then becoming, and is now, one of England's noblest Colonies, and much more within the range of shipping than the other). "There was much anxiety to know what succor or protection those that remained behind might expect thereafter—a point on which I was unable to afford positive information"—and Captain Freemantle *should* have been very specifically instructed by Sir William Denison, on that important subject. "George Adams, in particular, pressed hard that when a ship came to convey to Norfolk Island those who intended to proceed thither, the position of the others who were left, with respect to the British Government, might be explained them"—and the final result when that ship arrived, during the following year, was partly owing to the fact, that no such explanation was given. His Excellency was a very resolute Governor—one who carried out at all hazards the wishes of the Imperial authorities—but consideration for the feelings, or reasonable expectations of others, was not amongst the number of his virtues: "It was also suggested by them that the time of the removal of those who decided upon going should not take place during the winter months, that is, between March and July; and I think I could detect a general wish that the dissolution might be postponed till after, rather than precede, that season of next year." But it will be seen that the middle of the following winter was the time chosen by the considerate Governor for their transhipment.

"Subsequently to the meeting, I held some conversation with George Adams, and the others who are disposed to stay at Pitcairn; and, being asked for advice, I endeavored, without using any undue persuasion, to show it would be better that no separation should take place. The few that remained would probably find themselves very much isolated, without grown up men sufficient to work the plantations, or to man the boat, and without the means of controlling the crews of whalers which now frequently call off the island for water, and to barter clothing and other necessaries for fruit and vegetables; or to prevent their settling there. Much of the interest felt towards them would be transferred to Norfolk Island, whither the main body would be gone; and it was to be feared that, without a Clergyman, or teacher, the rising generation might not imbibe or retain those pious and moral principles which are now universal." These arguments were reasonable enough in themselves; but they were not verified by the actual occurrences, when, at a still later period than that of the proposed transfer, Pitcairn came to be occupied by a yet smaller band than desired to cling to it at the time of Captain Freemantle's mission. He then prophesies, "there is great reason to expect, that, when the time comes, not one of the islanders will adhere to the resolution of stopping behind; so affectionate, so attached are they to each other; and the ties of relationship are necessarily so interwoven that the moment of parting will, most probably, stifle all other considerations. . . . Meanwhile, the enthusiasm displayed by the officers, and by the ship's company for the islanders' welfare, was quite uncontrollable; they were ready to part with anything, everything, to supply or gratify the others; and equally anxious to carry away some object or token in remembrance of the place, even to the stones on the beach. And the girls, perceiving this, collected a quantity of toppa, sufficient to enable every man in the ship to receive a suitable material."

"The yam harvest having been recently gathered in, there was no deficiency of the ordinary means of subsistence; but their stock of animal food is very limited." (There is a mistake here; for Captain Morshead, writing from Valparaiso, in May, '56, states that, having, in the *Dido*, left the Pitcairners on 13th April, of that year, "they had lately been slaying many of their cattle; their stock having increased and thriven wonderfully.") But (proceeds Captain Freemantle) "a liberal contribution of salt meat was furnished by the men and officers of the *Juno*, from their messes, and the Paymaster was authorised to supply the islanders with four casks of beef on the part of the Government: They expressed their gratitude with frank simplicity; they especially prize any favor or attention which has its source from the Crown or Government of England; and they evince the greatest anxiety, and esteem it their highest privilege, to be recognized as subjects of Her Majesty."

The second visit (above referred to) of the *Dido* to Pitcairn, is thus chronicled by Mr. Nobbs, under date 10th April, '56:— "We were yesterday electrified by a shout from the 'Rope,' that a man-of-war was in sight!; and she made but slow progress. However, about 9 p.m. her boat anchored off the harbor of Bounty Bay; the officers landed in our boat; and the young moon was shining right into the bight. The ship proved to be the *Dido*, and right glad we are to see our friend Captain Morshead again. She sails on the 13th;" and her Commander adds, in the letter from which I have quoted, that he "had arranged for the people's departure for Norfolk Island"—in the latter end of July (as Mr. Nobbs subsequently writes).

But so far back as the 23rd Feb., '56, the *Morayshire* (a roomy vessel, hired for that purpose by Sir William Denison,) had been despatched from Sydney, to proceed to Pitcairn, in order to effect the removal to Norfolk Island. The *Morayshire* reached Pitcairn on 22nd April, and sailed thence for Norfolk Island on the 3rd May, '56; having taken on board, in the meantime, the entire population of the former—then consisting of 194 souls, viz., 40 adult males, 47 adult females, 54 boys, and 53 girls— together with all their goods and chattels. And in a letter to Mr. Murray, of 24th Sep., in that year, Mr. Nobbs, writing from Norfolk Island, thus describes the last days spent by them on their old, loved, abode, with the voyage to and landing at their new home:—"21st April, '56. While busily employed in the school this forenoon, a piercing and electric shout apprized me that a ship was in sight; but it was a long time before anyone came from the hill to say what she looked like. About 3 o'clock, it was ascertained she was a large merchant ship, standing in for the land. At 4, she rounded St. Paul's rock; and then we perceived she had a pennant flying. On this being made known, some one exclaimed, 'That is the ship come to convey us to Norfolk Island, and the pennant denotes she has a Naval officer on board.' It was the *Morayshire* (Captain Mathers). Having learned from the *Dido*, but little more than a week since, that the ship for removing us would not be here before the end of July, I could not believe this was the one until her boat landed, bearing her Commander, and Lieutenant Gregorie, of the *Juno*, who had been appointed to superintend the embarcation of all those who were now disposed to accept Her Majesty's gracious offer, to wit, Norfolk Island, and all that appertains thereto, for themselves and families. Such an unqualified offer of a spot so beautiful as that island is easier to imagine than realize.

"May, 3rd. Breakfast eaten with heavy hearts. My family being among those appointed to embark first, Mrs. Nobbs and I went previously to the grave-yard where lie the remains of our first born. Scarcely a word was spoken by either of us; but tears fell freely. Why? Not because we lamented the loss of a soul in Christ; but because we were about to leave a grave, and head-stone, those frail memorials, which had become unspeakably dear to us, never to behold them more. *Vale*, Reuben! till 'this corruptible shall put on incorruption.' And every family on the island had a like visit to pay, a like sorrow to endure, and a like hope to sustain them, as they parted from the home where nearly all of them had been born, and had lived since birth; where many of them had been married; and where each was leaving, amid the peaceful dead, a father or mother, brother or sister, child or sweetheart. Then, let New South Wales be ever thoughtful of, and tender towards, the trustful hearts, resolute men, and noble women, she thus incorporated with her own people; and let her evince for them, and their children, a little more sympathy and regard than is evidenced by one solitary visit to Norfolk Island, by each of her Governors, during the five or six years of his Vice-Royalty.! Nor, whenever it can be shown, should a like affection be withheld from those of them who afterwards re-sought, and now, with their offspring, re-occupy, the pleasant places of that early home, or "good land of the Pacific," which their old Pastor, and best earthly friend, has celebrated in song, adorned by his virtues, and (with Adams and Young—the mutineers) assimilated more nearly to the "mansions above," their peace, purity, and bliss, than has been ever attained in other spot throughout the world.

The arrival of a ship capable of bearing all of them to Norfolk Island, the absence of an assurance from Sir William Denison, such as George Adams had pressed for (as to the position of those who might remain at Pitcairn), the old dread of giving offence to the British Government by any opposition to its apparent wishes, after the solicitude it had evinced on the general behalf, and the grief that must have attended their separation from the rest, had overcome the reluctance of the 34 persons who had dissented from Captain Freemantle's proposal in the preceding August; and all the Pitcairners were now prepared to try their fortunes at Norfolk Island.

"At Bounty Bay" (continues Mr. Nobbs), "we joined those who were to embark in the same boat with my family. Passing safely through the surf, we commenced our departure; after a short pull we got on board the *Morayshire;* and were kindly received by Captain Mathers. Now my vocation commenced in reality." Through very culpable neglect on the part of those to whom the transhipment of nearly 200 persons, old and young, many women and little ones (most of whom had never been any distance from Pitcairn), neither Surgeon, nor other attendant for the sick, had been provided for the pending voyage—2,200 miles; "and scarcely had we reached the ship, when women and children became sadly affected by the motion, though the weather was very fine. So, placing them in the best positions available I hastened to the berth-deck and got the beds into their places. But the sufferers could not remain in these berths; field-beds had to be made on the deck: and, as the different boats came alongside, and were discharged, all the sea-sick folks were laid side by side. The best was done for their comfort that could be, under the circumstances. By 4 p.m., every person was on board, without any accident occurring; and the ship made sail with a fair breeze; carrying away not only what had been the whole population of the place, but all the property worth removal which each family had accumulated since 1789.

"In the dusk of the evening, Pitcairn Island receded from view. There were very few of our people on deck to take a last lingering look at the dear and ever to be remembered spot." Their hearts were too sad, and their miseries too great; "but very many of them wished themselves on shore again; for so intensely were they suffering from grief and nausea, that, could they have regained the land, they would most assuredly have remained there. During the whole night, I was continually employed in attempting to relieve their distress ; the few men who were not sick had to nurse the infants ; and old Arthur Quintall (assisted, occasionally by the Captain, and Lieutenant Gregorie), was employed in administering, under my direction, such remedies as seemed most appropriate. It was a comfortless, and to most of our people, a sleepless night. For several days did this state of things continue ;" and but for Mr. Nobbs' exertions, many of them (as another account states) "would have found a long home in the waters ;" so unusually severe and lengthened were their agony. The passage (the greater portion of which proved very boisterous) occupied 31 days. But on Friday, 6th June, there was the cry of "Land, ho!"; it was, however, "still a long way off; and the wind not being fair" (the Pastor continues), "we made but slow progress ; and night closing in upon us, hid the land from view. Next morning, it was some 25 miles distant; the weather cloudy; and a sail in shore; with which we exchanged signals at noon. She is H.M.S. *Herald* (Captain Denham), and is, no doubt, engaged sounding round the island, as she occasionally hove to.

"For picturesque beauty, Norfolk Island is not to be compared with Pitcairn. At sunset, we were pretty handy to Phillip's Island, which is a few miles distant from the former—that, by way of pre-eminence, is generally called the 'main land.' Another night must be passed on board ; but in all probability we shall land to-morrow. Squally weather through this night; and, being close to shore, it was one of anxiety to those on board. Sunday, 8th June: Close in with Norfolk Island ; very much disappointed in its appearance from the present point of view, which is directly off the settlement, and presents a succession of hillocks and shallow ravines, covered with short brown grass, but scarcely a tree to be seen. No doubt, other parts of the island have a better appearance; but this side certainly loses in comparison with our 'Rock of the West.' At eight o'clock, the anchor was let go; and preparations made for landing. The *Herald's* boats also came to assist in it. At 10 a.m. I left with my family, and some others, in the ship's lifeboat; but it blew fresh, and we were nearly two hours getting on shore, the wind being off the land. During our passage several squalls of rain occurred, and the boat leaking badly, we were thoroughly drenched; the women and children presenting a most forlorn appearance. The actual landing was not bad; and we had no difficulty in crossing the reef, and running alongside the pier, steered by one of our own people. We were kindly received by Captain Denham, and Mr. Stewart, the gentleman in charge of the Government establishment. Mrs. Stewart was also there, notwithstanding the rain; and conducted the different females, as they reached the shore, to the house prepared for their reception; where a large fire was made, and hot tea ready; and greatly the various parties needed these kind attentions, as they arrived from the ship; for they were so cramped by the rain and cold, that on landing, many of them found it difficult at first to walk. Being conducted by Mr. Stewart to his residence, I placed my wife there, and then returned to the pier. By 1 o'clock, all our people were landed, without any accident occurring; and, the weather clearing up, the boats returned for our bedding. During the entire time of our debarkation, Captain Denham remained on the pier, in spite of the heavy rain, welcomed the arriving parties to their new home, and showed the greatest anxiety for their comfort. (*a*)

Nearly 67 years had elapsed, since Fletcher Christian and his eight associates—outlaws all—had sought shelter at Pitcairn; and now their descendants, having been conducted to a new abode under the friendly auspices of the British Government, were received at the latter by a Queen's Captain, with a courtesy equally honorable to him, and to them; and (as we shall see) ample provision was made for their proper subsistence, and independence, there. But the Hand which had thus regulated their destiny was not forgotten. At sea, as on land, their daily thanksgivings had been

---

(*a*) He had considerately detained his vessel for several days, that he might help the Pitcairners, and cheer them by the sight of a man-of-war, on their arrival.

poured forth; and, towards the close of the eventful day of their landing on Norfolk Island (8th June, 1856), "We all" (pursues Mr. Nobbs) "assembled in a large upper room in the military barracks, and solemnly offered our thanks and praises to God, for His continued goodness and mercy in thus bringing us to our future earthly home—soon after which we retired to rest under the same roof.

"*Monday, 9th.*—All hands up early; and after prayers, the men of our community prepared to go on board for our luggage. Everything denotes that we are in a strange country—the size of the houses, their construction, and the great height of the rooms, the number of cattle feeding quietly about, the oxen yoked to the carts bringing our goods from the pier to the place where we reside; and the barracks, three stories high: Thus everything astonished our people. *Sunday, 15th*: For some days little could be done towards landing anything; the *Morayshire* being obliged, from bad weather, to go out;" and it was not until the 25th, that all their worldly possessions had been brought on shore: And within a few days afterwards, that vessel, as well as the *Herald*, and the *Juno* (which had made her appearance on the 23rd), got under weigh, and took their departure; " leaving the Pitcairners all alone in their new possessions." But they speedily applied themselves to the altered circumstances in which they were placed; for we read that, on the 29th, "some are employed tending sheep, some driving in the cattle, and two or three at the windmill, grinding maize. It is really wonderful with what facility our people comprehend the details of these complicated employments." (*a*)

Intermediately (on the 17th July), Mr. Nobbs thus notes the progress of work, to another correspondent: "We are now getting the houses, stores, cattle, &c., &c., transferred to us by Mr. Stewart. Some of our people are having lessons in ploughing, sheep-shearing, milking, and corn grinding; so that we are all very busy;" and the first step for future provision from the soil

---

(*a*) They were delighted and amazed at the sight of the horses—animals they had never seen before; but they were not long in becoming acquainted with their use. On the day after arrival, several took their turn in riding the overseer's horse about the island; from the severe exercise which they gave him, the poor beast was completely tired out by the evening; and Jacob Christian, riding with more courage than skill, had a bad fall.

was taken, "by planting their esteemed sweet potato." While the provision made by the Government of New South Wales (since it was so privileged), for their start in life, in other respects, was very bountiful. "Pending harvest time," says Captain Denham, "I leave this community of 194 persons provided with 45,500 lbs. of biscuit, flour, maize and rice, with groceries in proportion, and abundance of milk at hand. Their live stock and fodder consist of 1,300 sheep, 430 cattle, 22 horses, 10 swine, in sties, domestic fowls, 16,000 lbs. hay, 5,000 lbs. straw, and a number of wild pigs and fowls. And, lest the first crop (for the coming of which they give 6 months) should be retarded, or fall short, I have submitted a list of supplies (Irish potatoes, rice, and peas), which the Governor General will forward from Sydney to these islanders, as an extent in aid."

Sunday, the *15th June*, "was a day" (adds Mr. Nobbs) "which will long be remembered by us; it was our first meeting in the Church for public worship. After the morning's Service, I administered the Holy Communion, and in the evening committed to the earth a premature ear from our gradually ripening sheaf (an infant which had died since the landing). Think of us in the Church which had formerly been occupied with the vilest outcasts of society; and then imagine us in the graveyard, filled with mounds that contained hundreds of their bodies; and you will enter largely into, and partake of, the gratitude, joy, grief, and I had almost said terror, that pervaded our minds." In another passage (under date 7th July), the Chaplain mentions, "I went through the prisons and other departments of the disused establishment for convicts; but no sound was there of good or evil: They were merely mementoes of the past. Still, it was harrowing to pass amid those barriers of wood and stone, and to be continually stepping on bolts and shackles, and requiring to use much strength to swing on their hinges the ponderous doors of cells and dungeons, which, when closed, were impervious to the light of day. It seemed to me that even the very air was forbidden to enter, except in very insufficient quantities." The island that had been disgraced by the presence of those fearful holes, was designated by one who had lived upon it for nearly four years, the "Ocean Hell"; "but I doubt not" (says the first Bishop Selwyn, who refers to the circumstance) "that eventually the presence of the Pitcairn people will render it what nature intended it to be—an earthly Paradise;" and the virtues of that people, with the noble efforts of himself, his martyred successor, and devoted, chivalrous, son, have realized the expectation, in so far as mortals could.

The following letter from the Rev. Mr. Patteson, then Chaplain to that first Bishop, and who afterwards, filling the other's place, sealed with his blood the ties that now bind us to the Melanesian Mission, presents a pleasant picture of the Pitcairners almost immediately after their arrival at Norfolk Island. It was addressed to his sister, in July, '56, and states:—

"I know you will feel interested in receiving a note written amongst the Pitcairners in Norfolk Island. Yesterday we sailed up to that island; saw no signs of people being on it; and thought they were not yet arrived; but at 4 p.m., a boat came off through the swell, manned by six men. As they neared us, we saw they were not English—too dark colored. They came up; jumped on deck; and we shook hands heartily. Familiar names, John Quintall, Frederick Young, John Nobbs (son of the Clergyman), &c. The Bishop and Mrs. Selwyn, intending to come on shore to-day, sent me off with these islanders, at 4.30; the Pitcairners working their boat through the surf admirably. Met Mr. Nobbs, and plenty of men and women: 30 families; 60 married people; and 134 children, young men and women. I had tea at Mr. Nobbs' house; and afterwards asked to hear some young people sing—which they did beautifully, in parts. About 24 came to his house, and sang for two hours and a half, psalms and hymns; and ended with 'God Save the Queen,' admirably given. The simple, modest behaviour, the gentle look of all, men and women—everything about them—quite confirming all I had read; and I enjoyed the evening exceedingly.

"Their settlement, at the S.E. corner, at Norfolk Island, contains 18 or 20 houses of brick, with verandahs, nice gardens, paddocks, and plenty of good grass for cows and sheep; there is, besides, a large building, formerly the barracks. The men are darker than Italians; as dark as some of the lighter colored Maories, occasionally; but no shade of black—it is more of the bright copper tint. The women are scarcely distinguishable from European; and most of the young ones are nice looking. There are but eight or nine surnames in the island. They seem a fine, healthy race in all respects. The men wear shirts, serge jerseys, and a sailor costume, in general; many without shoes or socks. The women are chiefly dressed in loose kind of robes; all modest and quiet; but without any appearance of timidity—just the kind of simple, easy manners you would expect. . . . *They have all the dress of poor people, with the feelings of those gently born and nurtured. Two of John Adams' daughters—the oldest people on the island—are really magnificent women, like Queens; old Hannah's long black hair fell almost to her waist, though she is 65."*

In like manner, Mr. Augustus Robinson, who had gone from Sydney to aid in their transfer from Pitcairn to Norfolk Island, in '56, informs a friend:—

"*My sojourn amongst these interesting people extended over a period of two months (six weeks at Pitcairn, and two at Norfolk), during which I had every opportunity of becoming acquainted with their manners, habits, and general mode of life; and I can easily imagine they must have been supremely happy at Pitcairn. Their modesty of demeanor, urbanity of manner, affectionate disposition, and personal appearance, have won for them the esteem and admiration of all who have visited them. . . . The mode of salutation adopted by the females, especially after the first introduction, is by a kiss, which is given on their part with as great a degree of modesty as exists during the exchange of ordinary civilities amongst more enlightened communities. They appear more like one large family; and the indiscriminate attention shown towards each others' offspring, when any difficulty or danger exists, is very striking. I never witnessed anything approaching to ill-feeling, or anger, amongst them; and a passage of Scripture inculcated into their minds by old John Adams, 'Never to allow the sun to go down on your wroth,' seems to have become so completely a part of their duty that, I was informed by Mr. Nobbs, they might sometimes be seen, of an evening, issuing from their houses to meet one another, and make up any little differences that may have arisen during the day.*"

I have now described the Mutiny of the *Bounty*, and its causes; traced the fortunes of the mutineers, and pictured the deeds that marred, and the scenes that should immortalize, Pitcairn Island. The course of my story, therefore (having followed its people to Norfolk Island), is well nigh complete; for any elaborate account of their subsequent life on the latter would be beyond its scope. Nor (with a passing exception, which shows that courage and fidelity are still their characteristics—that the nerve of the mutineer, and the love of the Tahitan, still glow in the veins and animate the frame of their descendants—and a peep, in later days, at the "Rock of the West," whence they came), can I do more than allude, in general terms, to the allotment of lands at Norfolk Island, in a fifty-acre farm, to each of the families brought from

Pitcairn by the *Morayshire*, almost immediately on their arrival—to the still earlier visit of Bishop Selwyn, and the initiatory steps taken by him towards the centering of the Melanesian Mission in their new quarters (since perfected by his successors) —to the establishment of a whaling station there—to the return to Pitcairn, in Dec., 1858, of two families of the Youngs (16 persons in all); being dissatisfied with the new home, and yearning for the soft atmosphere, and untrammelled freedom, of the dear one of former years—to a second exodus (in Dec., 1863), when three other families (of the Youngs, and Christians, with a Buffett—and consisting of about 30 souls,) followed their example, and regained the old abode (*a*)—to the privations or crowning comforts, and material progress, " moving accidents," and increased population, in Norfolk Island, during the next 11 years—showing in 1869 about 326 persons belonging, strictly, to the old Pitcairn Colony, which it had absorbed, and of these, one son of Matthew Quintall, and one son and one daughter of John Adams (with one daughter of John Mills, in Pitcairn Island), were all that remained of the *children* of the mutineers, though there were 32 of the *second* generation (with *their* offspring)—and to the recorded fact, that when, in 1870, fourteen years had elapsed since the removal from Pitcairn, and the discomforts and disappointments which attended it had mainly passed away, the various descendants of that brotherhood evinced in Norfolk Island the same simplicity of manners, and the same adherence to truth and uprightness, as distinguished the race in Pitcairn.

Yet I may mention (as a proof of the "pluck" and devotion of the hardy whalers of Norfolk Island, and of the stock whence they spring,) the following incident, recounted to Admiral Moresby, by Mr. Nobbs, in Dec., 1868 :—" During the late season,

---

(*a*) In March, 1884, Mr. F. A. Nobbs, the present Chief Magistrate of Norfolk Island, writes me: "The heads of the families that first returned to Pitcairn, in 1858, are grandsons of Mr. Young, of the *Bounty* (Mayhew and Moses Young); the former married a relict of a McCoy, by whom he had four or five children; and she herself was a grand-daughter of the famous Christian, so you will observe what an admixture of three of the prominent names of the *Bounty* have re-established themselves on that isolated but beautiful island, for nearly six and twenty years. And the extended swarm, that imitated their example five years later, with the previous intermarriages of some of its members with other families, restored to Pitcairn a strain of the eager blood of all the mutineers."

a boat of Frederick Young, with himself and five others on board, was three miles from the shore; and imprudently fastened to a cow-whale, no other boat being then in sight (though that of Fletcher Nobbs was also "in search"); the great animal very quietly turned the boat bottom up, without staving a plank, and then went off some distance. The crew set about righting the boat, but could not free her from water; however, they got the oars lashed athwart, and, though the gunwale was level with the sea, commenced paddling homewards (each boat always carrying a set of paddles besides the oars). The current was against them, and they did not make much progress; still, they were gaining ground, when to their surprise they saw the wounded whale coming towards the boat—either supposing it to be her calf, which lay dead some two miles off, or actuated by a desire for vengeance. The crew leaped overboard; the irritated monster placed her head on the boat, and there remained motionless for some time. Then she retired to a short distance; and the head-man swam back, and got a lance ready, determined to use it if the whale came again within reach. She did return; and the dauntless Young, swimming up to her, thrust the lance several times into her 'spout hole.'! Feeling the smart, the whale settled down some fathoms, came up swiftly, and smashed the boat and oars into fragments.

"There was now no alternative but to strike out for the land. One of the crew, an English sailor, could not swim; but two of our people bid him put an arm on each of their necks, and they would not leave while life remained. The last time they saw the whale, she was in a very weak state from loss of blood, but still remaining by the *debris* of the boat. And now, for three long weary hours, did the immersed whalers exert their energies to the utmost, but the current setting off they had not gained more than a mile. The poor sailor was nearly exhausted, and most of the party began to think their ultimate safety doubtful. There was also a lad of 16, one of our own people, who was growing tired, so that the other, disengaged, men of the crew had to keep by his side, to encourage him. That which seemed to alarm the lad most was the presence of immense sharks, whose fins were continually coming in contact with his legs." [Can a more dreadful position be imagined?] "And all this time their perilous situation was unknown to the other boat, or to us on shore.

"At length my son Fletcher, seeing nothing of Young's boat for several hours, left off chasing whales, and went in quest of it. After a search of some time, he concluded the boat must have landed, and began to think of doing so himself; but while running leisurely along near to the shore, and standing up, steering, he fancied he heard something like a distant shouting, or calling. Having mentioned this to his boat's crew, they ceased pulling, and surveyed the adjacent ridge, which stretched down close to the water's edge, supposing the sound proceeded from some one desirous of apprising them in what direction the other boat was. They could not, however, see anyone; yet presently, the like sounds were again heard, and then, after a short interval, for a third time. Fletcher and his crew were now of opinion it was from seaward the voices came; the boat's head was therefore turned in that direction, and 'Spring boys! there's help needed somewhere!' was the prompt conclusion. They bent to their oars with a good-will, and after pulling nearly a mile, the steersman, who had perched himself on the gunwale of the boat, fancied he saw three black spots on the water, about the size and appearance of cocoa-nuts, and became assured they were human heads. Feeling these were the crew of Young's boat, and thinking none others were left, he became so affected that he sank down in the stern sheets, and could not utter a word. But he speedily recovered himself, and simply said, 'Pull, boys! there they are!' Soon they had three of the swimmers on board; but they were afraid to ask what had become of the other three, fearing they were either drowned, or eaten by the sharks; but one of the rescued men said, 'Pull on,! the others can't be far off;' and about half-a-mile further on, they were happily met with, but in a most exhausted state; humanly speaking, another half-hour would have sealed their fate.

"As to ourselves, who were on shore: Many of us, both men and women, were assembled on the pier; looking at a floating whale which had been killed the day before, when a boat appeared, rounding the 'Wind-mill point.' All eyes were directed towards her, and some one remarked, 'There are more than six people in that boat; an accident has happened.' Our faces blanched, and our hearts beat quick; after a few moments' silence, and as the boat drew nearer, we attempted to count the number on board; but, having no glass at hand, we could only perceive nine. Three are gone! was the mournful conclusion; but *whose* husband, son, or brother, were the missing? I now ventured to ask, but with bated breath, 'Who's steering the boat?' 'Fletcher,' was the prompt reply—the only son I had out that day. Did I feel a relief? Wasn't it selfish? I can answer the first query; let casuists decide the second.

"After a little further scrutiny of the quickly approaching boat, a tenth person was discovered, and then an eleventh; they were seated among the rowers. At last the twelfth was observed, stretched low in the stern, and with his head resting on the gunwale. Yes, they were all there; but this last undoubtedly injured. Well, the pier was soon rounded, and as they came within hail, 'All right?' was our half fearful interrogatory. 'All right, thank God!' was the subdued, but cheerful response. No one was hurt; though the English sailor (the man leaning on the side of the boat) was still weak and pallid: Our people had stuck by him, to the endangering of their own lives!"

Children of the mutineers! strong, indeed, were thine arms, and true thy faithful, loving, hearts, on that dread day; and it is something—much—to know, and feel, that they are now citizens of New South Wales—the parent Australian State.

CHAPTER XII.—Pitcairn Re-visited, and Revived.

1858—1884: Pilgrims to the olden shrine—Captain Montreson's, and Sir C. W. Dilke's, accounts of them, and it, in 1860 and 1866—that of the shipwrecked sailors of the *Khandeish*, in '75—Rosalind Young's letter; and Admiral De Horsey's report, in '78—A narrative of '82—And tidings in '84—Parting suggestions.

IT has been mentioned that two families, of the Youngs, consisting of sixteen persons, preferring their first to their second love, returned to Pitcairn from Norfolk Island in 1858 : They sailed in a small vessel hired for that purpose; and though Sir William Denison was very wroth at what he termed their "versatility and weakness," they went notwithstanding: Parting with the families that remained on Norfolk was a heavier trial; and they felt it keenly: But they thought they would be happier, leading the old life in the old home; and they sought both accordingly. It has also been seen that, in 1863, a still larger swarm of the Pitcairn islanders returned to it from Norfolk Island, under a like influence.

I have not been able to learn very much as to the result of those yearnings and steps; yet, in so far as tidings have been gleaned, his Excellency's anger might have been spared: For when, in 1860, Pitcairn was touched at, by H.M.S. *Calypso*, Captain Montresor found (though they had not as yet any recognised laws, or Magistrate,) it was the intention of the heads of the families which had re-occupied it, since '58, to establish, as their children grew up, the like rules as had been handed down to them from the time of their first "father;" that they had Church Service twice every Sunday, besides family prayer, each morning and evening; that the houses in which they lived were neat and clean, resembling in the interior the cabin of a merchant ship, with a row of bunks on one side; that their farms were stocked with well-bred swine, and "looked as if they belonged to thriving tenant farmers in England;" that wild cattle (from survivors of the original stock presented by Admiral Moresby, and others, in days gone by), had increased so greatly, and had become so fierce, that they were obliged to kill them off, and had shot 26 since their return; that wild goats and poultry were sufficiently plentiful to supply them with flesh and fowl for years; that bread-fruit, taro and peas, grew wild and in abundance; that the men appeared to be sensible, hard-working, steady, good fellows; the women, modest, pleasing, and homely in their manners; and the children neither shy nor bold: while all seemed healthy; and that, most probably, Pitcairn, with the nucleus it then possessed, would, in time, be obliged to throw off its swarm;" but that, meanwhile, as Captain Montresor shook hands with the women in parting, and asked if they were really glad they had returned to the isle, there was marked evidence of the affirmative; "for they instantly replied, 'Oh, yes, indeed!' with an unmistakable earnestness as to their happiness in being again at home."

In like manner, the present Chief Magistrate of Norfolk Island (Mr. F. M. Nobbs), informs me (31st March, 1884), that when the second band of *retournés* reached Pitcairn, from Norfolk Island (in 1863), they found the first arrivals "healthy, cheerful, and happy, and prospering as well as could be expected, separated as they were from the civilized world." He adds, "that great care was taken, both up to that time, and since, to instil into the minds of the young those principles of religion and morality which, in the earlier days, had been taught by the patriach John Adams, and subsequently by my own honoured father."

In keeping with this, is the following account of a comparatively recent visit to Pitcairn by Sir C. Wentworth Dilke, in the M.S. *Rakaia*, towards the close of 1866, as given in his "Greater Britain":—"Although at sea there was a calm, the ground swell beat heavily upon the shore; and we were fain to content ourselves with a view of the island from deck. It consists of a volcanic peak, hung with an arras of green, creeping plants, passion flowers, and trumpet vines. As for the people, they came off to us, dancing over the seas in their canoes, and bringing us green oranges and bananas; while a large Union Jack was run up on their flagstaff

by those who remained on the shore. As the first man came up
the side, he rushed to the Captain, and, shaking hands violently,
cried out in pure English, entirely free from accent, 'How do you
do, Captain?' How's Victoria?' There was no disrespect in the
omission of the title 'Queen'; the question came from the heart.
At the same time, the bright-eyed lads by whom he was accompanied, Adams and Young—descendants in the third generation of
the *Bounty's* mutineers—who next climbed our decks, announced
the coming of Moses Young, the then Magistrate of the isle,
who presently boarded us in state. He was a grave and gentle-
manly man, English in appearance, but somewhat slightly built,
as were, indeed, the lads. . . . . . He told us, that his people had
30 sheep, which were owned by each of the families in turn; the
household taking care of them, and receiving the profits of them,
for one year. Water, he said, sometimes fell short in the island,
but they then made use of the juice of the green cocoa-nut. Their
school is excellent; all the children can read and write; and in
the election of Magistrates, they have female suffrage."

"It was at first supposed (from her firing two guns as she stood
in towards Pitcairn), that the *Rakaia* was a ship of war; and Mr.
Young came on board for the purpose, amongst others, of taking
the opinion, and obtaining the decision, of her Commander upon a
question that had greatly 'exercised' the islanders since their
return to the old home, and which might have puzzled 'a Phila-
delphia lawyer': namely, whether upon that return, the different
families who shared in it stood remitted to the ownership of the
same portions of land as they had held before the migration to
Norfolk Island? or whether they started afresh, and each comer
acquired, by the new occupation, an equal share with the others in
the land generally? Fortunately for the Captain, his vessel was
not a man-of-war; he was thus saved from the necessity of adjudi-
cating upon such a difficult 'Case'; and he adroitly recommended
the Chief Magistrate to refer it to the decision of the then
Governor of New South Wales. In what manner his Excellency
dealt with it I do not know. But when the 'knotty point' had
been thus shelved by him, the Commander of the *Rakaia* made a
commercial treaty with the Magistrate, who agreed, on behalf of
the islanders, to supply the ships of the new line of steamers
(being then established), whenever daylight enabled them to call at

Pitcairn, with fruit and vegetables, for which the producers were to receive cloth and tobacco in exchange—tobacco being the money of the Polynesian Archipelago. . . . . . " And as we stood out from the bay into the lonely seas, the island peak showed a black outline against a pale green sky; but in the west, the heavy clouds that in the Pacific never fail to cumber the horizon, were glowing with a crimson cast under the now setting sun; and the dancing wavelets were tinted with reflected hues."

A still later visitor tells the same tale of place and people, as all his predecessors have done since 1608. For in 1875, a Liverpool ship, the *Khandeish*, was lost not far from Pitcairn; and one of the crew of 23 who reached it (after rowing in open boats for 70 hours), and resided upon it for nearly 8 weeks, writes as follows, when describing their landing and abode there—"Soon a boat was put off from the island, and came alongside of us; she was manned by seven fine young men, who brought us provisions; rightly presuming us to have been shipwrecked. They put one of their own hands into our boat, and piloted us to their island; where we were most hospitably received by all the inhabitants coming on to the beach to welcome us. The best beds in the houses were put apart for us; and we were in all respects treated more like brothers than a lot of sailors. The cocoa-nut, bread-fruit, pine-apple, and many other fruits grow in great abundance, especially oranges, lemons, and citrons. There are 73 inhabitants, all told; some being very handsome; the women having beautiful hair, and (allowing for the hot sun) have fairer skins than would be supposed, being hardly darker than Europeans. They depend on passing vessels for all their clothes and agricultural implements, &c.; always going barefoot, except on Sundays, when some few of them wear boots. They grow sweet potatoes, yams, cotton, arrowroot, and Indian corn, which they give in exchange for clothes. The chief person in the island is Simon Young, grandson of Mr. Midshipman Young, of the *Bounty*. He officiates in Church on Sundays, also at the day and Sunday schools; they use the Church of England Service; and a sermon is generally read from some volume. All have good ear for music, and sing most beautifully. When anything has to be decided, they call a general meeting, and go by the majority of votes. They still have one of the cannon which belonged to the *Bounty*, and a carpenter's vice. We were upon the island 52 days, before we sighted a ship, and were treated with the greatest kindness all the while. We left one of our crew behind us, as he married one of the girls during our stay. Consumption is the only disease known among them. There is a scarcity of water at times which, they sometimes fear, will eventually force them to leave the island. Crockery is much needed, as in cases of accident they cannot get it replaced; and musical instruments would be appreciated in their singing school. . . . They retain all their pristine innocence, love of England which they never saw, and of their English relatives."

Thus we see that the "old lines" were followed at Pitcairn, and the same favorable results experienced by those who re-sought it from Norfolk Island, in 1858 and 1863, and by their children, as distinguished it and them prior to the migration to the latter in '56: And this is further illustrated by the homely, graceful sketch of society and life in Pitcairn, which was furnished in the early part of 1878 by one of its own people, Rosalind Young, when writing to the Rev. W. B. Keen, Acting British Chaplain at Valparaiso, on receipt of a box of goods, and of a letter from him (accompanied by a communication from an old benefactor, Dr. Turnbull, of same place).

"*Pitcairn Island, May* 16, 1878.

"*Rev. Sir, and Dear Friend,—I write to express my sincere thanks to you for all your kindness, and for all the interest you have taken in our welfare. It is a week ago since Captain Avery brought your gifts to us. We read Dr. Turnbull's letter on the first night it was received, and so sent an immediate answer by way of Tahiti. Your own letter was not opened till after the schooner had sailed; having been mislaid somewhere aboard ship, and was not delivered on shore in time for us to write an answer.*

"*The Magistrate will, no doubt, send an acknowledgment, and also reply to your inquiries. But perhaps you will not be unpleased to have me write something about ourselves. We are a very simple people, and all our surroundings are so. Our houses have plain gabled roofs, covered with thatch—the dried leaves of our palm trees; but they are entirely waterproof, so that rain can never penetrate them. The covering lasts for seven or eight years before a fresh one is required. As regards the interior of our dwellings, it is all very plain; each house containing from two to four rooms. Bedsteads are not universally used, but the innermost* sides of the houses are lined with bed places, which answer every purpose. Chairs are not used, only benches, not from choice, as the former can not be so easily made as the latter. There are only about eight or nine chairs altogether on the island, and these are considered among the 'luxuries of life.' We furnish our homes in the best manner our very limited means will allow; though that is but poorly, yet enough so to be contented. We try to keep them as clean as possible, though sometimes it is very difficult to do so, as grass cannot grow around them; and as we have no verandahs the dust easily finds its way in if the weather is hot or dry; and if rainy, on the other hand, then mud would be very disagreeable. We have been abundantly supplied with rain for a few years back till now, so that there is no lack of water. Just now we are enjoying the most delightful weather, and everything is very pleasant.

"Our Sundays are always enjoyable. First of all, in the morning we have school from half-past nine o'clock, then Divine Service, which all attend, from half-past ten to four o'clock, including both Services and the intermission. Then school again in the afternoon, and after that, the young people attend a singing school at which hymns only are sung; but on Wednesday evenings, we assemble again to sing glees, catches, &c.

"Day school is taught from Monday to Friday. There are 31 children attending; the eldest just sixteen, the youngest about six years of age. Only the simple studies are given—reading, writing, arithmetic, and geography. School hours are from nine to two o'clock, being opened and closed by singing a hymn and prayer. My dear father conducts it, and he also officiates as Minister on Sabbath days. A Bible class is regularly held on Wednesdays; and we meet also on every first Friday in each month for praise and prayer, and for strengthening and confirming one another in the faith. And here I would entreat, dear Sir, that you will remember us in your prayers before the throne of Grace, that we may walk stedfastly in the Lord, and that we may show by a consistent life that our profession is not in vain.

"I could give more accounts of us, but shall leave the rest for Mr. McCoy, as he will doubtless give you full particulars; and I hope you will excuse the liberty I have taken in writing this. I must now close, after again thanking you, and all the other kind friends in Valparaiso, for what you and they have done for us; and when I add, 'May the blessing of the Lord rest upon you, and them,' I know that I only express the feeling which we all entertain. Very truly yours,—ROSALIND YOUNG."

When Admiral De Horsey came to and reported upon Pitcairn, in Sep., 1878, he has a like story to tell. The population then amounted to 90 of all ages (41 males and 49 females): There was but one survivor of the generation which immediately followed the Mutiny—Elizabeth Young, aged 88, and daughter of John Mills, gunner's mate of the *Bounty*. The oldest man upon the island sustained the name of Thursday October Christian, was aged 59, and grandson of Fletcher, the leader of the mutineers. During the preceding twelve years, the deaths on Pitcairn had numbered about 12; no contageous diseases visited it, nor were the animals subject to disease. The then Governor was James Russell McCoy; who was also steersman of the boat—the only one on the island at that time; it stood in place of one destroyed in saving the crew of another shipwrecked vessel (the *Cornwallis*): This " Magistrate and chief ruler " (like his predecessors in former days) is " in subordination to Her Majesty, the Queen of Great Britain," and not only administers the laws, but enacts them, with the advice and assistance of two Councillors; while the " heads of families are convened for consultation when required." The laws then in force on the island " bore no date, but were drawn up by the Chief Magistrate on accession to office, and were evidently compiled from former ones now destroyed " [more probably from the original code quoted in Chapter IX.]; and as the Admiral remarks, "the almost puerile simplicity of the existing laws is, perhaps, the best evidence that can be afforded of the good conduct of the people." Only three crimes are contemplated as possible; and no case of any of them had occurred since the enactment of those laws. As in the original code, the Chief Magistrate is elected annually (on New Year's Day), is capable of re-election, and both sexes, of and above the age of seventeen, have votes.

The Admiral adds, that family prayers are said in every house, the first thing in the morning and the last in the evening; and no food is partaken of without asking God's blessing before and after; and, as Captain Beechy wrote of their parents, 54 years ago, the same could be said of the children now—" these excellent people appear to live together in perfect harmony and contentment; to be virtuous, religious, cheerful, and hospitable; to be patterns of parental and conjugal affection; and to have few vices of any kind." Sunday was strictly observed, but in no pharisaical spirit; for the islanders find their chief pleasure in prayer and praise; and their walk in life and conversation were in keeping with their professions. The acting Chaplain and schoolmaster was then Simon Young; who was assisted by his daughter in the latter office. "The instruction comprises reading, writing, arithmetic, history, geography, and Scripture. The girls learn cooking, sewing, hat and basket making; and all are taught part-singing very effectively. English is the only language spoken or known." On the island were sheep, goats, pigs, fowls, cats and dogs. As there was generally rain once a month, they had usually sufficient water; though there had been years in which they suffered from drought. There was no money, except a few coins kept as curiosities. No alcoholic liquors were used except for medical purposes; "and a drunkard is as unknown as a doubloon." The men were mostly employed in house-building, canoe-fishing, and in growing vegetables and maize. Pine-apples, figs, custard-apples, &c., were common; but the bread-fruit tree, which was at one time plentiful, was rapidly dying out. All the inhabitants took their share in public work when required to do so. The only communication they had with the outer world was with passing ships, averaging about one a month. Most ships fetch to windward of the island; and many of those which do sight it—principally vessels on their way to or from San Francisco—are unable to touch. There was no communication with Tahiti; and very rarely any with Norfolk Island, or New Zealand. A few of the islanders had expressed a desire to reseek the former island—a not unnatural wish for a change—though Mr. Young thought none were likely to go. But "I believe the Queen does not"— concludes the Admiral — "possess, in any part of the world, more loyal and affectionate subjects than this little knot of settlers."

Since he thus wrote, some considerate persons, interested in their behalf, have procured a couple of new boats for the Pitcairners, and supplied them with the means of obtaining a few other necessaries which they required; and our gracious Admiralty has expressed its willingness "that a ship-of-war should now and then visit them."

An English navigator, of Dec., '82, carries down the narrative almost to the present date; but mentions circumstances which tend to show that the energies and fertility of resource, derived by their fathers from the blood of the mutineers, is somewhat on the wane amongst the present inhabitants of Pitcairn: He tells us that, on a voyage home from San Francisco, at the period above mentioned, he sighted their island, and staid a short while to communicate with its people. Eight of them came off to his ship, in a boat sent to them by the Board of Trade, some years ago, and brought with them fruit and vegetables. "They were a fine lot of young fellows; and five of them were great-grandsons of Fletcher Christian." They feared that the sweet potato, on which they chiefly depended for their food, would prove a failure during the coming season from the excessive drought they were then suffering; "and they expected to have a very hard time of it, as they had no cattle." It is added, "they cannot grow grain on account of the number of rats on the island." But there did not appear to have been any falling off in the warm-hearted, grateful feelings that distinguished the old race. "They spoke with great pride and delight of the organ given to them by the Queen, some time ago." And they are still remarkable for their musical accomplishments. "After descending the ship's side, and getting into their boat, the returning crew said, "We will sing to you, before we go!" And there they sat, and sang the "Life-boat!" and "Pull for the Shore!"; taking the different parts, and rendering them in admirable harmony. There were then 103 or 104 people on the island; 60 of them were females.

"We occasionally hear from Pitcairn" (resumes the Chief Magistrate of Norfolk Island, in his communication of March, '84). "Their letters reach us from all parts of the world; being taken by Masters of passing vessels, and, when they arrive at their destinations, posted to us, *via* Auckland or Sydney—whence they finally turn up here. We heard from them, thus, about three months ago; they seemed to be comfortable, and contented on the little 'spot' which God hath given them. Simon Young, one of the band who returned to it in 1863, acts as their Pastor and teacher—and very satisfactorily, so far as we can learn." And though the worthy Magistrate of Norfolk Island adds, "but it seems to me there must be a great void in such a life as theirs; deprived, as it is, of the higher ordinances of our Holy Church, as well as of the blessings of a more civilized home," it is less their misfortune, than the fault of Christian England (which will not spare them a licensed Pastor), that those ordinances are not fully enjoyed by them; and it is more than questionable whether their true happiness would not be diminished, rather than increased, by a nearer approach to the paths and ways of "civilization."

A word more—having permitted both Otaheite and Toubouai to pass into the hands of France, England's nearest possessions to Pitcairn are the Fiji Group, and New Zealand; and, as the intercourse with it is now merely preserved by means of an occasional visit from one of her ships-of-war, or a passing merchant-man, might it not be well if the old home of the *Bounty's* mutineers, and their children—of their wrongs and their sufferings, joys and noble character—were incorporated with one or other of those British Colonies? Or, if it be thought (as perhaps it ought) that the descendants of Fletcher Christian and his daring mates, whether they now reside on Pitcairn Isle, or Norfolk Isle, should at least be citizens of the *same* State, then let the Government of the one embrace the other as well; and let New South Wales have the honor of enrolling all of them as such—of fostering the surviving, and cherishing the memory of the dead, as the best proof that can be given of *its* detestation of the cowardly outrages that caused the "Mutiny in the *Bounty*," and its reverence for the pure and hallowed lives of the "Pitcairn Islanders," who sprung from it.

In either case, while Australia grows in wealth, power, and culture, let us prize those island brethren, whose outlawed fathers founded an English Colony, amid the Pacific waters, within two and twenty months from the establishment of the Port Jackson settlement, by all the might of England; and who for heroic courage, tender affection, and earnest faith, are the noblest offshoot of the British race in the Southern Hemisphere: And while the chant of psalm, and organ's peal, proudly swell through our Cathedral aisles and Temples fair, let kindly memory often stray to the simple worshippers, whose prayers and praises are wafted to heaven daily, by Pitcairn's mountain side, and the tall Norfolk pines.

Let us feel and know, too, that beneath the shadows of the same towering land-marks, sable children of many a darkened isle are now kindling the torch, that shall yet illumine them all; and let us, therefore, duly honor the devoted Mission that has gathered them there; and is prepared to seal with the blood of its best " the liberty with which Christ makes them free, indeed."

FINIS.

Gibbs, Shallard, & Co., Pitt Street, Sydney.